Achieving the Mind-Body-Spirit Connection

A STRESS MANAGEMENT WORKBOOK

Also by
Brian Luke Seaward, PhD

Quiet Mind, Fearless Heart: The Taoist Path
Through Stress and Spirituality

Hot Stones and Funny Bones: Teens Helping
Teens Cope with Stress and Anger

Health of the Human Spirit

The Art of Calm: Relaxation Through the Five Senses

Stressed Is Desserts Spelled Backward: Rising Above Life's
Challenges with Humor, Hope, and Courage

Stand Like Mountain, Flow Like Water: Reflections
on Stress and Human Spirituality

Health and Wellness Journal Workbook, Second Edition

Managing Stress: A Creative Journal, Third Edition

Managing Stress: Principles and Strategies for Health
and Well-Being, Fourth Edition

Achieving the Mind-Body-Spirit Connection

A STRESS MANAGEMENT WORKBOOK

BRIAN LUKE SEAWARD, Ph.D.

JONES AND BARTLETT PUBLISHERS

Sudbury, Massachusetts

BOSTON   TORONTO   LONDON   SINGAPORE

WORLD HEADQUARTERS

Jones and Bartlett Publishers
40 Tall Pine Drive
Sudbury, MA 01776
978-443-5000
info@jbpub.com
www.jbpub.com

Jones and Bartlett Publishers
 Canada
6339 Ormindale Way
Mississauga, ON L5V 1J2
CANADA

Jones and Bartlett Publishers
 International
Barb House, Barb Mews
London W6 7PA
UK

Jones and Bartlett's books and products are available through most bookstores and online booksellers. To contact Jones and Bartlett Publishers directly, call 800-832-0034, fax 978-443-8000, or visit our website at www.jbpub.com.

Substantial discounts on bulk quantities of Jones and Bartlett's publications are available to corporations, professional associations, and other qualified organizations. For details and specific discount information, contact the special sales department at Jones and Bartlett via the above contact information or send an email to specialsales@jbpub.com.

PRODUCTION CREDITS
Acquisitions Editor: Jacqueline Ann Mark
Senior Production Editor: Julie Champagne Bolduc
Assistant Editor: Nicole Quinn
Junior Editorial Assistant: Erin Murphy
Marketing Manager: Ed McKenna
Director of Interactive Technology: Adam Alboyadjian
Interactive Technology Manager: Dawn Mahon Priest
Manufacturing Buyer: Therese Bräuer
Composition: Interactive Composition Corporation
Cover and Interior Design: Anne Spencer
Cover Image: © Robert Harding World Imagery/Alamy Images
Printing and Binding: Courier Stoughton
Cover Printing: Courier Stoughton

ISBN-13: 978-0-7637-4573-8
ISBN-10: 0-7637-4573-1

6048

Printed in the United States of America
14 13 12 11 10   10 9 8 7 6 5 4

In honor of the spirit
of my mother and father,
Pat and Ed Seaward

Contents

Introduction: The Whole Is Always Greater Than the Sum of the Parts

Modern man is sick because he is not whole.
—Carl Gustav Jung

There is a huge crisis in the world today. It's so big that it barely gets noticed in the news headlines, yet it underlies nearly every topic of conversation among friends, family, co-workers, acquaintances, consumers, and even children. The crisis is an epidemic of stress, and it affects everything in our lives, from our eating habits to the most basic lifestyle behaviors of everyone with whom we interact. Sociologists tell us that stress is one of the few factors that knows no demographic boundaries. As the expression goes, "Stress is the equal-opportunity destroyer."

We are all greatly affected by stress. Moreover, it's no secret to say that the world itself is under a great amount of stress today. The waves of political issues, environmental problems, and global concerns crash upon the shores of our personal lives in ways that were unimaginable only a few decades ago. Despite the current issues of alarming divorce rates, chronic diseases, financial instability, global warming, corporate and political scandals, computer viruses, identity theft, genetic cloning, and terrorism, the solutions to these problems are within our grasp—if we make a concerted effort to use our inner resources to bring things back into balance.

Holistic stress management is based on the premise of ageless wisdom, where the whole is always greater than the sum of the parts. If you were to talk to the shamans, sages, mystics, and healers of all times, of all ages, and all languages regarding the topic of health and ask "What are the parts that make up the whole?" you would hear a unanimous voice among the wisdom keepers repeating these words: mind, body, spirit, and emotions. When asked to elaborate further, they would explain that holistic health is the divine alchemy derived from the integration, balance, and harmony of these four components.

Today the voice of ageless wisdom is often drowned out by the dull roar of the scientific community, which tends to look for, and associate a specific cause with, each effect. Rather than looking at the whole picture, Western culture has opted to dissect and study the pieces that make up the whole; curiously, however, it never gets around to putting the pieces back together. Moreover, Western culture often fails to recognize the significance of the unique unifying synergistic force that gives power to the whole that is greater than the sum of the parts. Herein lies the danger regarding our current health care system. Symptomatic relief, the cornerstone of the Western medical model, does not honor the code of holistic health, in which both the causes and symptoms of disease and illness are addressed and resolved together. Perhaps most important, holistic stress management honors the aspect of spiritual well-being, a component that has been long ignored or neglected entirely for nearly 400 years.

Paradigms are often slow to change. With a newly recognized national interest in various forms of complementary and alternative medicine, however, new insights into health and healing, based on ageless wisdom, are taking root in the American culture. In his acclaimed book *The Best Alternative Medicine: What Works and What Doesn't,* author Kenneth Pellitier notes that there are over 600 different modalities of holistic healing, from acupuncture to zero balancing. The purpose (implicit or explicit) of every modality of complementary and alternative medicine (now called CAM by the medical establishment) is to restore a sense of homeostasis through the integration, balance, and harmony of mind, body, spirit, and emotions. It's no coincidence that virtually every modality of holistic stress management is considered a member of this family of 600 healing modalities (from autogenics to Tai Chi). The purpose of all effective coping skills and relaxation techniques is the same: to return each person to a sense of homeostasis.

To understand, appreciate, and utilize the wealth of knowledge in the realm of holistic health, it is important to realize that the wisdom of mind-body-spirit stress management draws upon the disciplines of psychology, sociology, physiology, theology, anthropology, mythology, quantum physics, cosmology, and perhaps several more areas—all of which come together as a means to create the parameters of "the bigger picture." By and large, we live in a society in which experts focus their specialty on one discipline, rather than on a synthesis of all aspects of the human journey. The result is dangerous blind spots. In essence, this fragmented approach creates a very myopic view of life, particularly when trying to deal with the complexities that make up the human condition, none of which is held tightly in the domain of any one discipline.

Holistic stress management is more than just a theory, although many people end their journey there. In support of the premise that the whole is always greater than the sum of the parts, holistic stress management goes beyond the theory to include the daily application of this knowledge, so that effective coping skills and relaxation techniques become part of one's daily lifestyle rather than a simple first aid kit for crises.

I have been a follower of the holistic model of health all my life. Although the premise of the wellness paradigm is clearly intuitive, it is disappointing to me to see it not being more widely embraced. As has often been said, we don't have a health care system in this country, we have a sick care system, in which the focus is on symptomatic relief. It was in the mid-1970s that I made a decision to focus my efforts as a health educator on being an advocate for holistic health. Soon after I completed my master's degree in exercise physiology, a culmination of events opened the door to ensure this calling with relative ease, not the least of which was the distinct honor of meeting Dr. Elisabeth Kübler-Ross. She was the keynote speaker at the American Holistic Medical Association meeting held in La Crosse, Wisconsin, in 1981. Although she was renowned the world over for her work on the topic of death and dying, she gave a stunning presentation on the nature of holistic healing. Her presentation and my subsequent meetings with her galvanized the direction of my professional career.

Although Kübler-Ross is one of my mentors, the contents of this workbook are based on the collective wisdom of many additional 20th-century luminaries in the fields of psychology, physiology, sociology, theology, and mythology, including Carl Jung, Abraham Maslow, Ken Cooper, Albert Einstein, Candace Pert, Viktor Frankl, Andy Weil, Joseph Campbell, Wayne Dyer, Carolyn Myss, Richard Gerber, Matthew Fox, Deepak Chopra, Larry Dossey, and many, many others. The purpose of this book is to increase your awareness regarding the various aspects of wellness through the mind-body-spirit nexus, as well as to utilize any and all ideas so that you may fully integrate them into your life. By doing so, you begin to take an active role in the process of cultivating inner peace, rather than feeling like a passive victim in a crazy, frenetic world.

If there is one theme to this workbook (and actually, there are many), it is the theme of balance, for without balance in one's life, nothing else is really possible. Every skill and technique described in this workbook carries with it the premise of restoring a sense of balance, homeostasis, or inner peace to mind, body, spirit, and emotions.

An ancient proverb often quoted in the halls of Wall Street states, "To know and not do, is not to know." In simple terms what this means is that you can know all the information that supports a powerful strategy for holistic stress management, yet by not practicing these techniques and making them part of your daily routine, the knowledge is quite useless. Perhaps in simplest terms, holistic stress management is an adaptation process involving all aspects of the mind, body, spirit, and emotions to reach one's highest potential.

At the end of each chapter are a series of worksheets, exercises, and activities based on specific chapter contents. These exercises are designed to be stepping stones to your soul-searching efforts for balance. They have been created specifically to help you process the informational content for the most comprehensive understanding possible. Although you are encouraged to complete the exercises, you may find it best to read each exercise over first and then come back to each one when you are truly ready. Whereas some exercises were designed specifically for this workbook, the majority of them were created for workshop participants and college students over a period of two and a half decades. They have proven to be very valuable and, in some cases, life changing. It is my wish that you find them to be equally valuable in seeking that place of inner peace through mind, body, spirit, and emotions.

Acknowledgments

This book is a culmination of much wisdom and many exercises and homework assignments created for students and workshop participants over the past 25 years. I am deeply indebted to all of you who allowed me to share these exercises and meditations as a means for personal enlightenment, soul searching, and mind-body-spirit integration. Your feedback was (and is) greatly appreciated.

Heartfelt gratitude goes to my friends and colleagues Don Campbell, Donna Eden, David Feinstein, and Harriet Lerner for their wonderful endorsements of this book. I would also like to give profound thanks to those who have served as my teachers, mentors, and wisdom keepers over the many years whose keen insights have found their way into the magical synthesis of this book, including Carl Jung, Elisabeth Kübler-Ross, Viktor Frankl, Wayne Dyer, Leo Buscaglia, Abraham Maslow, M. Scott Peck, Joseph Campbell, Jean Houston, Larry Dossey, Deepak Chopra, Andy Weil, Bernie Siegel, Roger von Oech, Herb Benson, Dean Ornish, Jon Kabat-Zinn, Kenneth Pellitier, Caroline Myss, Richard Gerber, Hans Selye, Matthew Fox, Black Elk, Lao Tsu, Patricia Norris, Elmer Green, Mietek Wirkus, Albert Einstein, Ken Wilber, Norman Cousins, Jane Goodall, Robert Becker, Don Campbell, Donna Eden, Candace Pert, and Harriet Lerner.

A big thanks goes to my personal assistant, Marlene Yates, who, as always, was a real trouper in reading and rereading each and every page in the editing process, many times over.

The staff of Jones and Bartlett are nothing less than superlative, and I am eternally grateful for this and all our collaborative efforts. To Jacqueline Mark, Nicole Quinn, Julie Bolduc, and Anne Spencer, who believed in this project from the start, and everyone else at Jones and Bartlett, I am eternally thankful for your efforts and support.

A special word of thanks to the National Wellness Institute and American Holistic Nurses Association, who have supported my efforts to offer my holistic stress management instructor certification workshop over the years. Muchas gracias!

As always, thanks to my friends and family, too numerous to mention, who have always been such a tremendous support to me and my work over the course of my career.

Blessings to you all.

Best wishes and inner peace,
Brian Luke Seaward, Ph.D.
Boulder, Colorado
www.brianlukeseaward.net

One Quiet Night

One Quiet Night, a CD featured in this book, contains the most melodic, relaxing instrumental music ever compiled from the EverSound label. This CD features music by John Mills, Ron Clearfield, Lino, John Adorney, Manuel Iman, and Nigel Holton. Each song was selected by Brian Luke Seaward as a timeless musical prescription for relaxation and inner peace. This CD is available in all music outlets or through www.eversound.com.

PART I

The Wellness Mandala

CHAPTER

1

Stress: A Global Epidemic

Tension is who you think you should be. Relaxation is who you are.
—Ancient Chinese proverb

Are you stressed? If the answer is yes, then consider yourself to be in good company. Several Harris and Gallup polls taken over the past few years have noted an alarming trend in the psyche of the American public. Across the board, without exception, people admit to having an increasing sense of anxiety, frustration, unease, and discontent, particularly in the worksite, but generally in all aspects of their lives. Sadly, episodes of suicide, road rage, school shootings, and personal bankruptcies are so common that they no longer top the headline news. Ironically, in a country where the standard of living is said to be the highest anywhere in the world, nearly one-third of the American population is said to be on antidepressants. Moreover, it is estimated that the average person has accrued between $7,000 and $9,000 in credit card debt, and current estimates suggest that one in three people suffer from a chronic disease, ranging from cancer and coronary heart disease to rheumatoid arthritis, diabetes, and lupus. For a country with the highest standard of living in the world, something is very wrong with this picture.

Furthermore, since the events of September 11, 2001, a blanket of fear has covered much of the country, if not the world, keeping people in a perpetual state of anxiety. In fact, so pervasive is stress in the lives of all planetary citizens that the World Health Organization (WHO) refers to stress as "a global epidemic." Global problems only seem to intensify our personal stressors. Sadly, it doesn't make any difference where you live, what you do for a living, or how much money is in your checking account: Stress is the equal-opportunity destroyer.

Times of Change and Uncertainty

Today the words *stress* and *change* have become interchangeable, and the winds of change are certainly in the air. Changes in the economy, changes in technology, changes in health care, and dramatic changes in the weather are just some of the gale forces blowing in our collective faces. By and large the average person doesn't like change because change tends to disrupt one's comfort zones. It appears that the "known," no matter how bad, is a safer bet than the fear of the unknown. Change, it should be noted, has always been part of the human landscape. However, today the rate of change has become so fast and furious that it creates a perpetual sense of uneasiness in the hearts and minds of nearly everyone. Take a moment to reflect on how change affects your life.

At one time, getting married, changing jobs, buying a house, raising children, going back to school, experiencing the death of a friend or close relative, and suffering from a chronic illness were all considered to be major life events that would shake the foundations of anyone's life. Although these events still play a pivotal role in personal upheaval, a new crop of social stressors has added to the critical mass of an already volatile existence, throwing things further out of balance. Consider how these trends directly influence your life: the rapid acceleration of technology (from software upgrades to Internet downloads), the proliferation of cell phone use, an accessible 24-7 society, global economic woes (e.g., gasoline prices), global terrorism, genetically modified foods, and public health issues ranging from AIDS to the newest infectious virus. Moreover, there is a growing consensus that we have become addicted to a fast-paced consumeristic lifestyle that is globally unsustainable. Indeed, stress is a part of the human landscape! Today a rapidly paced lifestyle, for whatever reason, may be normal, but normal isn't necessarily healthy!

Times of change and uncertainty tend to magnify our personal stress. Perhaps the biggest looming concern facing people today is the issue of personal boundaries or the lack thereof. The advances of high technology combined with a rapidly changing social structure have eroded personal boundaries. These boundaries include home and work, finances, nutritional habits, relationships, and many more, all of which add to the critical mass of stress. Even the ongoing war on terrorism appears to have no boundaries! Ironically, the lack of boundaries combined with factors that promote a fractured society, in which people feel a lack of community and belonging, as well as conflicting values, leads to a greater sense of disconnection; this, too, intensifies our personal stress levels.

The Whole Is Always Greater

Several centuries ago a philosophy took hold in Western culture that tried to make sense of life, but in doing so, ended up blinding nearly everyone to the bigger picture. The philosophy is known as the Cartesian principle, proposed by René Descartes, who is credited with the separation (or fragmentation) of mind and body. His Cartesian principle is also known as the *reductionistic method of science*, in which, in order for something to be considered real and valid, it has to be measured repeatedly through the five senses. The premise of "divide and conquer" led to many areas of specialization—regrettably, at the expense of a unified vision.

This Cartesian principle works great for all things physical, but ignores, and to a large extent invalidates, the nonmaterial world. In the case of health and well-being, our physical health can be measured in terms of bone density, blood chemistry, and cell physiology, down to the molecular structure of our DNA. A specific focus on the body has proven beneficial for physical health. However, ignoring the mind, emotions, and spirit in favor of human physiology only leads to more serious problems. Although many good things have come from the scientific method, at best this focus on physical health offers only symptomatic relief. Rarely, if ever, does it address the cause of our problems. In the words of Dr. Elisabeth Kübler-Ross over two decades ago, "To ignore all aspects of health, including the spiritual dimension, only leads to dysfunction." Prophetically, today the word *dysfunctional* has become our national adjective.

Ageless wisdom shared by the sages and mystics of all times reveals that health is composed of the integration, balance, and harmony of four unique aspects: mind, body, spirit, and emotions, in which the whole (often expressed in the form of a circle) is always greater than the sum of the parts. The circle is a universal symbol of wholeness. From the taoist yin/yang symbol and the American Indian medicine wheel to the Tibetan mandala, the Christmas wreath, the labyrinth (Figure 1.1), the peace symbol, and the planet Earth itself, a circle represents wholeness. Like the mandala of the four seasons and the four directions, the mandala of human health is also composed of four quadrants: mind, body, spirit, and emotions, in which the whole is always greater than the sum of the parts (Figure 1.2). The

Figure 1.1

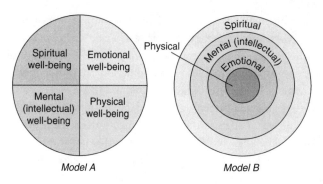

Figure 1.2

lines that separate or appear to fragment these four components are an illusion of sorts. They don't really exist. They are placed in the circle for theoretical or academic purposes. In truth, there is no separation of mind and body, body and spirit, or any of these aspects of the human condition. All parts come together to complete one beautiful, dynamic package. Indeed, the whole is always greater than the sum of its parts.

The Premise of Holistic Stress Management

Honoring the premise of this ageless wisdom, holistic stress management promotes the integration, balance, and harmony of one's mind, body, spirit, and emotions for optimal health and well-being. Indeed, stress affects all aspects of the wellness paradigm. To appreciate the dynamics of the whole, sometimes it's best to understand the pieces that make up the whole. What follows is a definition of each of the four aspects that constitute the human entity, and the effects that unresolved stress plays on each.

- **Emotional well-being:** The ability to feel and express the entire range of human emotions and to control them, not be controlled by them. Unresolved stress tends to perpetuate a preponderance of unhealthy or negative emotions (unresolved anger and fear), thus compromising emotional balance and leading to the inability to experience and enjoy moments of joy, happiness, and bliss.

- **Physical well-being:** The optimal functioning of the body's physiological systems (e.g., cardiovascular, endocrine, reproductive, immune). Unresolved stress creates wear and tear on the body: The association between stress and disease is approximately 80 to 85 percent. Ultimately, stress left unresolved can kill you.

- **Mental well-being:** The ability of the mind to gather, process, recall, and communicate information. Stress certainly compromises the ability to gather, process, recall, and communicate information. Like static on a radio station, stress jams the frequencies of a clear mind, decreasing attention span and increasing poor decision-making.

- **Spiritual well-being:** The maturation of higher consciousness as represented through the dynamic integration of three facets: relationships, values, and a meaningful purpose in life. Most, if not all, stressors involve some aspect of relationships, values (or value conflicts), and the absence, search, or fulfillment of a meaningful purpose in one's life.

The Nature of Holistic Stress Management

With the appreciation that the whole is always greater than the sum of the parts, here are some insights that collectively shine light on the timeless wisdom of holistic stress management:

- Holistic stress management conveys the essence of uniting the powers of the conscious and unconscious minds to work in unison (rather than opposition) for one's highest potential. Additionally, a holistic approach to effectively coping with stress unites the functions of both right and left hemispheres of the brain.

- Holistic stress management suggests a dynamic approach to restore one's personal energy, in which one lives consciously in the present moment rather than feeling guilty about things done in the past or worrying about things that may occur in the future.

- Holistic stress management uses a combination of effective coping skills to resolve issues that can cause perceptions of stress to linger and sound relaxation techniques to reduce or eliminate the symptoms of stress and return the body to homeostasis. This is different from the standard practice of merely focusing on symptomatic relief.

- Holistic stress management is achieving a balance between the role of the ego to protect and the purpose of the soul to observe and learn life's lessons. More often than not, the ego perpetuates personal stress through control and manipulation. With a holistic perspective, one responds rather than reacts.

- Holistic stress management is often described as moving from a motivation of fear to a place of unconditional love.

When all of these aspects are taken into consideration, the process of integrating, balancing, and bringing harmony to mind, body, spirit, and emotions becomes much easier, and arriving at the place of inner peace is easier to achieve. This is the clarion message of this workbook.

Definitions of Stress

A quick survey of experts reveals that there are many different definitions of stress. Each definition is succinctly framed from the expert's respective discipline, whether it be physiology, psychology, sociology, theology, or anthropology. Some say that stress is the inability to cope with demands. Others define stress as wear and tear on the body. Still others insist that stress is the loss of emotional control. Sages explain that stress is the absence of inner peace.

To some extent, all of these definitions hold merit; however, no one definition paints the entire picture of this unique phenomenon. Although there appears to be no exact agreement, there is a consensus among experts that stress is a "perceived threat" (real or imagined) that affects one's mental, emotional, physical, or spiritual well-being. It is important to underscore the word *perceived* here. Each situation goes through a process of interpretation, and two people can perceive the same situation quite differently. Moreover, the mind can create perceptions (sometimes even illusions) that perpetuate stress, giving credence to the adage of "making a mountain out of a mole hill."

Good Stress and Bad Stress

Like a coin with two faces, stress also has two sides: good stress and bad stress. Good stress is anything that makes you feel motivated, exhilarated, or inspired. Sitting in the audience to hear one of your favorite musical groups, falling in love, or being on the best vacation ever are examples of good stress. Although the body has some sympathetic neural activity, it also produces some very desirable neuropeptides. By and large, we don't experience enough of this kind of stress. Bad stress, also known as *distress*, is in no short supply today, and most everyone knows what this term means.

Using the coin metaphor once again, bad stress also has two sides. These include *acute stress,* which is very intense but doesn't last too long (about 20–30 minutes) and *chronic stress*, events that are not so intense but seem to last forever (e.g., days, weeks, months, or years). Examples of acute stress might include locking your keys in your car, being pulled over for a speeding ticket, or playing phone tag with someone. Acute stress also includes occasional daily hassles. Conversely, examples of chronic stress may include a troublesome boss, ex-spouse, co-worker, or mother-in-law, a tax audit, or being laid off and unable to find a job. These problems don't go away in 20 minutes! As you might have guessed, chronic stress is the real culprit with regard to one's health. Problems that are left unresolved eat away at your soul and ultimately wreak havoc on your body. Ultimately, the body becomes the battlefield for the war games of the mind. Exercises 1.1 and 1.2 invite you to survey your life in terms of behaviors and events associated with chronic stress as a means to begin to resolve them.

Fight or Flight: The Physiology of Survival

Using a high-tech metaphor, your body is equipped with a unique survival software package. It's called the *fight-or-flight response* (also known in some circles as the *stress response*), and it serves as your "bodyguard" for threats of physical danger. The mind, with the help of the ego, constantly processes an immense amount of information every day, through the doors of the five senses, looking for signs and signals of physical threats. The smell of smoke, the sight of flames, or the sound of wheels screeching are just a few examples of the sensory cues that the mind processes. Nonthreatening cues are quickly dismissed. In the event of possible danger, however, the body gears up to either defend one's territory or run like the blazes to escape harm. In the splendor of human physiology, your body prepares to do both simultaneously.

With the grandeur of human physiology, however, there is a hidden danger. What was once designed as a survival dynamic is now becoming a serious liability to our health. The fight-or-flight response, for the most part, has become antiquated. By and large, most people today have very little in the way of physical stressors. Most of our problems, issues, and challenges are of a mental, emotional, or spiritual nature rather than physical threats to our human existence. Still, the human body responds the same way, regardless of the problem—whether you are trying to escape from a burning building or vigorously attempting to creatively finance your next mortgage payment. Tightly woven in the fight-or-flight response is the role of the ego, whose purpose is to serve as your security guard for physical danger. Problems arise when the ego undermines this process with the intention to control and manipulate other aspects of your life. This is what the ancient Chinese proverb means by saying "Tension is who you think you should be, relaxation is who you are."

Tend and Befriend: The Female Endowment

Are women more evolved than men when it comes to dealing with stress? Physiologically speaking, the answer appears to be yes! Although women certainly have the fight-or-flight response hardwired into their nervous system, they also have what is now called the *tend-and-befriend response*. Under duress, not only do women produce different neurochemicals in the brain to help cope with the problems at hand, but they also seek out the company of other women to console and be consoled. Connectedness offers its own sense of security.

Over the course of history, this additional software package has proven to be an invaluable asset, and perhaps one reason why women tend to live longer than men. But don't be fooled, ladies. The cumulative effects of stress can overwhelm this system if adequate measures for stress relief are not taken. Remember, ultimately stress is the equal-opportunity destroyer.

From Burnout to Exhaustion

It wasn't long ago that stores were closed on Sundays (in some places, even Mondays) and television networks only broadcast from 6 A.M. to midnight. Not only has the pace of life speeded up, but it seems that nearly everyone and everything is accessible 24 hours a day, every day of the year. *Burnout* used to be a term reserved for job stress, but now it is being applied to life in general. Our infatuation with technology is only partly to blame. Poor eating habits, lack of exercise, and extremely poor boundaries also constitute other reasons why people show the following signs of burnout: fatigue, mood swings, irritability, insomnia, and exhaustion. The words *burnout* and *stress* are now frequently used interchangeably.

The Power of Adaptation

One of the greatest attributes of the human species is the ability to adapt to change. Adaptation is the number one skill with which to cope with the stress of life. Adaptation involves a great many human attributes, from resiliency and creativity to forgiveness, patience, and many others. Given the rapid rate of change in the world today, combined with the typical changes one goes through in a lifetime, the ability to adapt is essential. Those who incorporate a strategy to adapt positively will not only be healthier, but in the long run will be much happier. Adaptation to stress means making small changes in your personal lifestyle so that you can move with the flow of the waves of change and not feel personally violated or victimized. Sometimes, adaptation to change means merely fine-tuning a perception or attitude. In the best stress management program reduced to 27 words, the following quote by Reinhold Niebuhr speaks to this process: "God, grant me the serenity to accept the things I cannot change, the courage to change the things I can, and the wisdom to know the difference." The skills introduced in this workbook are designed to help you gracefully adapt to the waves of change, for whatever situation in which you find yourself.

The Focus of This Workbook

The purpose of this workbook is to help you address the issues of stress from a holistic perspective: mind, body, spirit, and emotions. The aim is to assist you to resolve the causes of your stress, as well as help you relieve and minimize the physical symptoms that accompany the general wear and tear of everyday life. The goal of this workbook is for you to live your life from a place of balance, rather than feeling as if you were teetering on the brink of disaster. Restoring and maintaining a sense of personal balance is the underlying theme of this workbook. It's very possible—it simply takes practice.

The next four chapters highlight the unique relationships between stress and one's physical, mental, emotional, and spiritual well-being, respectively. In Chapter 5, a special emphasis has been placed on the most neglected component of the wellness paradigm, spiritual well-being. Part II addresses the topic of effective coping skills to provide you tools with which to initiate the resolution process, and Part III provides insights regarding a host of relaxation techniques to restore personal homeostasis.

Reading and learning the time-tested theories of stress management is one thing, but putting this wisdom to use is quite another. As the adage states, "To know and not to do, is not to know." Therefore, at the end of each chapter you will find one or several exercises to assist you in the process of moving from theory to the direct application of this knowledge so that you can begin to integrate these concepts fully into your life. If you get one thing out of this book to make your life a little easier and help you adapt to one or more of the many life changes you are going through, then the time taken to do these exercises will be well worth it.

Additional Resources

Brown, L. *Plan B: Rescuing a Planet Under Stress and a Civilization in Trouble*. New York: Norton, 2004.
Carson, R. *Don't Sweat the Small Stuff*. New York: Hyperion Books, 1997.
McEwen, B. *The End of Stress as We Know It*. Washington, DC: Joseph Henry Press, 2002.
Sapolsky, R.M. *Why Zebras Don't Get Ulcers*. New York: W.H. Freeman, 1998.
Seaward, B.L. *Stressed Is Desserts Spelled Backward*. Berkeley, CA: Conari Press, 1999.
Selye, H. *The Stress of Life*. New York: McGraw-Hill, 1978.

Exercise 1.1 Are You Stressed?

Although there is no definitive survey composed of 20 questions to determine if you are stressed or exactly how stressed you really are, questionnaires do help increase awareness that, indeed, there may be a problem in one or more areas of your life. The following is an example of a simple stress inventory to help you determine the level of stress in your life. Read each statement and then either circle the word *Agree* or *Disagree*. Then count the number of "Agree" points (one per question) and use the Stress Level key to determine your personal stress level.

Statement		Agree	Disagree
1.	I have a hard time falling asleep at night.	Agree	Disagree
2.	I tend to suffer from tension and/or migraine headaches.	Agree	Disagree
3.	I find myself thinking about finances and making ends meet.	Agree	Disagree
4.	I wish I could find more to laugh and smile about each day.	Agree	Disagree
5.	More often than not, I skip breakfast or lunch to get things done.	Agree	Disagree
6.	If I could change my job situation, I would.	Agree	Disagree
7.	I wish I had more personal time for leisure pursuits.	Agree	Disagree
8.	I have lost a good friend or family member recently.	Agree	Disagree
9.	I am unhappy in my relationship, or am recently divorced.	Agree	Disagree
10.	I haven't had a quality vacation in a long time.	Agree	Disagree
11.	I relish the fact that my life has meaning and purpose.	Agree	Disagree
12.	I tend to eat more than three meals a week outside the home.	Agree	Disagree
13.	I tend to suffer from chronic pain.	Agree	Disagree
14.	I don't have a strong group of friends to whom I can turn.	Agree	Disagree
15.	I don't exercise regularly (more than three times per week).	Agree	Disagree
16.	I am on prescribed medication for depression.	Agree	Disagree
17.	My sex life is not very satisfying.	Agree	Disagree
18.	My family relationships are less than desirable.	Agree	Disagree
19.	Overall, my self-esteem can be rather low.	Agree	Disagree
20.	I spend no time each day dedicated to meditation or centering.	Agree	Disagree

Stress Level Key

Less than 5 points	You have a low level of stress and maintain good coping skills.
More than 5 points	You have a moderate level of personal stress.
More than 10 points	You have a high level of personal stress.
More than 15 points	You have an exceptionally high level of stress.

Exercise 1.2 Personal Stress Inventory: Top 10 Stressors

It's time to take a personal inventory of your current stressors—those issues, concerns, situations, or challenges that trigger the fight-or-flight response in your body. The first step to resolving any problem is learning to identify exactly what the problem is. Take a moment to list the top ten issues that you are facing at the present moment. Then place a check mark in the columns to signify whether this stressor directly affects one or more aspects of your health (mind, body, spirit, emotions). Next to each stressor, chronicle how long it has been a problem. Finally, check whether this stressor is one that elicits some level of anger, fear, or both.

Stressor	Mental	Emotional	Spiritual	Physical	Duration of Problem	Anger or Fear
1.						
2.						
3.						
4.						
5.						
6.						
7.						
8.						
9.						
10.						

Exercise 1.2

CHAPTER

2

The Body: The Battlefield for the Mind's War Games

The immune system does not reside solely in the body.
—Patricia Norris, Ph.D.

Here is a startling statistic: Over 80 percent of patients' visits to physician offices are associated with stress (unresolved issues of anger and fear). Here is another statistic: Researchers in the field of psychoneuroimmunology (PNI) and energy healing suggest that as much as 85 percent of illness and disease is not only associated with stress, but is also causally linked. Anyone who has ever suffered a tension headache knows intuitively how strong the mind-body connection really is. Today, it is well documented that stress aggravates several health conditions, notably type II diabetes, for example. Furthermore, many diseases are now thought to have an autoimmune component to them, such as lupus, fibromyalgia, Epstein-Barr, rheumatoid arthritis, and type I diabetes. The list of stress-related illness continues to grow, from herpes and hemorrhoids to the common cold, cancer, and practically everything in between. Pharmaceuticals and surgery are the two tools of trade used in Western (allopathic) medicine, yet the trade-offs can include severe side effects. This is one reason why so many people are turning to complementary forms of alternative healing for chronic health problems. Every stress management technique is a form of complementary medicine.

Prior to the discovery of vaccinations and antibiotics, the leading cause of death was infectious diseases. Today the leading causes of death are lifestyle diseases (e.g., cancer, diabetes, obesity, strokes, and coronary heart disease), all of which have an undesirable stress component to them. The Western model of health care (which some people label "sick care") places a strong focus on symptomatic relief rather than prevention and healing restoration. As we are now learning, the most advantageous approach appears to combine the best of allopathic and holistic healing to address both the causes and symptoms of stress and return one to homeostasis, turning the battleground into a peaceful landscape. Exercise 2.1 is a personal stress inventory to help you determine any association between stress and symptoms of stress in your body.

Stress and Chronic Pain

In addition to issues related to chronic disease, an increasing number of Americans suffer from debilitating chronic pain, ranging from bothersome discomfort to complete immobility. Muscular pain associated with the lower back, hips, shoulders, and neck is a constant nightmare, so much so that it can steal your attention away from practically everything you try to focus on. The connection between stress and chronic pain cannot be ignored. Neither can the connection between stress and obesity. All of these factors are tightly integrated. Perhaps as no surprise, many of the coping and relaxation techniques in the toolkit of holistic stress management that are used to maintain health and well-being are well-documented means to help restore a sense of homeostasis for chronic pain as well.

Your Human Space Suit

Renowned inventor and philosopher Buckminster Fuller once said that the human body is our one and only space suit in which to inhabit the planet Earth. It comes with its own oxygen tank, metabolic waste removal system, a sensory detector system to enjoy all the pleasures of planetary exploration, and an immune defense system to ensure the health of the wearer in the occasional harsh environments. This specially designed space suit also is equipped with a unique program for self-healing. Factors associated with this self-healing process are enhanced by the basic common health behaviors associated with longevity: regular physical exercise, proper nutrition, adequate sleep, the avoidance of drugs, and a supportive community of friends and family. Unfortunately, most people don't take good care of their space suits, and under the influence of stress, many have forgotten the means to activate the program for self-healing.

Fight or Flight with a Bite

The fight-or-flight response may begin with a perception in the mind, but this thought process quickly becomes a series of neurological and chemical reactions in the body. In the blink of an eye, the nervous system releases epinephrine and norepinephrine throughout the body for immediate blood redistribution and muscle contraction. At the same time a flood of hormones prepares the body for immediate and long-term metabolic survival. Similar to the cascade of a waterfall, hormones are secreted from the brain's pituitary and hypothalamus glands as messengers, moving quickly downstream to the adrenal glands (cone-shaped organs that sit atop each kidney). Upon command, cortisol, aldosterone, and other glucocorticoids infiltrate the bloodstream to do their jobs, all in the name of physical survival.

What works well for short-term hassles can cause serious problems with long-term issues. Repeated synthesis and release of these stress hormones day after day can literally wreak havoc on the physical body. In essence, the body becomes the battlefield for the war games of the mind.

Gross Anatomy and Physiology

Your body is composed of a network of several amazing systems that work together as an alliance for the necessary functions of all daily life activities. For centuries, these aspects were identified as nine separate systems existing within the anatomical structure of the human body. Now most health experts agree (through the wisdom of PNI) that the body is truly one system, with the whole always being greater than the sum of the parts. The parts include the musculoskeletal system, nervous system, cardiovascular system, pulmonary system, endocrine system, reproductive system, renal system, digestive system, and the immune system. If you have a health problem with one of these systems, very quickly all other systems become directly affected. In union with this "one system" are the many anatomical organs responsible for the integrity of their work, including the heart, lungs, kidneys, liver, stomach, pancreas, brain, and lymph nodes. Physical well-being is often described as the optimal functioning of all of these physiological systems.

What comes to mind when you hear the expression "the picture of health"? For most people this conjures up an image of a physically fit person consistently enjoying some rigorous outdoor activity well into his or her later years. Unfortunately, this has now become an image to which few people can relate. Stress can not only affect the optimal functioning of all of these physiological systems to tarnish if not destroy the picture of health, but can also literally shut down the entire body. Simply stated: Left unresolved, stress kills! Exercise 2.2 is a questionnaire that brings to your attention the health habits that make a composite of your health picture.

Subtle Anatomy and Physiology

Equally important, yet often less obvious than gross anatomy, are three other systems critical to the operations of the human space suit. These are more commonly known as *subtle anatomy and physiology* and comprise the human energy field, the meridian system, and the chakra system. A holistic perspective of health would be incomplete without mention of this aspect of health. The following is a more detailed look at the aspects of our subtle anatomy and physiology.

The Human Energy Field

Western science has recently discovered that the human body has a unique field of electromagnetic energy that not only surrounds but permeates the entire body. Often called the *human aura* by mystics, it is the basis of Kirlian photography and of the diagnosis of disease through magnetic resonance imaging (MRI). Ageless wisdom notes that there are many layers of the human energy field, with each layer associated with some aspect of consciousness (e.g., instinct, intellect, intuition, emotions). This and other scientific findings support the timeless premise that our mind isn't located in our body. Instead, our body is located in our mind!

Each layer of consciousness in the human energy field is considered a harmonic vibration. Like keys on a piano keyboard, the frequency of the body's vibration and those of the emotional, mental, and spiritual fields are set at different octaves, yet are within the harmonic range of each other. If a thought coupled with an emotion is left unresolved, it can cause dissonance or imbalance within the layers of energy in the aura. Distortion first appears in the aura outside the physical body. When left unresolved, these emotional frequencies cascade through the layers of energy (which include the chakras and meridians) to pool within various cell tissues. The end result is dysfunction of the corresponding area in the physical body. Dissonance (the opposite of resonance) eventually appears at the cellular level, and the once-harmonic vibration is no longer tuned to homeostasis, hence setting the stage for disease and illness.

Medical intuitives such as Dr. Mona Lisa Schultz, Dr. Judith Orloff, Caroline Myss, Donna Eden, Mietck Wirkus, and others describe the initial stage of illness and disease as unresolved emotions (e.g., anger or fear). In this model of well-being, disease develops outside the body and filters down through the layers of energy. Ironically, physical symptoms in the body are not the first signs of illness, but the last. The body, indeed, becomes the battlefield for the war games of the mind.

The Meridian System

The physical body holds 12 rivers (*meridians*) of energy or chi, which were first brought to the world's attention by the ancient Chinese. Each meridian connects to one or more vital organs (e.g., heart, lungs, liver, kidneys). When energy is blocked or congested in any meridian, the health of the associated organ will suffer. Acupuncture is the primary modality used to ensure the free flow of energy through these meridians, by placing tiny bulblike needles at various gates (acupuncture points) along the meridian pathways to unblock energy congestion. Acupressure (also known as *shiatsu*) is another method used for energy regulation. Although Western medicine doesn't quite acknowledge the concept of chi or meridians, it does recognize the many remarkable outcomes of acupuncture (without side effects, no less) in the treatment of chronic illnesses for which Western medicine itself has proven less than effective.

The Chakra Energy System

The human body is said to have seven major energy portals. The ancient Sanskrit word for these energy portals is *chakra*, which translates to mean "spinning wheel." Chakras look like small tornadoes attached to various organs in the body. Like the meridian energy system, each chakra is associated with the health of vital organs specific to the region to which it's attached. When the chakra shows signs of congestion or distortion, then the life force of energy through the chakra cannot be maintained in its specific region. Ultimately, the health of these organs is greatly compromised. Each chakra is not only associated with a body region, but with a layer of consciousness in the human energy field as well, directly linking mind, body, and spirit. Exercise 2.3 explores the concept of chakras and your health status.

The science behind subtle energy provides valuable insight into a problem that has vexed Western health experts who study the area of stress and disease—specifically, why is it that two people who go through a similar stressful experience can contract different chronic illnesses? The answer may appear to be strongly associated with the dynamics of the chakra energy system. The following is a brief summary of the seven primary chakras.

First Chakra.   The first chakra is commonly known as the *root chakra* and is located at the base of the spine. The root chakra is associated with issues of safety and security. There is also a relationship with our connectedness to the earth and feelings of groundedness. The root chakra is tied energetically to some organs of the reproductive system, as well as the hip joints, lower back, and pelvic area. Health problems in these areas, including lower-back pain, sciatica, rectal difficulties, and some cancers (e.g., prostate) are thought to correspond to disturbances with the root chakra. The root chakra is also known as the seat of the Kundalini energy, a spiritually based concept yet to be understood in Western culture.

Second Chakra.   The second chakra is also known as the *sacral chakra*, located two inches below the belly button. It is recognized as being associated with the sex organs, as well as with personal power in terms of business and social relationships. The second chakra deals with emotional feelings associated with issues of sexuality and self-worth. When self-worth is viewed through external means such as money, job, or sexuality, this causes an energy distortion in this region. Obsessiveness with material gain is thought to be a means to compensate for low self-worth and is hence a distortion to this chakra as well. Common symptoms associated with this chakra region may include menstrual difficulties, infertility, vaginal infections, ovarian cysts, impotency, lower-back pain, prostrate problems, sexual dysfunction, slipped discs, and bladder and urinary infections.

Third Chakra.   Located in the upper stomach region, the third chakra is also known as the *solar plexus chakra*. Energetically, this chakra feeds into the organs of the gastrointestinal (GI) tract, including the abdomen, small intestine, colon, gallbladder, kidneys, liver, pancreas, adrenal glands, and spleen. Not to be confused with self-worth, the region of the third chakra is associated with self-confidence, self-respect, acceptance, and empowerment. The wisdom of the solar plexus chakra is more commonly known as a gut feeling, an intuitive sense closely tied to our level of personal power, as exemplified in the expression "This doesn't feel right." Blockages to this chakra are thought to be related to ulcers, cancerous tumors, diabetes, hepatitis, anorexia, bulimia, and all stomach-related problems. Issues of unresolved anger and fear are deeply connected to organic dysfunction in this body region.

Fourth Chakra.   The fourth chakra is affectionately known as the *heart chakra* and is considered to be one of the most important energy centers of the body. The heart chakra represents the ability to express love. Like a symbolic heart placed over the organic heart, the feelings of unresolved anger or expressions of conditional love work to congest the heart chakra, which in turn has a corresponding effect on the anatomical heart (atherosclerosis), as noted by renowned cardiologist Dean Ornish. The heart, however, is not the only organ closely tied to the heart chakra. Other organs include the lungs, breasts, and esophagus. Symptoms of a blocked heart chakra can include heart attacks, enlarged heart, asthma, allergies, lung cancer, bronchial difficulties, circulation problems, breast cancer, and problems associated with the upper back and shoulders. Also, an important association exists between the heart chakra and the thymus gland. The thymus gland, so instrumental in the making of T cells, shrinks with age.

Fifth Chakra.   The fifth chakra lies above the fourth chakra and is connected to the throat. Organs associated with the *throat chakra* are the thyroid, parathyroid glands, mouth, vocal chords, and trachea. As a symbol of communication, the throat chakra represents the development of personal expression, creativity, purpose in life, and willpower. The inability to express oneself in feelings or creativity or to freely exercise one's will inevitably distorts the flow of energy to the throat chakra and is thought to result in chronic sore throat problems, temporomandibular joint dysfunction, mouth sores, stiffness in the neck area, thyroid dysfunction, migraines, and even cancerous tumors in this region.

Sixth Chakra.   The sixth chakra is more commonly known as the *brow chakra* or the *third eye*. This chakra is associated with intuition and the ability to access the ageless wisdom or bank of knowledge in the depths of universal consciousness. As energy moves through the dimension of universal wisdom into this chakra it promotes the development of intelligence and reasoning skills. Directly tied to the pituitary and pineal gland, this chakra feeds energy to the brain for information processing. Unlike the solar plexus chakra, which is responsible for gut-level intuition regarding personal matters, the wisdom channeled through the brow chakra is more universal in nature, with implications for the spiritual aspect of life. Diseases caused by dysfunction of the brow chakra (e.g., brain tumors, hemorrhages, blood clots, blindness, comas, depression, and schizophrenia) may be caused by an individual's not wanting to see something that is extremely important to his or her soul-growth process.

Seventh Chakra.   If the concept of chakras is foreign to the Western mind, then the seventh chakra may hold promise to bridge East and West. Featured most predominantly in the Judeo-Christian culture through paintings and sculptures as the halo over saintly beings, the seventh chakra, also known as the *crown chakra,* is associated with matters of the soul and the spiritual quest. When the crown chakra is open and fully functioning, it is known to access the highest level of consciousness. Although no specific disease or illness may be associated with the crown chakra, in truth, every disease has a spiritual significance.

Although not everyone can see the human energy field, meridians, or chakras, you can be trained to do so. Exercise 2.4, "Energy Ball Exercise," is an introductory session to the perception of the human energy field. Exercise 2.5, "Subtle Energy System Vitamins," includes several ideas for maintaining a healthy flow of personal energy.

Stress and the Immune System

It's no surprise to learn that under chronic stress, the immune system is greatly compromised, beginning with the immunoglobins in the saliva down to the natural killer cells that scan the body for unwanted pathogens and mutant cancer cells. Chances are that if you were to look back to the most recent time you became ill, right before it (days, even weeks) you would find a stressful experience that triggered a cascade of unresolved stress emotions and washed a flood of stress hormones through your body.

What physiological factors are responsible for a suppressed immune system? At first, the finger was pointed at the central nervous system (e.g., epinephrine and norepinephrine). Then attention soon turned to cortisol, the stress hormone secreted by the adrenal glands responsible for a host of metabolic survival activities. Apparently, when cortisol gets done with its fight-or-flight duties, for some unknown reason it has a nasty habit of attacking and destroying white blood cells, the frontline defense of the immune system. Recent research suggests that cortisol is not the only culprit when it comes to an immune system compromised by stress. Landmark research by Candace Pert and others determined that various neuropeptides, secreted by the brain and other cells in the body, are triggered by emotional responses. Pert calls these "molecules of emotion," and they can either enhance or detract from the efficacy of the immune system. In essence, thoughts are energy; they can kill or heal.

Through the lens of holistic wellness, it is important to realize that the immune system does not reside solely in the body. The aspects of consciousness that comprise your subtle anatomy also constitute your immune system.

The Stress and Disease Connection

Through the eyes of Western science, which views each human being as a machine, stress is often described as "wear and tear" of the physical body. Like a car that has over 200,000 miles, the body is viewed as having parts that typically break down and need to be fixed or replaced. In this paradigm, these parts are often called *target organs,* because they seem to be specifically targeted by neurochemical pathways produced by chronic stress. Any organ can be a target organ: hair, skin, blood vessels, joints, muscles, stomach, colon, and so on. In some people, one organ may be targeted, whereas in others, many organs might be affected. We'll first take a look at disease and illness from a Western perspective and then conclude with a holistic view of the healing system.

Western science has categorized stress-related disorders into two classifications: nervous system–related disorders and immune system–related disorders. It's good to understand this perspective when employing the techniques of mental imagery, art therapy, and self-regulation. The following is a brief listing of chronic diseases from each of these two categories.

Nervous System–Related Disorders

Tension Headaches.   Tension headaches are produced by contractions of the muscles of the forehead, eyes, neck, and jaw. Increased pain results from increased contraction of these muscles. (Lower-back pain can also result from the same process.)

Migraine Headaches.   A migraine headache is a vascular headache. Symptoms can include a flash of light followed by intense throbbing, dizziness, and nausea. Migraines are associated with the inability to express anger and frustration.

Temporomandibular Joint Dysfunction.   Excessive contraction of the jaw muscles can lead to a phenomenon called *temporomandibular joint dysfunction,* or TMJD. In many cases, people are unaware that they have this illness because the behavioral damage (grinding one's teeth) occurs during sleep. Like migraines, TMJD is often associated with the inability to express feelings of anger.

Bronchial Asthma.   Bronchial asthma is an illness in which a pronounced secretion of bronchial fluids causes a swelling of the smooth-muscle tissue of the large air passageways (bronchials). The onset of asthmatic attacks is often associated with anxiety.

Irritable Bowel Syndrome (IBS).   IBS is characterized by repeated bouts of abdominal pain or tenderness, cramps, diarrhea, nausea, constipation, and excessive flatulence. One reason IBS is considered so directly related to stress is that the hypothalamus, which controls appetite regulation (hunger and satiety), is closely associated with emotional regulation as well.

Coronary Heart Disease (CHD).   Elevated blood pressure (hypertension) is a significant risk factor for CHD. Stress hormones are often responsible for increasing blood pressure. When pressure is increased in a closed system, the risk of damage to vascular tissue due to increased turbulence is significantly increased. This damage to the vessel walls appears as small microtears, particularly in the intimal lining of the coronary heart vessels, which supply the heart muscle (myocardium) itself with oxygen. As a way of healing these tears, several constituents floating in the blood bind with the damaged vascular cell tissue. Paradoxically, the primary "healing" agent is a sticky substance found floating in the blood serum called *cholesterol,* resulting in atherosclerosis that can eventually lead to a heart attack.

Immune System–Related Disorders

The Common Cold and Influenza.   Stress hormones (specifically cortisol) tend to destroy members of the white blood cell family, suppressing the immune system and hence leaving one susceptible to colds and flu.

Allergies.   An allergic reaction is initiated when a foreign substance (e.g., pollen, dust spores) enters the body. However, in some people, allergic reactions can occur just by thinking about a stimulus that provoked a previous attack. Allergic reactions are also more prevalent and severe in people who are prone to anxiety.

Rheumatoid Arthritis.   Rheumatoid arthritis, a joint and connective tissue disease, occurs when synovial membrane tissue swells, causing the joint to become inflamed. In time, synovial fluid may enter cartilage and bone tissue, causing further deterioration of the affected joint(s). The severity of arthritic pain is often related to episodes of stress, particularly suppressed anger.

Ulcers and Colitis.   Over 75 percent of ulcers are caused by the bacteria known as *Helicobacter,* creating an open wound that stomach acids only worsen. Treatment with antibiotics is now shown to be highly effective for a large percentage of people who have ulcers, yet two questions remain: What makes some people more vulnerable to the *Helicobacter* bacterium than others? and Why are antibiotics only effective in 75 percent of the cases of people with ulcers? Stress (in the form of anger) is considered to be one answer.

Cancer.   Cancer has proved to be one of the most perplexing diseases of our time, affecting one of every three Americans. The body typically produces an abnormal cell about every 6 hours, but the immune system (e.g., natural killer cells) roams the body to search and destroy these mutant cells. Stress hormones tend to suppress the immune system, allowing some mutant cells to become cancerous tumors. Stress emotions also trigger various neuropeptides to suppress the immune system.

The Dynamics of Self-Healing

All things being equal, the body craves homeostasis and will do all it can to maintain a sense of balance. The body has a remarkable ability to heal itself—when given the chance to do so. Exercise and nutrition play an essential role in the healing process, but so do our thoughts and feelings. Ultimately, disease, in all its many forms, is a sign that something is clearly out of balance. Chronic illness suggests that the body's attempt to regain that inner balance is compromised, most likely by lifestyle behaviors and belief systems that don't support the healing process.

In his book *Spontaneous Healing,* Dr. Andy Weil documents the unique self-healing process of the human body, from the body's wisdom in killing germs by raising the body's core temperature to the role of a specific enzyme (polymerase I) in repairing damaged DNA. Deepak Chopra approaches the topic in a similar way in his book *Quantum Healing.* Chopra explains that every cell in the body regenerates itself—some within a matter of days, others in years. The life span of red blood cells, for instance, is approximately 37 days. Nerve cells, it seems, take the longest. We know now that even brain cells have the capacity to regenerate. Consequently, within a seven-year time period, you have a completely new body of cells.

Most cancerous tumors take years, even decades, to grow. So why is it that with a new body, we still have old tumors? Perhaps the answer resides in the vibrations of consciousness that surround and permeate each and every cell and which get passed on from generation to generation of cells through a process called *entrainment.* Entrainment is a physics term used to describe sympathetic resonance between two objects. It's commonly known in physics circles as the law of conservation of energy. The classic example of human entrainment is observed when women who live or work together begin to see a synchronization of their menstrual periods. Where there are neighboring energies, there is entrainment as well. Every cell vibrates with energy, as do tumors.

Conventional wisdom states that only brain cells hold some level of consciousness, but it now appears that every cell in the body contains a vibration of consciousness. It is suggested that this imprint of conscious frequency is then transferred via entrainment from cell to cell, thus allowing a tumor to develop and keep growing long after the original mutant cells have died off. Can changes in one's thoughts change the vibration of cells? The answer appears to be yes, in a critical mass of people—those who demonstrate "spontaneous remission."

Which emotions are prone to compromise the integrity of the immune system? In simplest terms, any lingering unresolved emotion associated with the fight-or-flight response. It would not be too hard to single out anger and fear as the main culprits; however, both of these serve as umbrellas for literally hundreds of other emotions, which, along with joy, love, and happiness, constitute the full spectrum of feelings. As was mentioned earlier, when used properly, none of these emotions is bad, not even anger or fear. However, when left unresolved, anger, or fear and all the many ways in which these two survival emotions manifest, will suppress the immune system over time. In doing so, these emotions open the door wide to a multitude of health-related problems.

Just as a preponderance of unhealthy emotions can suppress the immune system, so positive thoughts and feelings can enhance it. Although all aspects of the inherent self-healing program are not fully understood, one thing is clear: Effective coping skills that help to resolve the causes of stress in tandem with effective relaxation skills that strive to return the body to homeostasis offer the best opportunity to engage the healing process to its fullest potential.

Additional Resources

Chopra, D. *Quantum Healing*. New York: Bantam Books, 1989.
Eden, D. *Energy Medicine*. New York: Tarcher/Putnam, 1998.
Gerber, R. *Vibrational Medicine,* 3rd ed. Rochester, VT: Bear & Co., 2001.
McTaggart, L. *The Field*. New York: Harper Collins, 2002.
Ornish, D. *Love and Survival*. New York: Harper Collins, 1998.
Pert, C. *Molecules of Emotion*. New York: Scribner Books, 1997.
Sarno, J. *The Mindbody Prescription*. New York: Warner Books, 1999.
Weil, A. *Spontaneous Healing*. New York: Knopf Books, 1997.

Exercise 2.1 Physical Symptoms Questionnaire

Please look over this list of stress-related symptoms and circle how often they have occurred in the past week, how severe they seemed to you, and how long they lasted. Then reflect on the past week's workload and see if you notice any connection between your stress levels and possible stress-related symptoms.

		How Often? (number of days in the past week)	How Severe? (1 = mild, 5 = severe)	How Long? (1 = 1 hour, 5 = all day)
1.	Tension headache	0 1 2 3 4 5 6 7	1 2 3 4 5	1 2 3 4 5
2.	Migraine headache	0 1 2 3 4 5 6 7	1 2 3 4 5	1 2 3 4 5
3.	Muscle tension (neck and/or shoulders)	0 1 2 3 4 5 6 7	1 2 3 4 5	1 2 3 4 5
4.	Muscle tension (lower back)	0 1 2 3 4 5 6 7	1 2 3 4 5	1 2 3 4 5
5.	Joint pain	0 1 2 3 4 5 6 7	1 2 3 4 5	1 2 3 4 5
6.	Cold	0 1 2 3 4 5 6 7	1 2 3 4 5	1 2 3 4 5
7.	Flu	0 1 2 3 4 5 6 7	1 2 3 4 5	1 2 3 4 5
8.	Stomachache	0 1 2 3 4 5 6 7	1 2 3 4 5	1 2 3 4 5
9.	Stomach/abdominal bloating/distention/gas	0 1 2 3 4 5 6 7	1 2 3 4 5	1 2 3 4 5
10.	Diarrhea	0 1 2 3 4 5 6 7	1 2 3 4 5	1 2 3 4 5
11.	Constipation	0 1 2 3 4 5 6 7	1 2 3 4 5	1 2 3 4 5
12.	Ulcer flare-up	0 1 2 3 4 5 6 7	1 2 3 4 5	1 2 3 4 5
13.	Asthma attack	0 1 2 3 4 5 6 7	1 2 3 4 5	1 2 3 4 5
14.	Allergies	0 1 2 3 4 5 6 7	1 2 3 4 5	1 2 3 4 5
15.	Canker/cold sores	0 1 2 3 4 5 6 7	1 2 3 4 5	1 2 3 4 5
16.	Dizzy spells	0 1 2 3 4 5 6 7	1 2 3 4 5	1 2 3 4 5
17.	Heart palpitations (racing heart)	0 1 2 3 4 5 6 7	1 2 3 4 5	1 2 3 4 5
18.	TMJD	0 1 2 3 4 5 6 7	1 2 3 4 5	1 2 3 4 5
19.	Insomnia	0 1 2 3 4 5 6 7	1 2 3 4 5	1 2 3 4 5
20.	Nightmares	0 1 2 3 4 5 6 7	1 2 3 4 5	1 2 3 4 5
21.	Fatigue	0 1 2 3 4 5 6 7	1 2 3 4 5	1 2 3 4 5
22.	Hemorrhoids	0 1 2 3 4 5 6 7	1 2 3 4 5	1 2 3 4 5
23.	Pimples/acne	0 1 2 3 4 5 6 7	1 2 3 4 5	1 2 3 4 5
24.	Cramps	0 1 2 3 4 5 6 7	1 2 3 4 5	1 2 3 4 5
25.	Frequent accidents	0 1 2 3 4 5 6 7	1 2 3 4 5	1 2 3 4 5
26.	Other (please specify)_____	0 1 2 3 4 5 6 7	1 2 3 4 5	1 2 3 4 5

Score

Look over this entire list. Do you observe any patterns or relationships between your stress levels and your physical health? A value over 30 points most likely indicates a stress-related health problem. If it seems to you that these symptoms are related to undue stress, they probably are. Although medical treatment is advocated when necessary, the regular use of relaxation techniques may lessen the intensity, frequency, and duration of these episodes.

Exercise 2.2   Your Picture of Health

We all have an idea of what ideal health is. Many of us take our health for granted until something goes wrong to remind us that our picture of health is compromised and less than ideal. Although health may seem to be objective, it will certainly vary from person to person over the entire aging process. The following statements are based on characteristics associated with longevity and a healthy quality of life (none of which considers any genetic factors). Rather than answering the questions to see how long you may live, please complete this inventory to determine your current picture of health.

3 = Often	2 = Sometimes	1 = Rarely	0 = Never			
1.	With rare exception, I sleep an average of 7 to 8 hours each night.		3	2	1	0
2.	I tend to eat my meals at the same time each day.		3	2	1	0
3.	I keep my bedtime consistent every night.		3	2	1	0
4.	I do cardiovascular exercise at least three times per week.		3	2	1	0
5.	My weight is considered ideal for my height.		3	2	1	0
6.	Without exception, my alcohol consumption is in moderation.		3	2	1	0
7.	I consider my nutritional habits to be exceptional.		3	2	1	0
8.	My health status is considered excellent, with no preexisting conditions.		3	2	1	0
9.	I neither smoke nor participate in the use of recreational drugs.		3	2	1	0
10.	I have a solid group of friends with whom I socialize regularly.		3	2	1	0

Total Score ☐☐☐☐

Score

26–30 points	Excellent health habits
20–25 points	Moderate health habits
14–19 points	Questionable health habits
0–13 points	Poor health habits

Exercise 2.3 Subtle Anatomy Energy Map

The accompanying figure is an outline of the human body highlighted with the seven primary chakras. Note the body region associated with each chakra and then take a moment to identify any health issues or concerns associated with this specific region of your body. Once you have done this, refer back to pages 12–14 and ask yourself honestly if you happen to recognize any connection between the important aspects of the chakra(s) associated with the region(s) you have indicated and a specific health concern.

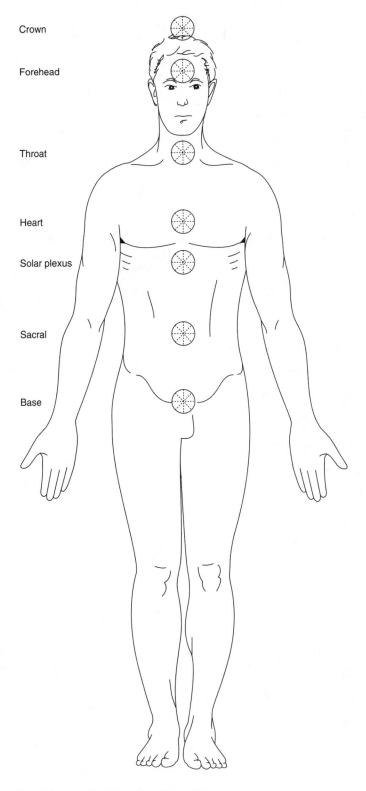

Crown

Forehead

Throat

Heart

Solar plexus

Sacral

Base

Chakras	Body Region	Health Issue

Exercise 2.4 Energy Ball Exercise

This relaxation technique was taught to me by the renowned bio-energy healers Mietek and Margaret Wirkus. I have adapted and taught this technique many times in classes and workshops throughout the country with great success. Although it was introduced to me as the first of many healing techniques in bio-energy healing, first and foremost this is a relaxation exercise. This technique is done through the following steps.

1. Begin by sitting comfortably with your legs crossed and your back straight. You may wish to sit up against a wall. In this exercise, it really helps to keep your back straight. Close your eyes and focus your attention on your breathing. Take a moment to clear your mind of distracting thoughts and feelings. Place your attention on your breathing. If it helps to have some soft instrumental music in the background, then try this as well. Sometimes, to set the tone, it helps to think of a happy moment in your life, when you were filled with utter joy. Allow this feeling to resonate within every cell in your body. Then take a couple of comfortably slow, deep breaths to let the feeling be absorbed.

2. Unlike the belly breathing that is typically taught in relaxation workshops, this particular exercise requires that you focus your attention on the upper lobes of your lungs. Take a moment to place your hands on your upper chest to become fully conscious of your upper lungs. Then take five breaths, breathing comfortably slow and deep into your upper lungs.

3. Once you have completed this, place your hands on your knees and repeat this breathing style by taking five slow, deep breaths. As you exhale, repeat this phrase to yourself: "My body is calm and relaxed." As you say this, feel a deep sense of relaxation throughout your body with each exhalation.

4. Next, being fully conscious of your hands resting on your knees or thighs, take five more deep breaths, but this time as you exhale, repeat this phrase to yourself: "I am my hands." With each breath, place all of your concentration, all of your attention, on your hands. Sense what your hands feel like. Are they warm? If so, where? On the palms, fingertips, or backs of your hands? Again remind yourself of the phrase "I am my hands."

5. Using your imagination, picture a small window in the center of each palm, about the size of a dime. Imagine now that as you breathe, air not only comes into your nose or mouth but into your hands as well. If you prefer, you may use the image of light coming into your palms. Imagine that as you inhale, air or light enters your palms and moves up your arms, to the center (heart space) of your upper chest. As you exhale, feel the energy return from where it entered through your hands. Try repeating this several times, again taking several slow, deep breaths and repeating to yourself, "I am my hands."

6. Next, slowly lift your hands off your knees or thighs so that they rest comfortably in the air, suspended in front of your chest, with the palms face open, toward the ceiling.

7. Next, fully conscious of your hands, take five more deep breaths. As you exhale each breath, repeat the phrase "I am my hands." With each breath, place all of your concentration, all of your attention, on your hands. Again sense what your hands feel like. Are they warm? If so, where? On the palms, the fingertips, the backs of your hands? Do your hands feel heavy? If so, how heavy? What other sensations do you feel? Again remind yourself as you exhale, "I am my hands." As you do this, notice if you see any colors.

8. Now, keeping your hands about 10 to 12 inches apart, allow the palms of each hand to face each other. Again using your imagination, picture or sense that between your hands is a large sponge ball. As you hold this ball, slowly press in and then release. What do you feel as you do this? Again, bring your hands closer together without touching, then begin to separate them farther apart. Ask yourself, what do I feel? At what distance is the sensation the strongest?

9. Now, placing the palms of your hands about 6 to 12 inches apart, imagine that there is a beam of light from palm to palm, window to window. Take a slow, deep breath and as you exhale, slowly compress the beam by slowly bringing your palms together without touching. Then, during the next inhalation, allow your hands to separate again slowly. What do you feel as you do this? Is the sensation between your hands stronger when you inhale or exhale?

10. Again, return to the sensation between your hands. Between your hands is a ball of energy, the healing energy ball. Take this ball of energy and place it into a region of your body that feels stressed or desires healing. If you are completely relaxed, try placing this energy in your heart. Take five slow, deep breaths and repeat the phrase "My body is calm and relaxed." Feel a sense of relaxation throughout your entire body. Take one final slow, deep breath and enjoy this sensation again.

11. When you are done, slowly place your hands back on your knees or thighs. Recognize that although you feel relaxed, you also feel energized. When you are ready, open your eyes to a soft gaze in front of you. Then make yourself aware of your surroundings so that you may continue on with your daily activities.

Exercise 2.5   Subtle Energy System Vitamins

Donna Eden is a renowned energy healer with a gift for, author of *energy medicine,* observing subtle energies. She also teaches others how to regulate their subtle energy for enhanced health and well-being. Integrating the flow of energy through the human aura, chakras, and meridians, Donna combines a variety of self-help techniques so that, in her words, "You keep your energies humming and vibrant." The following are ideas and suggestions that Donna teaches in her energy medicine workshops—exercises that she calls *energy system vitamins.* She recommends that you do this short routine daily.

Three Body Taps
There are various acupuncture/acupressure points that, when stimulated, will help direct the flow of energy and thus increase your vitality and help boost your immune system.

1. **Chest bone tap:** Gently tap on the top of your chest bone just below where the two clavicles meet for about 15 to 20 seconds. This point is known to acupuncturists as K27 (from points on the kidney meridian).

2. **Thymus gland tap:** Your thymus gland (an important gland of the immune system) resides between your throat and your heart, but the point to tap is in the center of your chest bone about 2 inches below K27. Once you have found this point, tap on it with your fingers for about 15 to 20 seconds.

3. **Spleen points tap:** The spleen is also an essential organ to your immune system. The spleen points are located on the rib cage, directly below your nipples. Once you have found these two points, tap vigorously with your fingers for about 15 to 20 seconds.

Cross-Crawl Movements
To do the cross crawl, first you must understand that the left side of the brain controls the right side of the body, and vice versa. Many people's energies are not vibrant or harmonized due to a lack of neural energy moving from the right to the left or from the left to the right sides of the brain. Poor energy movement is referred to as a *homolateral pattern* and will affect thought processes, coordination, and vitality.

Sitting or standing, raise your right knee and your left arm (you can touch knee to elbow if you'd like). Follow this by raising your left knee and your right arm. Twist your torso so that your arms cross the midpoint of your body. Try this movement pattern for about 30 to 60 seconds.

The Crown Pull
Placing your hand on top of your forehead and crown of the head, imagine that your fingers are pulling from the center down to your ears, in a motion starting from the front of your head and working to the back of your skull. The purpose of this exercise is to move stagnant energy from the top of your head and open the crown chakra. This exercise can be helpful in relieving headaches too.

Zip Up
The central meridian (in the front of your body) can easily become congested, open, or exposed to other's energy. This technique invites you to close your auric field as a means of health and protection. Start by tapping the K27 point again and then reach down to the top of your thighs with your right (or left) hand, take a deep breath, and pull up as if you were pulling up a zipper, clear up to your chin. Repeat this three times. By pulling up, you trace the directional flow of the central meridian and strengthen the flow of energy. This technique is recommended before making speeches or dealing with someone who is very angry.

CHAPTER
3

The Emotions: From a Motivation of Fear to a Motivation of Love

Until you extend the circle of compassion to all living things,
you will not find inner peace.
—Albert Schweitzer, M.D.

Love. Anger. Grief. Happiness. Anxiety. Bliss. Sorrow. Guilt. Mirth. Compassion. Despair. Joy. Emotional well-being can best be described as the ability to feel and express the entire range of human emotions and to control them, not be controlled by them. This may sound like a tall order, but it's not impossible. The spectrum of human emotions spans the continuum from anger to love and everything in between. Humans are thought to be unique among all the earth's creatures in our capacity to exhibit such an array of emotions. This gift comes with a price. We also seem to be the only species on the planet that can become a slave to our emotions and become spiritually immobilized in the process.

Healthy Emotions

Given this definition of emotional well-being, all emotions are considered part of the spectrum. Yet the question begs to be asked: What constitutes a healthy emotion? From a holistic perspective, the expression of all emotions is considered healthy, because to deny the ability to feel and express any emotion suggests a serious emotional imbalance. Each sensation in the spectrum of human emotions is included in the software of the human mind for a reason—to feel and express ourselves in every possible way. The expression of each emotion also allows a release of feelings, or what is more commonly known as a *catharsis*.

Many people consider joy, bliss, euphoria, and love to be the healthy emotions, whereas anger and fear are labeled as unhealthy. In truth, anger and fear are also healthy emotions—when they are used specifically for their intended purposes. Both anger and fear are considered to be survival emotions and therefore essential for human life; however, each is only meant to last long enough to get us out of harm's way. Healthy emotions quickly become unhealthy or negative when they last longer than the purpose for which they were meant to serve. Unhealthy emotions appear like a black cloud hanging over our heads. Left unresolved, they can cause serious problems in the mind-body-spirit dynamics of optimal health.

Unhealthy Emotions

Ideally, anger, fear, and all the many ways in which they manifest in the spectrum of human emotions serve one purpose: to protect you. Upon the slightest inkling of danger, they summon the stress alarm to move rapidly into a state of physical survival. Both anger and fear are only meant to last long enough to get a person out of danger, which typically takes seconds, perhaps minutes, but not much longer. When feelings of anger or fear linger longer than the amount of time required to reach a place of safety, then we do not control our emotions—they control us! As such, our emotional well-being is greatly compromised, which in turn affects all components of the wellness paradigm.

When we hang on to feelings of anger or fear rather than letting them go, we literally give our power away. To feel "emotionally drained" is the hallmark of when a healthy emotion becomes unhealthy. Prolonged anger, fear, grief, and depression are not only classic but all too common examples of unhealthy emotions reflected on the faces of Americans almost everywhere today.

The Stress Emotions: Anger and Fear

Simply stated, anger and fear are the two primary stress emotions. Anger is the fight response. Fear is the flight response. Anger is exhibited in a great many ways, including impatience, guilt, envy, indignation, intimidation, intolerance, frustration, rage, prejudice, and hostility. Like anger, the color of fear also comes in many hues, including doubt, embarrassment, anxiety, apprehension, insecurity, and paranoia, to name a few. A quick glance at the headlines on any given day reveals the extreme level of stress in the world, with anger and fear underscoring nearly every news story. From school shootings and suicides to road rage and acts of international terrorism, anger has increasingly become part of the human landscape. For this reason, it merits considerable attention.

Mismanaged Anger Styles

Every episode of anger is the result of an unmet expectation. On average, the typical person gets angry about 15 to 20 times per day. When one realizes how anger can manifest, from impatience to rage, perhaps this number begins to make more sense. Given the number of expectations one has in the course of a day, this number may appear quite low. Although anger can be felt and expressed in a great many ways, there are four specific behavior patterns through which people from all global cultures tend to mismanage their anger. Typically, we tend to exhibit all of these, but it has been noted that one mismanaged anger style often seems to dominate our personality. Please read through this list and note any signs of familiarity.

- **The somatizer:** The somatizer is best described as a person who doesn't express anger. Instead, he or she suppresses it. Unexpressed emotions carry a price, and in this case the body (*soma*) takes a toll of serious physical problems, including migraine headaches, TMJD, ulcers, liver problems, hypertension, and rheumatoid arthritis, to name a few. Women, more than men, tend to be somatizers.

- **The self-punisher:** The self-punisher feels guilty about feeling angry; hence, he or she tends to substitute feelings of anger with some obsessive behavior, including excessive eating, drinking, exercise, shopping, and sex. Sadly, self-mutilators (cutters) also fall in this category.

- **The exploder:** The exploder's main outlet of anger is intimidation. Like a volcano, such people erupt, spewing their hot lava in the direction of the intended threat. Road rage, foul language, acts of violence, and hostility top the list of this mismanaged anger style. Explosive behavior is more common in men, but women can exhibit it as well.

- **The underhander:** Revenge is a motive for some in what they perceive to be considered socially acceptable behavior, particularly at the worksite. Sarcasm is the most common form of underhanded behavior, but there are other passive-aggressive behaviors in this style of mismanaged anger as well.

In each of these mismanaged anger styles, prolonged anger results in people trying to control themselves (somatizer and self-punisher) or others (exploder and underhander). Instead, they are being controlled by their anger and giving their power away. We now know that if we wish to change our behavior, we first have to identify what we are doing so we can learn to behave differently. These mismanaged anger styles are merely labels to help you identify undesirable behaviors associated with unresolved issues. Exercises 3.1 and 3.2 are inventories to help you identify which mismanaged anger style dominates your personality. Exercise 3.3 invites you to think of ways to creatively manage your anger so that you can begin to control it, and not have it control you.

Depression: The Black Cloud of Stress

It's no secret that depression is a huge problem in American culture, with nearly one-third of the population taking prescribed antidepressants. Although there are many factors involved with depression, including an imbalance of the neurochemicals serotonin and dopamine, a holistic approach to stress suggests that there is a strong relationship between an emotional imbalance and chemical imbalance. Is there a connection between depression and anger? Most holistic practitioners believe so. As the joke goes, "Depression is anger without the enthusiasm." Although pharmaceuticals may assist in bringing balance to one's brain chemistry, medications don't heal emotional wounds. As the Food and Drug Administration (FDA) announced in 2004, in some cases they may actually make things worse, including suicidal urges.

Facing Your Fear

Simply stated, fear is a response to physical danger. Rarely in this day and age, however, do we encounter physical danger that requires us to run away and hide. In any such event, the emotion of fear is there in case we do. Self-promoted feelings of fear and worry are extremely prevalent in today's society for reasons that have more to do with a perceived sense of failure, rejection, and fear of the unknown than any real physical danger. Credit card debt, struggling relationships, loss of a job, and terminal illnesses tend to top a long list of common chronic stressors associated with fear and anxiety.

If rational fears are triggered by physical danger, then one might assume that fear under any other prolonged circumstance is irrational. In truth, any fear that is not quickly resolved is often referred to as *unwarranted* or *irrational fear;* this type of fear can certainly become emotionally draining. Unlike anger, which is a very energizing emotion, fear is energy depleting. However, just like unresolved anger, over time, fear can be very toxic to the body.

For fear to be fully resolved, it must be confronted diplomatically. This means that each circumstance where fear surfaces must be faced—without a loss of self-esteem. As the expression goes, "Face your fear and it will disappear." If other people are involved, then the confrontation must not make them defensive or angry, because this will only perpetuate the problem. Big or small, diplomacy is essential with each confrontation. Exercise 3.4, "Confrontation of a Stressor," addresses this issue of making peace with fear.

From a Motivation of Fear Toward a Motivation of Love

One of the primary areas of study in the field of psychology is the aspect of motivational behavior: why we do the things we do. A conclusion by many is that, by and large, most of our behaviors are fear-based thoughts and actions (anger being considered an aspect of fear). This perspective suggests that humans operate from a fight-or-flight response the majority of time. Although this may sound preposterous, a quick glance through the annals of human history supports this theory. From a personal perspective, consider making a habit of observing your thoughts and behaviors to determine the source of motivation behind your actions. You may be quite surprised at the outcome.

Moving from fear to love means responding rather than reacting to stress. It means showing tolerance rather than anger, patience rather than hostility, forgiveness instead of resentment, and humor rather than arrogance. Ultimately, it means not placing yourself first all the time, and viewing the bigger picture with an open heart rather than a closed mind. All humans are capable of this endeavor!

Joy and Happiness: The Other (Eustress) Emotions

As was discussed in Chapter 1, not all stress is bad. Good stress is a necessary part of life, as well as all the emotions associated with it. Joy, happiness, love, compassion, and all the feelings that hearty laughter brings are essential to optimal health. These emotions generate a whole pharmacopoeia of beneficial neuropeptides that enhance the immune system. Emotional well-being is truly a balance of emotional experiences. By not seeking a balance to the full emotional spectrum, with frequent exposure to the emotions associated with good stress, all aspects of our personal wellness paradigm are affected, if not compromised. Therefore, it's in our best interest to seek out the peak experiences, the joyful moments, and the comic relief that give balance to our lives. Moreover, as you will see in later chapters, it is these emotions that, when combined with a host of coping skills and relaxation techniques, create very powerful results.

Additional Resources

Britten, R. *Fearless Living*. Berkeley, CA: Perigee Books, 2001.

Cox., D., Bruckner, K., and Stabb, S. *The Anger Advantage*. New York: Broadway Books, 2003.

Fleeman, W. *Pathways to Peace: Anger Management Workbook*. Alameda, CA: Hunter House, 2003.

Lerner, H. *The Dance of Anger*. New York: Harper & Row, 1985.

Skog, S. *Depression: What Your Body's Trying to Tell You*. New York: Wholecare, 1999.

Tavris, C. *Anger: The Misunderstood Emotion*. New York: Touchstone, 1989.

Warren, N.C. *Make Anger Your Ally*. New York: Simon & Schuster, 1983.

Williams, R. *Anger Kills*. New York: Harper Collins, 1994.

Exercise 3.1 Anger Recognition Checklist

He who angers you, conquers you.
—Elizabeth Kenny

The following is a quick exercise to help you understand how anger can surface in the course of a normal working day and how you *may* mismanage it. Please place a check mark in front of any of the following that apply to you when you "get angry" or "feel frustrated or upset." After completing this section, please estimate, on average, the number of anger episodes you experience per day.

When I feel angry, my anger tends to surface in the following ways:

_____anxious

_____depressed

_____overeat

_____start dieting

_____trouble sleeping

_____excessive sleeping

_____careless driving

_____chronic fatigue

_____abuse alcohol/drugs

_____explode in rage

_____cold withdrawal

_____tension headaches

_____migraine headaches

_____use sarcasm

_____hostile joking

_____accident prone

_____guilty and self-blaming

_____smoke or drink

_____high blood pressure

_____frequent nightmares

_____tendency to harp or nag

_____intellectualize

_____upset stomach
     (e.g., gas, cramps, IBS)

_____muscle tension
     (neck, lower back)

_____swear or name call

_____cry

_____threaten others

_____buy things

_____frequent lateness

_____never feel angry

_____clenched jaw muscles, TMJD

_____bored

_____nausea, vomiting

_____skin problems

_____easily irritable

_____sexual difficulty

_____sexual apathy

_____busy work (clean, straighten)

_____sulk, whine

_____hit, throw things

_____complain, whine

_____cut/mutilate myself

_____insomnia

_____promiscuity

_____help others

_____other _____

My average number of anger episodes per day is _____.

Exercise 3.2 Mismanaged Anger Style Indicator

Part I

Check the statements that are true for you the majority of the time.

_____ 1. Even though I may wish to complain, I usually don't.

_____ 2. When upset, I have a habit of slamming, punching, or breaking things.

_____ 3. When I feel guilty, I have been known to contemplate self-destructive behaviors.

_____ 4. I can be real nice to people, but then back-stab them when they're not around.

_____ 5. I have a habit of grinding my teeth at night.

_____ 6. When I am really irritated or frustrated by others, I tend to intimidate them.

_____ 7. When I am frustrated, I feel like going shopping and spending money.

_____ 8. I can manipulate people without them even knowing it.

_____ 9. It's fair to say that I rarely, if ever, get angry or mad.

_____ 10. I have been known to talk back to people of authority.

_____ 11. Sleeping in is a good way to forget about my problems and frustrations.

_____ 12. Watching TV or playing video games offers a good escape from my frustrations.

_____ 13. If I complain, I feel people won't like me as much, so I usually don't.

_____ 14. When driving at times, I feel like I want to run over people with my car.

_____ 15. When I get mad or frustrated, I have been known to eat to calm my nerves.

_____ 16. I plan a script or rehearse what I am going to say to win a conflict.

_____ 17. It's hard/uncomfortable for me to say the words "I am angry."

_____ 18. I usually try to get the final say in situations with others.

_____ 19. I have been known to use alcohol and/or drugs to deal with my anger feelings.

_____ 20. By and large, I tend to agree with the statement "Don't get mad, get even."

_____ 21. I tend to keep my feelings to myself.

_____ 22. When I get angry, I have been known to swear a lot.

_____ 23. I usually feel guilty about feeling angry, frustrated, or annoyed.

_____ 24. It's OK to use sarcasm to make a point.

_____ 25. I am the kind of person who calms the waters when tempers flare at home or work.

_____ 26. It's easy to say the words "I am angry" or "I am pissed" and really mean it.

_____ 27. On more than one occasion, I have imagined taking my own life.

_____ 28. I think of various ways to put people down.

_____ 29. Typically, I place the needs of others before myself.

_____ 30. I suffer from migraine headaches, TMJD, rheumatoid arthritis, or lupus.

(continued)

Part II: Score Sheet

Write down the numbers of the statements that you checked off in Part I:

_____ .

As a rule, we all tend to engage in all of these behaviors at some time; however, some behaviors are very common to us while others are more occasional, suggesting that when certain predominant behaviors are grouped together they reveal a specific style of mismanaged anger. Mismanaged anger leads to a host of serious problems for both ourselves and others. By learning to recognize series of behaviors that fall into one or perhaps two categories, we can more easily identify this pattern and then make a strategy to change or modify it so that stress is reduced rather than perpetuated. Labels are good to identify behaviors, but they are not meant to serve as mismanaged scarlet letters.

- If you have four or more answers from choices 1, 5, 9, 13, 17, 21, 25, 29, or 30, your mismanaged anger style strongly suggests you might be a somatizer.

- If you have four or more answers from choices 3, 7, 11, 12, 15, 19, 23, or 27, your mismanaged anger style strongly suggests you might be a self-punisher.

- If you have four or more answers from choices 2, 6, 10, 14, 18, 22, or 26, your mismanaged anger style strongly suggests you might be an exploder.

- If you have four or more answers from choices 4, 8, 16, 20, 24, or 28, your mismanaged anger style strongly suggests you might be an underhander.

Exercise 3.2

Exercise 3.3   Creative Anger Management Skills Action Plan

Dealing with anger effectively means working to resolve the issues and expectations that surfaced from the anger episode. There are many ways to creatively resolve anger so that you reclaim your emotional sovereignty. The following is a synthesis of suggestions from a variety of sources. Read through each suggestion and below it write a description of what steps you can implement to creatively manage your anger and keep each episode of anger within a healthy time period.

- Know your anger style. What is your most predominant mismanaged anger style?

_____

_____

- Learn to self-monitor your anger. Reflect on the past day's events (including listening to the news) and estimate the number of times you felt anger.

_____

_____

- Learn to de-escalate your anger. List three ways to let off steam (e.g., leave the room, take a big sigh, count to ten).

  1._____   2._____   3._____

- Learn to out-think your anger. Many times anger results from insufficient information. Identify an anger situation and reprocess the information to neutralize your anger feelings.

_____

_____

- Get comfortable with all your feelings. Some people have a hard time saying the words "I am angry," or "I feel angry."

_____

_____

- Plan in advance. Although avoidance is not advocated, making plans to work around a problem is known as the path of least resistance. Identify a current frustration and then list three things you can do as an action plan to rise above the occasion.

  1._____   2._____   3._____

- Develop a strong support system. List three people to whom you can turn to vent your frustrations as well as listen to as an objective voice regarding your stressful situation.

_____

_____

- Develop realistic expectations for yourself and others. Pick one anger situation you have had today (or yesterday), identify the expectation that wasn't met, and then refine the expectation.

  Unmet expectation: _____

  Refined expectation: _____

- Turn complaints into requests. As the expression goes, you get more flies with honey than vinegar. Script a phrase that you can use to incorporate the magic of request.

_____

_____

- Make past anger pass. Letting go of anger begins with forgiveness. List three people whom you feel have violated you in some way for which the steps of forgiveness need to be taken to bring closure to this situation.

  1._____   2._____   3._____

Exercise 3.4   Confrontation of a Stressor

It happens to us all the time. Someone or something gets us frustrated, and we literally or figuratively head for the hills, either avoiding the person or thing altogether or ignoring the situation in the hope that it will go away. But when we ignore situations like this, they typically come back to haunt us. In the short run, avoidance looks appealing, even safe. But in the long run, it is bad policy—really bad policy! We avoid confrontation because we want to avoid the emotional pain associated with it, the pain our ego suffers. Handled creatively, diplomatically, and rationally, the pain is minimal, and it often helps our spirits grow. After all, this is what life is all about: to achieve our full human potential.

The art of peaceful confrontation involves a strategy of creativity, diplomacy, and grace to ensure that you come out the victor, not the victim. In this sense, *confrontation* doesn't mean a physical battle but rather a mental, emotional, or spiritual battle. Unlike a physical battle where knights wear armor, this confrontation requires that you set aside the shield of your ego long enough to resolve the fear or anger associated with the stressor. The weapons of this confrontation are self-assertiveness, self-reliance, and faith. There is no malice, spite, or deceit involved. Coping mechanisms that aid the confrontation process include, but are not limited to, the following strategies: communication, information seeking, cognitive reappraisal, social engineering, and values assessment and clarification.

We all encounter stressors that we tend to run away from. Now it is time to gather your internal resources and make a plan to successfully confront your stressors. When you initiate this confrontation plan, you will come out the victor with a positive resolution and a feeling of accomplishment. First, reexamine the list of your top ten stressors. Then, select a major stressor to confront and resolve. Prepare a plan of action, and then carry it out. When you return, write about it: what the stressor was, what your strategy was, how it worked, how you felt about the outcome, and perhaps most important, what you learned from this experience.

The Stressor (State the stressor you plan to confront here.)

_____

_____

_____

_____

_____

Action Plan (State your plan of diplomatic confrontation here.)

_____

_____

_____

_____

Emotional Processing (After you have faced your fear, describe here what happened and how you now feel having done this. Also, what did you learn from this experience?)

_____

_____

_____

_____

_____

_____

_____

CHAPTER

4

The Mind: The Psychology of Stress

And yet the mind seems to act independently of the brain in the same sense that the programmer acts independently of the computer.
—Wilder Penfield, *The Mystery of the Mind*

For eons, philosophers, scientists, theologians, and psychologists as well as countless planetary citizens have all wondered, hypothesized, and speculated on the topic of the human mind. What is it? Where is it? How does it work? Why do identical twins have different minds? Where does the mind go when we die? What is a premonition? Can the mind be trained? What is intelligence? What is conscience? How fast can the mind travel? What is a thought? And what thoughts are really mine?

As we begin the 21st century, some scientists are now beginning to confirm what the mystics stated long ago: The mind is a reservoir of conscious energy that surrounds and permeates the human body. From a holistic perspective, the mind and the brain are not the same thing. The mind, the quintessential seat of consciousness, merely uses the brain as its primary organ of choice. New revelations from organ transplant recipients suggest that the mind uses other organs as well. In fact, new research suggests that every cell has consciousness, giving rise to a new term, *cell memory*.

The study of the mind (and the brain) has led to a deeper understanding of human consciousness, yet it's fair to say that despite this vast exploration of dreams, cognitive inventories, hypnosis, meditation, DNA, EEGs, and MRIs, our knowledge, at best, is still embryonic. Current research in the field of consciousness reveals interesting insights about a phenomenon that only grows more fascinating with further study. For example, distant healing, remote viewing, premonitions, synchronicities, near-death experiences, out-of-body experiences, spontaneous healings, and much more only begin to substantiate that mind, as consciousness, is certainly not a simple consequence of brain chemistry, although there are many who still believe this.

This much we do know: Much like a laptop computer, mental well-being is the ability to gather, process, recall, and communicate information. We also know that stress greatly compromises the mind's ability to do all of these functions. Information is constantly gathered and processed through the portals of the five senses for a variety of reasons (from threats to simple curiosity). Yet it's no secret that information also comes into the conscious mind in other ways, including intuition, meditation, and what can only be explained as extrasensory perception. Just as we know that the mind can generate stress without any outside stimulus, so too we know the power of the mind to heal the body. Although no one book can begin to elaborate on the psychology of stress or the secrets to mental well-being, this chapter offers some keen insights into the psychology of stress from renowned leaders in the field who have shared the greatest wisdom to date on the mysteries of the mind.

The Anatomy of Ego

When it comes to the mind, one cannot look at stress without first examining the role of the ego. Many claim that the ego is the cause of both personal and worldly problems, and although this may not be far from the truth, it must also be recognized that the ego is not always bad either. A healthy ego generates high self-esteem. As Freud accurately pointed out, the ego serves the role of protection. It also constitutes one's identity (or as Freud stated, "Id entity"). Perhaps more accurately, the ego is the mind's bodyguard and censor. In an effort to protect you from harm, the ego sounds the alarm of imminent danger from not only physical threats but also mental, emotional, and spiritual threats. Sometimes the ego goes overboard in its role as the mind's bodyguard and blows things completely out of proportion. Experts in the field of psychology call this *cognitive distortion,* and it becomes a real problem when coping with stress.

The ego has many tricks up its sleeve for protection. Freud called these *defense mechanisms:* thoughts and behaviors that act to decrease pain and perhaps even increase pleasure to the mind and body. He said, by and large, that we use more than one at a time and for the most part are not even aware of it. Here is a quick overview of some of the more common defenses of the ego:

- **Denial:** I didn't do it!

- **Repression:** I don't remember doing it!

- **Projection:** He did it!

- **Displacement:** He made me do it!

- **Rationalization:** Everyone does it!

- **Humor:** I did it, and a year from now maybe I'll laugh about this.

At its best, the ego serves as the bodyguard for the mind, body, and soul. At its worst, the ego tries to control and manipulate everything (and perhaps everybody). When ruled by fear and anger, the ego transitions from a place of power to one of control, or what some people refer to as an unhealthy ego. Freud might have been the first person in the West to study this aspect of the mind, but he certainly wasn't the first to acknowledge it. Philosophers as far back as Ancient Greece, India, China, and Tibet often spoke of the mind's shadow side. In Eastern culture, the ego is called the *small mind* (also called the *false self*), and ancient traditions suggest that the best means for mental well-being is to "domesticate" the small mind so that it can work in harmony with the larger mind of the universe. Psychologist Carl Jung described this process as "embracing the shadow." Ultimately, this means moving beyond a motivation of fear toward a motivation of love and compassion, a process that is not impossible, but requires great mental discipline.

In terms of coping with stress rather than using a defense mechanism to avoid it, the holistic approach to stress management suggests following advice from the Eastern tradition by learning to domesticate the ego. Meditation (as discussed in Chapter 15) is the premier skill to accomplish this goal.

The Power of Two Minds

Metaphorically speaking, you have not one, but two minds: the conscious mind and the unconscious mind. The conscious mind is best described as an awareness; it is like that which appears on a computer screen at any one time, and it receives nearly all of the attention of the ego. Conversely, the unconscious mind is analogous of not only all that which appears on the computer's hard drive, but some would say the entire Internet as well. Like an iceberg with nearly 90 percent of its entirety below water, the total mind is vast. It contains a wealth of information that often is never realized, yet is the model for today's typical computer. Unlike the conscious mind, which shuts down when you sleep, the unconscious mind works 24 hours a day, every day of your life. It, too, offers a sense of awareness. The unconscious mind is a container of all your personal memories as well as a reservoir of endless wisdom (Figure 4.1).

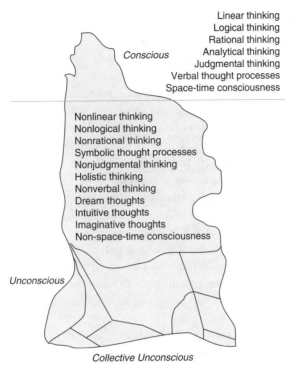

Linear thinking
Logical thinking
Rational thinking
Analytical thinking
Judgmental thinking
Verbal thought processes
Space-time consciousness

Conscious

Nonlinear thinking
Nonlogical thinking
Nonrational thinking
Symbolic thought processes
Nonjudgmental thinking
Holistic thinking
Nonverbal thinking
Dream thoughts
Intuitive thoughts
Imaginative thoughts
Non-space-time consciousness

Unconscious

Collective Unconscious

Figure 4.1

It would be simple if these two minds spoke the same language, but unfortunately this is not the case. Whereas the conscious mind is fluent in verbal skills, linear thinking, judgmental thinking, analytical thinking, rational thinking, and many other cognitive functions that are now associated with the left hemisphere of the brain, the unconscious mind is fluent in intuition, imagination, acceptance, and many other cognitive skills associated with the right brain. Like a virus scanner on your computer, the ego serves in the role of censor and gatekeeper, making sure nothing bubbles up to the surface of the conscious mind that might prove to be a threat. Unfortunately, in this process, much of the wisdom of the unconscious mind never passes through the gates of the ego. In no uncertain terms, stress can be defined as the conflict between the conscious and unconscious minds.

It was Carl Jung, one-time protégé of Sigmund Freud, who began to study the workings of the unconscious mind in earnest, particularly through dream analysis, but also through artwork and other nonverbal means of communication. Jung was of the opinion that if we took the time to learn the language of the unconscious mind, often expressed in archetypal symbols, and, in turn, gathered the wisdom that is there for the asking, then as a whole, we would have a lot less stress in our lives.

Jung was also of the belief that the mind was a gateway to the soul. Anxiety, he suggested, was not merely a consequence of physical survival but an evolutionary process of the human spirit. In other words, when we take the time to learn from our life experiences, then stress offers an opportunity for spiritual growth. The mind and the soul share a common space in the landscape of the human spirit. The word *psyche,* from which the word *psychology* is derived, means "soul." It goes without saying that just as there there is tremendous overlap between the quadrants of mental well-being and emotional well-being, there is the same with spiritual well-being. Carl Jung was quick to note this association when he stated that every crisis over the age of 30 is a spiritual crisis. Jung also noted that although we each have a personal unconscious composed of personal thoughts and memories, we are each connected to a larger reservoir of wisdom that he called the "collective unconscious," where time and space play by different rules. In fact, it was a conversation with Albert Einstein about his theory of relativity that seeded the idea of the collective unconscious in Jung's mind. Much of Jung's work can be found at the roots of many stress management therapies, including dream therapy, mental imagery, and art therapy.

The Death of Expectations

Anger (fight) and fear (flight) make up the two primary stress emotions from which all other stress-related emotions derive. Over the past century, anxiety stole the spotlight, primarily because Freud thought this was the easier of the two instinctual emotions to work with. Meanwhile, anger, in all its many manifestations, began to boil over on the back burner on the world stage, from road rage and the Columbine massacre to child and spouse abuse and international acts of terrorism. First and foremost, every episode of anger, no matter how big or small, is the result of an unmet expectation. Behind every episode of anger (no matter how small) lurk the feelings of remorse and grief.

Death is perhaps the hardest concept for the ego to be reconciled with. In an effort to maintain control, the ego does everything in its power to keep the upper hand. Dr. Elisabeth Kübler-Ross observed the progression of thoughts and behaviors one experiences through one's own personal death and dying process. It has now become such common knowledge that it can be found everywhere from greeting cards to cereal boxes. The stages include the following: denial, anger, bargaining, withdrawal, and acceptance. Grieving is a natural part of the human experience. All of these stages constitute the fine art of grieving. (It should be noted that the stage after acceptance is adaptation.) Prolonged grieving, however, is not healthy and only serves to perpetuate chronic stress, yet many people never move beyond anger to acceptance, a crucial step in the resolution of all stressors.

You don't have to come down with terminal cancer to experience this progression of thought processes. Most likely you experience this same linear process with the death of each expectation, no matter how big or small, whether it's a dent in your new car or the breakup of your marriage. The next time you find yourself angry, ask yourself what expectation wasn't met, and therein may lie the answer to your problem.

Finding the Meaning of Life

There is a wise proverb that states, "Pain is inevitable, suffering is optional." *Suffering* is another word for stress, and chronic stress proves to be quite common for those who find themselves in an existential vacuum, living a life that seems to have no purpose or meaning. Angst is a common plight among those who find themselves retired from a lifelong career, roaming an empty house made vacant by the last teenager to leave home, or mourning the sudden loss of a loved one, or even of Olympic athletes who walk off the podium with a bronze medal. Angst is also common among people who dislike their jobs. Interestingly, more heart attacks occur on Monday mornings than at any other time of the week, suggesting a link between the purposeful meaning of life and one's health. Depression, the hallmark cry of the soul, is a common malady in our stress-filled world.

How can suffering be optional? The voice of ageless wisdom, as echoed by Nazi concentration camp survivor Viktor Frankl in his classic book *Man's Search for Meaning,* suggests that to ease the angst of suffering, one must create a new meaning in one's life. To do this, one must find a new passion, make a new goal or goals, and make a commitment in deciding how to spend one's life energy, rather than letting it drain away. The voice of ageless wisdom advises the weary traveler to acknowledge the past and learn from it, but not dwell on it. Rather, one must set one's eyes on the future, one day at a time, one step at a time, until one regains balance and can move forward on the human journey.

Energy Psychology

Perhaps because the field of psychology has worked so hard to establish its credibility as a hard science, it has stayed clear of all things metaphysical, especially those things regarded as paranormal. However, a handful of maverick scientists and luminaries in the field of psychology have taken the initiative to integrate various aspects of ageless wisdom with many theoretical principles of modern psychology. The result has forged a path with many offshoots of this discipline, starting with humanistic psychology, health psychology, and transpersonal psychology and leading to the emerging field of energy psychology—a field of study that honors the mind-body-spirit dynamics and offers techniques to help counsel patients and clients through a wide range of psychological conditions. The premise of energy psychology is based on the ageless wisdom of the human energy matrix of subtle anatomy, including the auric field (layers of consciousness), chakras, and meridians. By using the human energy grid to detect congestion and distortions associated with mental and emotional disturbances, great gains can be made at the spiritual, mental, emotional, and physical levels to restore one to optimal health.

In the field of energy psychology, just as each layer of the auric field is associated with a specific layer of consciousness, so each of the primary chakras is associated with one or more aspects of one's personality. By recognizing the various aspects of each chakra, one can begin to process and resolve issues that tend to manifest as physical symptoms. (Consider rereading the section on chakras in Chapter 2.)

Stress-Prone and Stress-Resistant Personalities

No discussion of mental well-being would be complete without some discussion of the personality types that make up the collective persona of the human species. It's fair to say that the topic of personalities is as complex as it is popular to discuss and demystify. Personality is composed of attitudes, behaviors, values, philosophies, opinions, belief systems, and perhaps much, much more. Character, a component of one's personality, is often said to be how you behave when no one else is looking. The Myers-Briggs personality type inventory (based on the work of Carl Jung) is one of many personality profiles used to determine and predict how people will get along with each other. The Enneagram personality type is another. Perhaps because there are so many variables, personality assessments still remain more of an art than a science. Nonetheless, they offer keen insight into the complexities of the mind and how we deal with stress.

Whereas hard science points to genetic aspects (nature) that constitute aspects of one's personality, the softer sciences suggest a host of environmental factors (nurture) associated with the make-up of one's thoughts, attitudes, behaviors, and beliefs. Still others add a third dimension, ranging from astrological aspects to spiritual (karmic) considerations—all of which, to some extent, play a part in the complexities of the personality of each individual.

Although using a questionnaire to determine one's personality may be limiting, observations of specific character traits under stressful conditions can be quite revealing. Based on several decades of work, the following personality types have been assessed as being either stress prone or stress resistant.

Stress-Prone Personalities

These personality types not only do poorly in stressful situations, but when combined with periods of low self-esteem, they actually tend to attract more stress into their lives.

Type A.   Once labeled as the impatient personality, Type A behavior is now regarded as actions based on a sense of latent anger that manifests in explosive, competitive, and impetuous behaviors.

Codependent.   The codependent personality is composed of many traits that coalesce as a collective defense mechanism to cope with alcoholic parents or loved ones. The codependent personality is also known in rehabilitation circles as the *enabler*. Approval-seeking super-overachievers with poor boundaries, codependents live with a constant level of fear (primarily the fear of rejection). Exercise 4.1 is an example of a survey to help identify traits associated with this stress-prone personality.

Helpless-Hopeless.   The helpless-hopeless personality style best describes someone who, for whatever reason, has met failure at most every turn (e.g., child abuse, sexual abuse). Self-esteem is at rock bottom, and the individual feels a lack of personal resources to help cope with problems both big and small. Depression and feelings of helplessness and hopelessness are often associated with each other, in what sometimes can be described as a downward spiral.

Stress-Resistant Personalities

These people tend to let small things roll off their backs and to deal with big problems in a very positive way. Exercise 4.2 is an example of a survey to assess your stress-resistant personality traits.

Hardy Personality.   People who exhibit the hardy personality (1) demonstrate commitment to seeing a problem through to resolution, (2) challenge themselves to accomplish a goal or crisis with honor, and (3) control their emotions in a balanced way.

Survivor Personality.   Survivors are true everyday heroes who exhibit a balance of right- and left-brain skills so that problems can be approached creatively and solutions executed with confidence. Additional traits include being flexible, empathetic, playful, optimistic, and very creative.

Calculated Risk Taker.   This personality type is a person who approaches life with courage rather than fear—someone who sees danger and may even thrive on it, but only after surveying all options and choosing the most level-headed approach. Such people are spontaneous but grounded. A streak of thrill-seeking runs through this personality as well.

The evidence is quite clear that changing one's personality is impossible, yet we can begin to change our thoughts, attitudes, beliefs, and perceptions that either influence or negate various personality traits. Although you may demonstrate traits associated with the Type A or the codependent personality, it doesn't mean that you cannot change your thinking patterns to stop those behaviors and adopt stress-resistant traits instead.

The Power of the Mind

Holistic stress management honors the ageless wisdom of the power of the mind—the collective spirit of both conscious and unconscious minds to work in unison, as partners rather than rivals. History is punctuated with unfathomable stories of men and women who have harnessed the power of their minds to perform truly remarkable human feats. Lance Armstrong, six-time winner of the Tour de France; Ernest Shackleton, the captain of the *Endurance;* Rosa Parks, civil rights leader; and Aron Ralston, mountain climber, are but a few of the people who have harnessed the power of their minds to overcome extreme adversity. Their secret of success is really no secret. You too have the means within you to harness the power of your mind to deal with day-to-day stress. Meditation, music therapy, visualization, mental imagery, humor therapy, and positive affirmations are just a few of the many ways that the power of the mind can be disciplined and utilized to not only cope with the stress of life, but rise to one's highest human potential. Exercise 4.3 offers you a unique opportunity to cultivate the powers of your mind.

Additional Resources

Beattie, M. *Codependent No More*. Center City, MN: Hazelden Books, 1992.
Eden, D. *Energy Medicine*. New York: Tarcher/Putnam Books, 1998.
Seligman, M. *Authentic Happiness*. New York: Free Press, 2002.
Shackleton, E. *South: The Last Antarctic Expedition of Shackleton and the* Endurance. New York: Lyons Press, 1919.
Siebert, A. *The Survivor Personality*. New York: Perigee Books, 1996.

Exercise 4.1 Stress-Prone Personality Survey

The following is a survey based on the traits of the codependent personality.

	3 = Often	2 = Sometimes	1 = Rarely		0 = Never		

		3	2	1	0
1.	I tend to seek approval (acceptance) from others (e.g., friends, colleagues, family members).	3	2	1	0
2.	I have very strong perfection tendencies.	3	2	1	0
3.	I am usually involved in many projects at one time.	3	2	1	0
4.	I rise to the occasion in times of crisis.	3	2	1	0
5.	Despite problems with my family, I will always defend them.	3	2	1	0
6.	I have a tendency to put others before myself.	3	2	1	0
7.	I don't feel appreciated for all the things I do.	3	2	1	0
8.	I tend to tell a lot of white lies.	3	2	1	0
9.	I will help most anyone in need.	3	2	1	0
10.	I tend to trust others' perceptions rather than my own.	3	2	1	0
11.	I have a habit of overreacting to situations.	3	2	1	0
12.	Despite great achievements, my self-esteem usually suffers.	3	2	1	0
13.	My family background is better described as victim than victor.	3	2	1	0
14.	I have been known to manipulate others with acts of generosity and favors.	3	2	1	0
15.	I am really good at empathizing with my friends and family.	3	2	1	0
16.	I usually try to make the best impression possible with people.	3	2	1	0
17.	I like to validate my feelings with others' perceptions.	3	2	1	0
18.	I am an extremely well-organized individual.	3	2	1	0
19.	It's easier for me to give love and much more difficult to receive it.	3	2	1	0
20.	I tend to hide my feelings if I know they will upset others.	3	2	1	0

Total Score

Score A score of more than 30 points indicates that you most likely have traits associated with the codependent personality, a personality style known to be stress prone.

Exercise 4.2 Stress-Resistant Personality Survey

The following survey is composed of statements based on the hardy, survivor, and risk-taking personality traits—all of which share common aspects that resist rather than attract or promote stress in one's life.

		4 = Always	3 = Often	2 = Sometimes	1 = Rarely			0 = Never	
1.	I wake up each morning ready to face a new day.			4	3	2	1	0	
2.	I tend not to let fear run my life.			4	3	2	1	0	
3.	I would consider myself to be an optimist.			4	3	2	1	0	
4.	I tend to see "problems" as opportunities for personal growth and success.			4	3	2	1	0	
5.	Although I like to be in control of my fate, I know when to go with the flow when things are out of my control.			4	3	2	1	0	
6.	Curiosity is one of my stronger attributes.			4	3	2	1	0	
7.	Life isn't always fair, but I still manage to enjoy myself.			4	3	2	1	0	
8.	When things knock me off balance, I am resilient and get back on my feet quickly.			4	3	2	1	0	
9.	My friends would say that I have the ability to turn misfortune into luck.			4	3	2	1	0	
10.	I believe that if you don't take risks, you live a boring life and won't get far.			4	3	2	1	0	
11.	I like to think of myself as being a creative person.			4	3	2	1	0	
12.	I believe in the philosophy that "one person truly can make a difference."			4	3	2	1	0	
13.	I am both organized and flexible with my life's day-to-day schedule.			4	3	2	1	0	
14.	Sometimes having nothing to do is the best way to spend a day.			4	3	2	1	0	
15.	I trust that I am part of a greater force of life in the universe.			4	3	2	1	0	
16.	I believe in the philosophy that "you make your own breaks."			4	3	2	1	0	
17.	I approach new situations with the idea that I will learn something valuable, regardless of the outcome.			4	3	2	1	0	
18.	When I start a project, I see it through to its successful completion.			4	3	2	1	0	
19.	I am strong willed, which I see as a positive characteristic to accomplish hard tasks.			4	3	2	1	0	
20.	I am committed to doing my best in most everything in life.			4	3	2	1	0	

Total Score

Score A score of more than 30 points indicates that you most likely have traits associated with the hardy, survivor, and calculated risk-taker personalities, personality types known to be stress resistant.

Exercise 4.3   Mind over Matter: Harnessing the Power of Your Mind

Spoon bending may seem to be in a different league than the spontaneous remission of a cancerous tumor, but in reality, the premise of each is the same. Most likely you've heard the expression "mind over matter," yet few people actually put this philosophy into play. Mind over matter simply means using the power of your mind (both conscious and unconscious minds) to accomplish a task. Mind over matter isn't a means to control others. Conversely, it's a means of becoming empowered rather than giving your power away. Those who teach mind power often use the spoon-bending exercise as the first stepping stone toward the goal of other, seemingly larger, but no less challenging goals.

Mind over matter isn't magic, an illusion, or a cute parlor trick. It's merely the manifestation of an inherent power that we each hold in the center of our own minds. The process of mind over matter involves the following three distinct steps.

1. **Focus your mind:** The first step of mind over matter requires that your mind be focused completely and entirely on the task at hand. A wandering mind is analogous to irritating static on your favorite radio station making the transmission inaudible.

2. **Believe:** Once the mind is clear of distracting thoughts and is completely focused on the task at hand, the heart and mind (conscious and unconscious minds) must be aligned. This means that all doubt must be cast aside and faith must galvanize to a sense of absolute knowing that you will, indeed, accomplish the deed (whatever it happens to be). To reinforce the belief process, use the power of your imagination to picture the event as having already occurred. Feel the exhilaration of completing the task.

3. **State the command:** State the command to complete the desired action. To bend a spoon, you might simply state, "Bend!" To dissolve a tumor, state the command "Dissolve away!"

Spoon Bending 101

Locate an old spoon (or fork) from the silverware drawer (one that you don't intend to use again). Hold the base of the utensil in one hand and with a slight effort with the free hand apply a little pressure simply to test the strength of the metal. Follow steps 1 to 3 above. After stating the command "Bend!" once again hold the top of the utensil and bend it at the neck. If possible, bend the neck of the spoon or fork into a loop. Sometimes it helps to visualize the neck of the spoon as molten red, right before you apply pressure to bend the spoon. Once the utensil is transformed, consider keeping it in a place where you can see it often as a symbol to remind you of the power of your mind.

Spoon bending is really nothing more than a simple metaphor of the power of mind over matter. Once you have mastered this task, consider trying this technique in other areas of your life.

Exercise 4.4 Creative Altruism: The Power of Unconditional Love

Love, it is said, is the glue that holds the universe together. The expression of love can be made manifest in a great many ways. The following questions encourage you to explore the concept of unconditional love as an alternative to the motivation of fear.

1. Write your best definition of love.

   _____

   _____

   _____

   _____

   _____

2. If love is the energy that moves the human spirit, then fear is the metaphorical brake that stops love in its tracks. How does fear impede your ability to express love?

   _____

   _____

   _____

   _____

   _____

3. The slogan "Practice random acts of kindness" was coined by a woman who was searching for a way to make the world a better place in which to live. She created this catchphrase as a means to express heartfelt altruism. The idea of performing a random act of kindness means to give anonymously without the expectation of receiving anything back. Compose a list of five ways to "give" altruistically (at least three ways should not involve money).

   a. _____

   b. _____

   c. _____

   d. _____

   e. _____

4. Service! One cannot speak on the topic of altruism without speaking of the concept of service, yet service is an idea that has fallen on deaf ears lately. It's hard to feel sorry for yourself when you are helping others who are less fortunate. Over the past decade, the Institute of Noetic Sciences has given the Creative Altruism Award to those unique individuals who demonstrate the spirit of selfless service. If you could create an altruistic nonprofit organization to help others, what would you do? Explain it here:

   _____

   _____

   _____

   _____

   _____

CHAPTER
5

The Spirit: The Health of the Human Spirit

We are at this moment participating in one of the very greatest leaps of the human spirit—to a knowledge not only outside but also our deep inward mystery—the greatest leap ever.
—Joseph Campbell

How does one describe the indescribable? The topic of human spirituality has been pondered, discussed, and argued for eons. Yet even though many libraries are filled with volumes of books pontificating on the nature of spirituality, this unique concept defies a clear-cut definition or explanation because of the limitations of human language. It is safe to say that we as a human race don't possess the vocabulary to give the concept of spirituality an adequate definition or description. This, in turn, has led to frustration and confusion among a great many people around the world, who desire something tangible to comprehend. Undoubtedly, spirituality includes the aspects of higher consciousness, transcendence, self-reliance, love, faith, enlightenment, community, self-actualization, compassion, forgiveness, mysticism, a higher power, grace, and a multitude of other qualities.

In reality, no one word alone is sufficient to describe the essence of human spirituality, and herein lies the dilemma. To define a term or concept is to separate and distinguish it from everything else long enough to gain a clear focus and understanding of its true nature. However, it appears that human spirituality encompasses so many factors—possibly everything—that to separate anything out, even if only momentarily, denies a full understanding of this unique phenomenon.

This we do know: Spirituality is not the same thing as religion, although these two concepts do share some common ground, specifically, a union with the divine. Spirituality is inclusive, whereas religions tend to be exclusive (e.g., you cannot be Jewish and Baptist at the same time). Spirituality is a unique and personal experience with a dynamic force greater than oneself. Religions are based on rules and dogma, whereas spirituality has no dogma. Religions are based on faith. Spirituality is

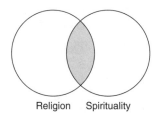

Religion   Spirituality

Figure 5.1

based on a personal knowledge. In the words of renowned theologian Houston Smith, "Religions are very organized, spirituality is a mess."

In nearly every culture around the globe, the words *spirit* and *breath* are synonymous, suggesting that spirit is a life force of energy that circulates through us and around us. Mystics say that this life force of energy is greatly affected by our thoughts and feelings. In essence, joy, happiness, and love keep the spirit vibrant, whereas unresolved issues of anger and fear can choke the human spirit. Health of the human spirit, therefore, is a metaphorical expression of keeping the spirit free-flowing, balanced, and vibrant.

Although the words of English, Arabic, Chinese, Navajo, and all other languages come up short when describing the nature of human spirituality, there is one language that begins to do justice to this topic—the language of metaphor. We use the language of metaphor and simile to help explain the unexplainable, to make the intangible tangible, if only long enough to gain a better glimpse of it. It's no exaggeration to say that the language of human spirituality is loaded with metaphors. Journeys, mountain tops, roadblocks, and distractions are but a few of these commonly used analogies. Perhaps by no coincidence, these archetypal metaphors are similar in all languages and cultures.

Sometimes in order to understand a concept, you just have to experience it, and experiences will certainly vary, as will the interpretation of these experiences. As the expression goes, there is no substitute for direct experience. Typically, people tend to describe their collective experiences of this nature as a "journey" or "path." Most important, for a path to enhance the maturation or evolution of your spiritual well-being, it must be a creative, not destructive path; a progressive, not regressive path. It must stimulate and enhance the human spirit, not stifle spiritual well-being. From this premise, remember too, that there are many paths to enlightenment and no one path holds dominance over the others. It matters not which path you take, but only that you keep moving forward (growing) on the path you have chosen. In the words of Carlos Castenada from the *Teachings of Don Juan,* "Look at every path closely and deliberately. Try it as many times as you think is necessary. Then ask yourself, and yourself alone, one question. Does this path have a heart? If it does, the path is good; if it doesn't, it is of no use."

The Neglect of the Human Spirit

Perhaps because spirituality is impossible to define and even harder to measure, it has taken a back seat in the paradigm of health in Western culture for the past 380 years, due in large part to the influence of René Descartes, the creator of the Cartesian principle or paradigm. To ignore the aspects of human spirituality, however, only leads to an incomplete picture of the human experience. To ignore the role of spirituality in the process of coping with stress tends to create a sense of victimization and helplessness rather than empowerment. In the past decade, theologians, scientists, teachers, physicians, and scores of other professionals have come together to make a stance that the spiritual component can no longer be ignored or neglected in terms of the wellness paradigm. Today there is a clarion call for a new paradigm (which is actually a very old paradigm) that honors the integration, balance, and harmony of mind, body, spirit, and emotions and recognizes that human spirituality is the cornerstone of health and well-being.

The Dance of Stress and Spirituality

At first glance, it might appear that the concepts of stress and human spirituality are mutually exclusive. Indeed, there are many people who believe that these two words cannot be used in the same sentence. In reality, stress and spirituality combine to form a unique alchemy. Quite literally, they are partners in the dance of life. When we are willing to learn from each human experience, stress provides an opportunity for spiritual growth. Like a precious gemstone with rough edges, the wisdom gained from each experience, both good and bad, smoothes our rough edges to bring out our inherent beauty. Stressors are resolved when the life force of spirit is allowed to help you move through the situation rather than become stuck in it.

Through the perspective of ageless wisdom, stress is defined as "a perceived disconnection from our divine source"—whatever we conceive this to be. In truth, we are never disconnected or separated from the divine source. Moreover, we are never betrayed by it either. Yet, unresolved issues of anger and fear begin to cloud our vision so that we feel as though we have been cut off, abandoned, or betrayed (the proverbial "day from hell"). In Eastern culture this is known as the veils of illusion. Despite our greatest fears, we can never be separated from our divine source. If you are still unsure if stress and human spirituality are partners in the dance of life, consider filling out Exercise 5.1.

Times of Spiritual Hunger

There comes a time in everyone's life when he or she begins to search for answers to life's most difficult questions. What begins as soul searching for life's meaning quickly grows into a spiritual hunger for more answers—a search for truth that often lies well beyond the reach of each individual to encompass a much larger perspective of the universe and our role in it. The goal of this quest is to seek answers that help guide us further along our own life journey.

In past generations, people often sought spiritual refuge in their religious traditions. However, today many people have become a little disenchanted with their standard religious practices, perhaps because they don't seem to offer insights and answers to problems looming on the horizons of humanity, such as cloning or discovery of new planets (and life) in our galaxy. With an appetite greater than that which can be satisfied by existing institutions, people have begun to look beyond their own back yards to seek the answers to life's questions. The advent of the Internet has only been one of many means to satisfy this hunger. Books, workshops, and *Oprah* often become stepping stones on this quest. Ageless wisdom notes that setting out to appease this hunger is an essential part of the spiritual journey, for we each must question truth to fully understand it.

Windows of the Soul

If you were to take the time to listen to the shamans, sages, mystics, and healers—the wisdom keepers of all times, all cultures, and all languages—you would hear them say that a circle is a universal symbol of wholeness, in which all parts come together to form the whole, yet the whole is always greater than the sum of the parts. Implicit in this message is that divinity resides in the power of the circle. We see this in the taoist yin/yang symbol. We are reminded of this in the Tibetan mandala, in the beauty of the Native American medicine wheel, Stonehendge, the Mayan calendar, the labyrinth, the peace symbol, and even a Christmas wreath. In the words of Hermes Trismegistus, "God is a sphere whose center is everywhere and whose circumference is nowhere."

In a stress-filled world, it is easy to become distracted and forget the sacredness of the circle. Moreover, we often forget our own inherent connection to the divine. In the event that you ever forget your wholeness, your divine connection, all you need do is take a look in the nearest mirror, into the reflection of your own eyes. There, in the iris of each eye, is a beautiful sacred circle to remind you of your own divinity. Indeed, as Shakespeare once said, "The eyes are the windows of the soul."

Within the power of the circle, the number 4 is very significant (e.g., the four corners of the earth, the four seasons, the four chambers of the heart, and the four parts that make up the human entity: mind, body, spirit, and emotions). If you were to converse once again with the shamans, sages, and mystics of all times and ask them to share their wisdom on the concept of human spirituality, you would hear them mention four aspects that unite to create a formidable essence. All four components transcend the boundaries of all religions and cultures. The first three—relationships, values, and a meaningful purpose in life—can be linked directly to every stressor you will encounter on the human odyssey. The fourth pillar speaks to the appreciation of the divine mystery of life itself. Exercise 5.2 invites you to walk through the mandala of the human spirit to gain a full perspective on the power of the whole being greater than the sum of the parts in all aspects of your life.

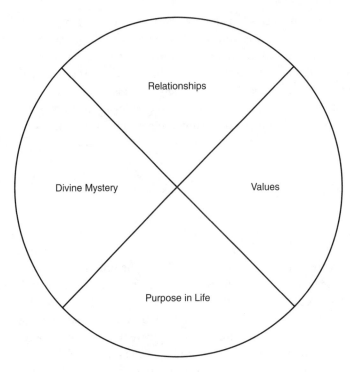

Figure 5.2

Relationships, Values, and a Meaningful Purpose in Life

A short prayer from the Lakota nation states, "Mitakuye oyasin." The translation means "All my relations." Nearly all the indigenous cultures around the world have a similar prayer, honoring the connectedness of life. Indeed, all life is relationship, and the health of the human spirit honors this connection. Two types of relationships coexist in this pillar of human spirituality to form the cornerstone of this paradigm. The first is an *internal relationship* that each individual has with himself or herself and one's higher self. The second is *external relationships,* the connection to all people and things outside of oneself. Many stressors involve the relationship we hold with ourselves as well as those we maintain among family, friends, peers, and colleagues.

The second pillar of human spirituality involves a personal value system. *Values* are abstract concepts of importance that we tend to make tangible through symbols. For instance, wealth is a value. Money is a symbol of wealth. Education is a value. A degree or diploma is a symbol of this value. It is believed that we each hold a strong set of core values and a larger set of supporting values that support the core values. Tension often arises when shifts occur in our value system, such as the tension between freedom and responsibility.

A meaningful purpose in life constitutes the third pillar of human spirituality. It represents who we are and why we are here. There is a general consensus that over the course of our existence, we will begin and complete many purposes. Yet, in between the completion of one and the start of another resides the potential for suffering. Exercises 5.3 to 5.6 take you through these pillars as a means to gain a better understanding of them.

Roadblocks on the Spiritual Path

Metaphorically speaking, every stressor we encounter on the human journey holds the potential to obstruct our safe passage, if we let it. Some stressors are nothing more than potholes on the road of life and can be easily sidestepped. Others seem like insurmountable roadblocks. The common tendency upon reaching a huge roadblock is to turn around and find another route. This behavior tends to promote avoidance, which can prove to be an extremely ineffective coping skill. Although the path of least resistance is often encouraged, avoidance is not. Wisdom reminds us that when we avoid roadblocks, we will almost certainly see the same obstacle (perhaps with a different name) 5, 10, or 20 miles down the road, waiting for us. On the human journey, roadblocks are meant to be dismantled, circumnavigated, or transcended, but never avoided completely. Remember, the first step to dismantling a roadblock is to recognize it for what it is: an obstruction on your life's journey. Exercise 5.7 invites you to look at any stressors disguised as roadblocks that may be impeding your life journey.

Distractions on the Spiritual Path

Everyone has heard the expression "Stop and smell the roses." By and large this is wonderful advice. Life was never meant to be a sprint to the finish line. Taking time to enjoy the simple things in life, as well as resting to enjoy the view, is considered by many to be as much a part of the journey as the arduous trek itself. There are many attractions along the road of life, but when attractions become distractions, then problems soon develop. Distractions pull one off the path, sometimes indefinitely. Today, distractions are some of our biggest health problems—from drugs and alcohol addiction to an obsessive need to answer voice mail and email. Distractions begin as attractions; like Rip van Winkle, who pulled off the side of the road for a drink one night and slept for 20 years, we too can fall victim to the lure of attractions if we are not careful. Falling asleep on the spiritual path is a common metaphor in literature. Likewise, becoming distracted on the spiritual path is extremely common. Moreover, stress tends to cast a spell that lures one farther off the path. Exercise 5.8 invites you to look at any distractions you may have in your life, so that they can be identified and resolved.

The Divine Mystery

While relationships, values, and a meaningful purpose in life constitute the framework for human spirituality, shamans, sages, mystics, and wisdom keepers will also tell you that there is a fourth aspect to human spirituality. In many circles, this aspect is called the *divine mystery,* and it speaks to all of the things that can never possibly be explained rationally or scientifically. Sadly, Western culture not only ignores this aspect, but often ridicules it. Until recently, most people who had a mystical experience kept it to themselves for fear of looking stupid (embarrassment is a form of stress). More recently, though, there has been a greater acceptance of mystic experiences in American culture. Moreover, some brave souls in the academic disciplines have tried to create a scientific methodology that begins to elucidate a clearer understanding of the divine and to widen the perspective of human understanding. Studies on prayer, subtle energies, and spontaneous remissions are just some of these areas of current research.

Indeed, there are many things that remain outside the domain of the five senses. Renowned philosopher and inventor Buckminster Fuller once said that 80 percent of reality could not be observed or detected through the five senses. Western culture ascribes to the Cartesian principle, or the mechanistic paradigm of reality, and therefore ignores all things outside the realm of the five senses. Oddly, things that cannot be ignored are often labeled as the "ghost in the machine." What are some examples of these unexplained ghosts? The list is rather long, but some examples include spontaneous healings, bizarre synchronicities, angelic encounters, near-death experiences, faith healings, and legitimate crop circles. Wisdom keepers never try to explain these events and happenings in rational terms. Rather, they simply suggest that it is better to become a mystic, meaning that one appreciates the mystical nature of the universe, rather than to deny its existence. To be a good mystic doesn't mean you understand unexplained phenomena. It simply means you have come to appreciate their mystery!

Another aspect of the divine mystery is the feeling of exuberance upon experiencing a sense of oneness with the world. Abraham Maslow called this a "peak experience," a unique type of eustress that takes your breath away and in which feelings of euphoria simply cannot be expressed in words.

So much emphasis is placed on distress these days that we tend to forget the other side of the coin: good stress. Some people call this experience a *natural high,* where the culmination of all five senses, perhaps in tandem with a sixth sense, provides a unique, exhilarating, ineffable sensation of a loving oneness. Everyone has had this experience at least once in his or her life. Maslow was of the opinion that peak experiences would be more common if basic needs were met (e.g., food, clothing, shelter, companionship). This, he believed, would allow for a quicker pace toward self-actualization, where peak moments are commonly experienced. Not only do we all have the potential to experience these peak moments, but we also hold the consciousness to be a good mystic. To be a good mystic means simply to appreciate the mystical aspects of the divine universe. Exercise 5.9 invites you to share your thoughts and feelings on this unique aspect of human spirituality.

Of Ego and Soul

The relationship between stress and spirituality is a lifelong dance. The dancers found within each individual are the ego and the soul. The partnership between ego and soul is as wonderful as it is baffling (and perhaps annoying). The soul, the spark of divine creation that resides in the core of our being, has but one purpose: to learn to give and receive love. Perhaps the real purpose of the ego is to serve as a bodyguard for the soul. Problems arise when the agenda of the ego (e.g., control and manipulation) overrides the soul's purpose, hence leading to an inherent tension within the mind and heart of each individual. Although all issues of unresolved stress can be traced to the ego, as was mentioned in Chapter 4, the ego is not necessarily the bad guy. Self-esteem and self-worth are very much tied to the purpose of the ego as well. Without an ego, the soul would be unprotected to do its work. The tension between ego and soul is often called a dance. At best, it's a romantic tango; at worst, it's a continual body slam. Like anyone taking dance lessons, the ego can be trained to step in a coordinated rhythm.

Seasons of the Soul

The planet Earth is a large mandala distinguished by four unique seasons: autumn, winter, spring, and summer. Like the planet Earth, of which we are very much a part, we too go through four specific seasons of the soul-growth process, much like the earth's seasons. Wisdom keepers from all corners of the earth speak of four distinct phases of the soul-growth process. These seasons go by many names, yet their similarities are undeniable. The seasons of the soul include the centering, emptying, grounding, and connecting processes. Let's take a closer look at each.

The Centering Process (Autumn).   The centering process is a time of soul searching and introspection. It is a time to go inside and cultivate the relationship you have with yourself and your higher self. The centering process is identified with autumn because just as the earth spins on its axis, allowing less light in the course of each day, so too we go inside earlier. The centering process is an invitation to turn off the sensory stimulation from the outside world and go within. The word *center* contains the word *enter,* and the purpose of the centering process is to enter the heart.

The Emptying Process (Winter).   Once the centering process has been initiated, the emptying process begins. The emptying process is a time to clear out, let go of, and release any and all thoughts, attitudes, behaviors, and perceptions that at one time may have helped you but now only hold you back. In no uncertain terms, the emptying process is the void. It's a time to let go, release, or detach and then step into the unknown, unencumbered by the things that we have accumulated along the journey. The purpose of the emptying process is to make room for new thoughts, insights, and ideas that will guide us further along on the human journey.

Due to our emotional attachments, letting go can seem quite painful in some cases. The emptying process goes by a few different names: *the winter of discontent* and, perhaps most notably, *the dark night of the soul.* Although this season isn't meant to be tortuous, it can seem like that for many people who have a hard time letting go of things. With letting go comes grieving. Sadly, many people get stuck in this season and see no way out. The void can seem like a lonely place; however, it's not meant to be a final destination. Rather, it is merely a necessary transition to the next season.

The Grounding Process (Spring).   Once room has been made for new insights, then the grounding process begins by attracting those things that are necessary in order to continue along the human journey. Just as winter turns to spring, so too does the clearance of space allow for new insights and shades of enlightenment. Nature abhors a vacuum! Surely, when room is made, something new will come to fill the space. New insights come in small pieces of information. It might be an intuitive thought. It might be a coincidence. Or it could be something that you hear mentioned by several different people in the course of a few days. In the customs of the Native Americans, the grounding process is the vision in the vision quest. This season is called the grounding process because when a nugget of insight arrives, it provides a sense of security and stability.

The Connecting Process (Summer).   When you think of summer, it's likely that you think of family reunions, picnics, family barbecues, and social get-togethers. Summer is a time of coming together and being together with friends and family. It is a time of bonding—nurturing old connections and ties and creating new ones. At a spiritual level, the connecting process is much the same. It's a time of sharing whatever insights you picked up in the grounding process so that everyone can benefit, because greed is not a spiritual value. The premise of the connecting process is nurturing our connections through unconditional love. This season is often compared to Disney World, and indeed, this season is as glorious as the emptying process seems daunting. It's compelling to want to stay here forever, but the rhythm of the seasons never allows for anyone to stay in one place too long.

What makes life interesting, if not complicated, is that in truth we have many seasons going on at one time. We could be in the emptying season with regard to a relationship and in the connecting process in our professional lives. Moreover, friends and family going through similar stressors tend to rotate through the seasons of the soul at different times, making it hard to relate to each other and hence possibly causing more stress. Exercise 5.10 challenges you to reflect on the seasons of your life at this time.

Muscles of the Soul

There are two ways to get through a stressful experience. The first is to become a victim. People who do this constantly remind themselves and others of how badly they have suffered from whatever ordeal they have encountered. Rather than letting go and moving on, they hang on to feelings of resentment, which only perpetuates the feelings of victimhood. The second (and best) way to emerge from a bad situation is to come through gracefully. People who do this show no sign of anger, animosity, or resentment from their ordeal. They have learned whatever they can from the experience and have moved on with their lives. When asked how they got through their situation, these people often have a similar answer. They say that it was their sense of faith, sense of courage, or sense of humor. Some mention that it was their sense of patience; others speak of a sense of optimism. These inner resources, which include but are not limited to humor, intuition, patience, honesty, imagination, integrity, forgiveness, humbleness, and compassion, are not gifts for a chosen few—they are birthrights for everyone.

In his study of several hundred remarkable people, renowned psychologist Abraham Maslow searched for personality traits that culminated into what he called the *self-actualized* person: an individual who was able to rise above the stressors of everyday life and reach his or her highest human potential. There are several traits that allow you to stand tall, yet go with the flow, particularly after experiencing a life-threatening event that can best be described as "a trip to hell and back." Exercise 5.11 invites you to focus on these muscles to be exercised as you work to dismantle your roadblocks. The following is a brief description of several "muscles of the soul" for this exercise.

Compassion.   To love without reciprocation, to care for someone or something without recognition or reward, constitutes the hallmark of compassion. Compassion is the ability to feel and express love when fear is an easier choice. Mother Teresa was compassion personified. You don't have to be a saint to feel compassion. Love is the fabric of our soul.

Courage.   The word *courage* comes to the English language via two French words, meaning "big heart." Courage often brings to mind the idea of bravery, and this is certainly a hallmark of courage. Perhaps courage is best thought of as the opposite of fear, for it is courage that allows one to go forward, whereas fear holds one back. Courage is a brave heart.

Creativity.   Creativity is two parts imagination, one part organization, one part inspiration, and one part perspiration. Creativity is not a right-brain function, it is an inner resource that requires both hemispheres of the brain. Creativity starts with imagination and then makes the ideas happen. Creativity is the synthesis of imagination and ingenuity (see Chapter 10, "Creative Problem Solving").

Curiosity.   In the effort to learn, the soul has a wide streak of curiosity. Some may call this an inquiring mind, while others call it information seeking. Either way, seeking options, answers, and ideas to learn makes life's journey more interesting.

Faith.   Faith is one part optimism, one part love, and two parts mystery. Faith is more than a belief that things will work out OK; it is an innate certainty that all will end well. Faith is an inherent knowing that we are part of a much bigger whole and that the whole has a loving, divine nature to it.

Forgiveness.   Forgiveness is the capacity to pardon those who we feel have violated us, as well as the capacity to forgive ourselves for our mistakes and foibles. Forgiveness is not letting someone off the hook when we feel violated or victimized. Forgiveness is a gift of compassion we give ourselves so that we can move on. If someone else benefits, great, but forgiveness isn't done for someone else. It is done for ourselves. Moreover, we must learn to forgive ourselves as well.

Humbleness.   The ego begs to go first. The soul is content going last. Humbleness is a trait that is called upon when we are reminded to serve others by allowing them to be served first. Humbleness is manifested in acts of politeness, yet it never undermines self-esteem. Humbleness is based on the Golden Rule, which states that you should treat others as you would have them treat you. In a fast-paced world where rudeness prevails, acts of humbleness are greatly appreciated.

Humor.   Humor is often described as a perception or insight that makes us giggle and laugh. Humor isn't a mood, but it certainly can promote a positive mood of happiness. Between parody and irony, between double entendres and slapstick humor, there are literally hundreds of things to make our lips curl and faces laugh. Mark Twain once said that humor is mankind's greatest blessing. There are many people who insist that a sense of humor is what truly saved their lives in times of stress. (Please see Chapter 7, "Comic Relief.")

Integrity.   When you meet someone of integrity, the first thought that comes to mind is honesty. Although this is certainly the cornerstone of integrity, there is more. Integrity is honesty over time. It is a code of conduct with a pledge to the highest ideals in the lowest of times. Integrity means taking the high road when the low road looks easier. In truth, integrity means the integration of many muscles of the soul.

Intuition.   This muscle of the soul may not help you win lottery tickets, but it is useful in sensing good from bad, right from wrong, and up from down. Research delving into the lateralization of left- and right-brain hemispheres suggests that intuition is a right-brain function. Intuition is an inherent knowing about something before the ego jumps in to confuse things. Premonitions, sudden insights, intuitive thoughts, inspiration, and pure enlightenment are examples of how this level of consciousness surfaces in everyday use if we let it.

Optimism.   Optimism is an inherent quality of being positive. This is not to say that every stressor is meant to be a Pollyanna moment. Rather, optimism is seeing the best in a bad situation, learning from each lesson offered. A great definition of an optimist is someone who looks at a pessimist and sees hope.

Patience.   Patience is the ability to wait and wait and wait until some sign acknowledges that it is time to move on. Just as there is strength in motion, there is power in stillness. Western culture is big on immediate gratification, the antithesis of patience. Impatience often leads to intolerance and anger. Patience quells an angry heart.

Persistence.   A persistent person is someone who doesn't take "no" for an answer until he or she has exhausted every conceivable option. (There are variations on this theme. Some people stretch the meaning of persistence to cover aggressive, in-your-face tactics.) The spiritual approach is one of being pleasantly persistent (not aggressive), like flowing water that ever so slowly softens the hardest rock.

Resiliency.   Some people call resiliency the ability to bounce back; specifically, bouncing back from horrendous adversity. Resiliency is a trait that combines self-reliance, faith, optimism, and humor, yet resiliency is undeniably greater than the sum of these parts.

Unconditional Love.   To extend love and compassion from your heart without conditions or expectations is the hallmark of this muscle of the soul. There are some who say that humans are not capable of unconditional love, but just ask any mother of a newborn baby and you will learn quite quickly that indeed we possess this attribute. Unconditional love is egoless.

Spiritual Potential and Spiritual Health

Within the heart and soul of each person lies the means to solve any problem and move beyond any roadblock, no matter how big or small. Just as everyone has the muscles to flex their arms and bend their knees, so too do we have spiritual muscles that are ready to be used to dismantle roadblocks of any size whenever called upon to do so. Spiritual potential is the potential that resides in each one of us to use these muscles of the soul when needed. Unfortunately, many people never meet their potential; instead, allowing these muscles to atrophy with disuse, they circle continuously in the whirlpool of stressful currents and are unable to lift themselves out. When individuals do begin to flex these muscles of the soul and make the effort to break down, circumnavigate, or transcend the roadblocks in front of them, they have moved from a place of spiritual potential to one of spiritual health.

The Hero's Journey

From all four corners of the earth, the spiritual path is described as a journey or lifelong rite of passage. It is an odyssey that can be measured in neither years nor miles—and certainly not possessions. Some say that this journey can be measured in experiences, whereas others say that it cannot be measured at all. Sages will tell you that the spiritual journey is no more than 12 to 14 inches, the distance from one's head to one's heart.

One wisdom keeper who dedicated his life to understanding the nature of the spiritual journey is Joseph Campbell. Leaving no stone unturned, Campbell compared the myths, legends, and fables of all societies only to find that regardless of the culture, the storyline is consistent: A person leaves the known to venture into the unknown, he or she encounters all kinds of problems, and with rare exception he or she fully resolves these problems, followed by a return home to a hero's welcome. In his classic book *Hero with a Thousand Faces,* Campbell referred to this template as "the hero's journey." These classic stories serve not only as a reminder but as a guide for our human sojourn—when we take the time to listen to the wisdom. It was Campbell's opinion that each and every one of us is on the hero's journey, and that every life span encompasses many, many journeys within the grand journey.

The template of the hero's journey involves three distinct stages: (1) the departure, (2) initiation, and (3) the return home. Let's take a closer look at each stage and at classic examples that illustrate the parts of the hero's journey.

The Departure

In the departure stage, the character leaves the familiar (usually home) and enters the unknown. Sometimes there is a call to adventure, whereas other times there is a great reluctance to venture out into the unknown. It was Campbell's belief that every hero is called to adventure, even if he or she is pushed unwillingly out the door. Examples include Frodo Baggins leaving the Shire and Dorothy leaving Kansas. In contemporary times, departure can occur each time you step out the front door to go to work. The departure can be any change in your life!

The Stage of Initiation

Initiation can be considered another word for *stressor.* Initiations are tests that the hero must pass or overcome so that he or she can move on to complete the quest. This stage goes by many names, including rites of passage, baptism by fire, or the road of trials. In this stage, every hero faces a challenge and is called upon to complete the challenge. If he or she fails, another will appear until it is mastered successfully. Frodo had to get rid of the ring, and Dorothy had to aquire the Wicked Witch's broom. Every hero must fulfill a task—a mission to accomplish or a stressor to resolve—as this apparently thickens the plot. The stage of initiation also contains what Joseph Campbell calls "spiritual aids," a helping hand from the divine source, whether it be angels, fairies, wizards, or the culmination of inner strength found within the soul of each hero. Dorothy had the help of the Good Witch of the North, Frodo had Gandalf, and you have assistance too!

The Return Home

Upon completing the challenge, the character returns home to be recognized as a hero. Often, but not always, the hero returns with a symbol of his or her strength, such as the golden fleece or the Medusa's head. Also called *incorporation,* the return home is a point where the hero becomes a master of two worlds: the world he conquered and the world he returns to. Sometimes returning home doesn't mean a literal return, but rather a symbolic return. In essence, the return home is symbolic of coming to a place of inner peace or homeostasis. Ulysses made it home, as did Jason and the Argonauts, and Frodo and Dorothy. The promise of the hero's journey is that you will too.

If you look closely, you will see the storyline of the hero's journey as the foundation for every great story, from Ulysses, King Arthur, and Dorothy (*Wizard of Oz*) to Frodo Baggins and Harry Potter. Through the same eyes, you can see that the hero's journey is told through countless stories of real-life heroes such as Lance Armstrong, Rosa Parks, and Maria Von Trapp. Whether you know it or not, you are the central character in the hero's journey of your life.

Campbell did note this word of caution: On rare occasion, the hero may lose sight of his or her goals and ultimately fail to return home. Greed, apathy, lust, or some other aspect of the ego may override the soul's intention, derailing the journey's completion. Metaphorically speaking, the character becomes distracted and falls asleep on the spiritual path. Rip Van Winkle is a classic example of this. There are many others. Please consider using Exercise 5.12 as a means to view your life through the template of your hero's journey.

Health of the Human Spirit

Taking steps to ensure the health of the human spirit is as important as steps to ensure physical health. In some people's minds, it's even more important because spiritual well-being is the cornerstone of the entire wellness paradigm. Health of the human spirit ensures a continuous healthy flow of the life force of universal energy, unencumbered by unresolved feelings of anger or fear. Moreover, at best, health of the human spirit fully acknowledges a relationship with the divine, however you choose to define this. In doing so, actions to ensure the health of the human spirit honor the sacredness of life and our connection to it. Ultimately, health of the human spirit means moving from a motivation of fear toward a motivation of love: unconditional love. Exercise 5.13 challenges you to consider ways to enhance the health of your human spirit.

Additional Resources

Campbell, J. *The Hero with a Thousand Faces*. Princeton, NJ: Princeton University Press, 1968.

Dossey, L. *Recovering the Soul*. New York: Bantam New Age Books, 1989.

Peck, M.S. *The Road Less Traveled*. New York: Touchtone Books, 1978.

Seaward, B.L. *Quiet Mind, Fearless Heart: The Taoist Path of Stress and Spirituality*. New York: John Wiley & Sons, 2005.

Seaward, B.L. *Stand Like Mountain, Flow Like Water: Reflections on Stress and Human Spirituality*. Deerfield Beach, FL: Health Communications, 1997.

Tolle, E. *The Power of Now*. Novato, CA: New World Library, 1999.

Zukav, G. *Seat of the Soul*. New York: Fireside Books, 1989.

Exercise 5.1 Stress and Human Spirituality

It may seem as though stress is the absence of human spirituality, but where there is stress, there is a lesson to enhance the soul-growth process. Take a moment to make a list of your top ten stressors. If you have less than ten, that's fine. If you have more than ten, simply list the top ten concerns, issues, or problems that are on your mind at this time. When you get done, place a check mark next to each stressor that involves issues concerning yourself or other people. Next, place a check mark next to all stressors that involve values or value conflicts (e.g., time, money, privacy, education). Finally, place a check mark next to all stressors that involve or are related a meaningful purpose in life (e.g., family, education, career, retirement). It is fine to have a stressor with more than one check mark. We'll come back to this theme in upcoming exercises.

Stressor	Relationships	Values	Purpose in Life
1.			
2.			
3.			
4.			
5.			
6.			
7.			
8.			
9.			
10.			

Exercise 5.2 Mandala of the Human Spirit

A *mandala* is a circular-shaped object symbolizing unity, with four separate quarters that represent directions of the universe, seasons of the years, or four points of reference. The origin of the mandala can be traced to the dawn of humankind. Mandalas vary in size, design, colors, and symbolism. They are often used in meditation as a focal point of concentration. In addition they are used as decorations in many cultures, from the Native American medicine wheel to art from the Far East.

The mandala of the human spirit is a symbol of wholeness. It is a tool of self-awareness to allow you the opportunity to reflect on some of the components of the human spirit: a meaningful purpose in your life, personal values, and the implicit chance to learn more about yourself in precious moments of solitude. Each quadrant represents a direction of your life, with a symbol of orientation. The east is the initial point of origin. It represents the rising sun, the point of origin for each day. The focus of the mandala then moves southward, then to the west, and finally to the north.

Each focal point of the mandala of the human spirit provides questions for reflection (see the accompanying figure). Take a few moments to reflect on the directions of the mandala to get a better perspective on the well-being of your human spirit. Then fill in the answers to the respective questions in the mandala on the following page, creating a mandala of your very own human spirit.

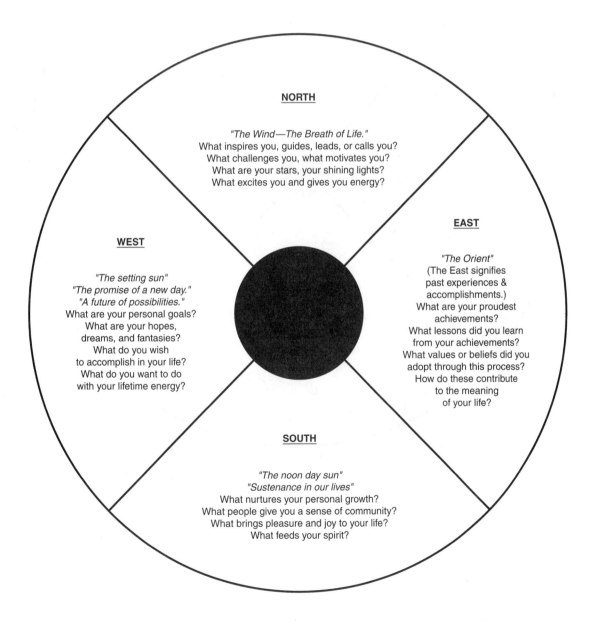

NORTH

"The Wind—The Breath of Life."
What inspires you, guides, leads, or calls you?
What challenges you, what motivates you?
What are your stars, your shining lights?
What excites you and gives you energy?

WEST

"The setting sun"
"The promise of a new day."
"A future of possibilities."
What are your personal goals?
What are your hopes,
dreams, and fantasies?
What do you wish
to accomplish in your life?
What do you want to do
with your lifetime energy?

EAST

"The Orient"
(The East signifies
past experiences &
accomplishments.)
What are your proudest
achievements?
What lessons did you learn
from your achievements?
What values or beliefs did you
adopt through this process?
How do these contribute
to the meaning
of your life?

SOUTH

"The noon day sun"
"Sustenance in our lives"
What nurtures your personal growth?
What people give you a sense of community?
What brings pleasure and joy to your life?
What feeds your spirit?

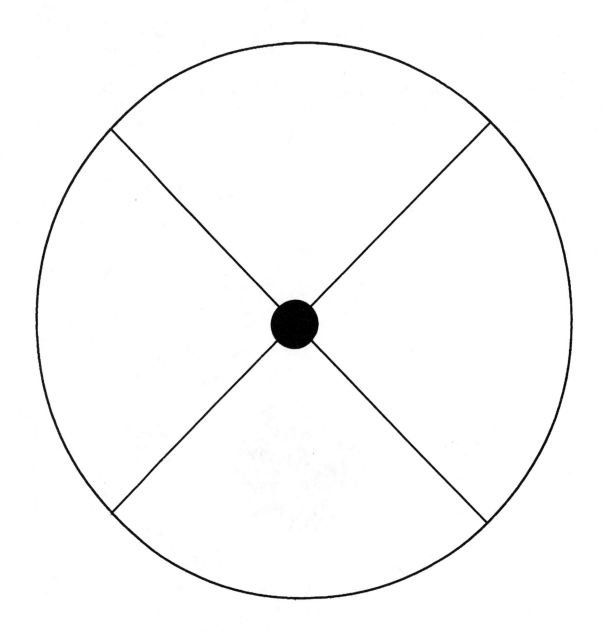

Exercise 5.3 Pillars of Human Spirituality

Every crisis over the age of 30 is a spiritual crisis.
Spiritual crises require spiritual cures.
—Carl Gustav Jung

The shamans, healers, sages, and wisdom keepers of all times, all continents, and all peoples say that human spirituality is composed of three aspects: relationships, values, and purpose in life. These three components are so tightly integrated that it may be hard to separate them from each other. But if this were possible, take a moment to reflect on these aspects of human spirituality to determine the status of your spiritual well-being.

Relationships
All life is relationship! In simple terms, there are two categories of relationships: internal (domestic policy), which is how you deal with yourself, how you nurture the relationship with yourself and your higher self; and external (foreign policy), which is how you relate, support, and interact with those people (and all living entities) in your environment. How would you evaluate your internal relationship, and what steps could you take to cultivate it? Moving from the aspect of "domestic policy" to "foreign policy," how would you evaluate your external relationships?

_____

_____

_____

_____

Your Personal Value System
We each have a value system composed of core and supporting values. Core values (about four to six) are those which form the foundation of our personal belief system. Supporting values support the core values. Intangible core values (e.g., love, honesty, freedom) and supporting values (e.g., education, creativity, and integrity) are often symbolized in material possessions. Quite regularly, our personal value system tends to go through a reorganization process, particularly when there are conflicts in our values. What are your core and supporting values?

Core Values	Supporting Values
1.	1.
2.	2.
3.	3.
4.	4.
5.	5.

A Meaningful Purpose in Life
A meaningful purpose in life is that which gives our life meaning. Some might call it a life mission. Although it is true that we may have an overall life mission, it is also true that our lives are a collection of meaningful purposes. Suffering awaits those times in between each purpose. What would you say is your life mission, and what purpose are you now supporting to accomplish this mission?

_____

_____

_____

_____

Exercise 5.4　Personal and Interpersonal Relationships

It is often said that all life is relationship—how we deal with ourselves and how we relate to everything else in our lives. It's no secret that relationships can cause stress. For this reason alone, all relationships need nurturing to some degree. Reflect for a moment on all the many relationships that you hold in your life, including the most important relationship—that which you hold with yourself. Relationships also constitute the foundation of your support system. Relationships go further than friends and family. This core pillar of human spirituality also includes our relationship with the air we breathe, the water we drink, and the ground we walk on. How is your relationship with your environment?

　　Write your name in the center circle of the accompanying figure and then begin to fill in the circles with the names of those people, places, and things that constitute your relationship with life. Finally, place an asterisk (*) next to those relationships that need special nurturing and then make a strategy by which to start this process.

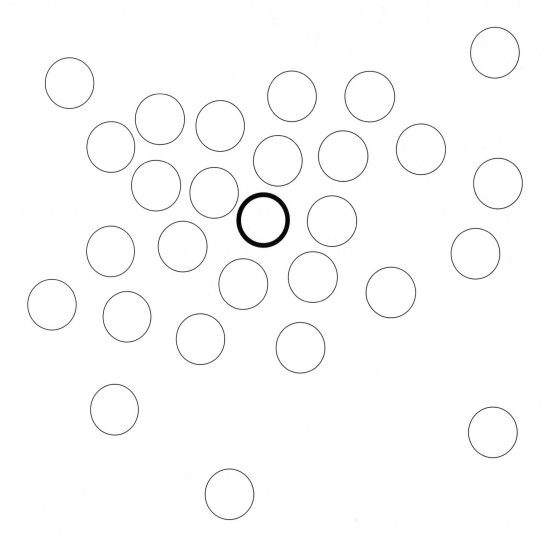

Exercise 5.5   Your Personal Value System

We all have a personal value system: a core pillar of the human spirit that is constantly undergoing renovation. What does your value system currently look like? Perhaps this diagram can give you some insights and, in turn, help resolve some issues that might be causing stress. The circle in the center represents your core values—abstract or intangible constructs of importance that can be symbolized by a host of material possessions. It is believed that we hold about four to six core values that constitute our personal belief system, which, like a compass, guides the spirit on our human journey. Give this concept some thought and then write in this circle what you consider to be your current core values (e.g., love, happiness, health). The many circles that surround the main circle represent your supporting values—those values that lend support to your core values (these typically number from five to twelve). Take a moment to reflect on what these might be and then assign one value per small circle. Also inside each small circle include what typically symbolizes that value for you (e.g., wealth can be symbolized by money, a car, a house, etc.). Finally, consider whether any stress you feel in your life is the result of a conflict between your supporting and core values.

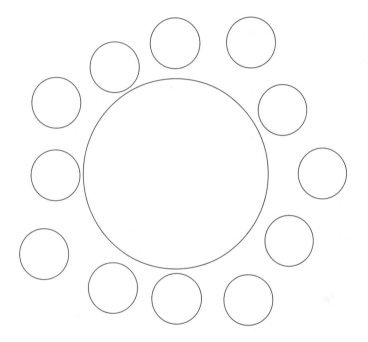

Exercise 5.6 Your Meaningful Purpose in Life

Knowing that your purpose in life may change many times in the course of your life, for this exercise, first write down (in a few words to a sentence) what you consider to be your life purpose now, at this point in time. Then take a moment to briefly describe what you considered to be your purpose in life at the start of each decade of your life (e.g., at age 20 it might be or have been to graduate with a college degree, at age 30 it might be or have been to raise a family or start a business, etc.).

NOW _____

_____

_____

_____

Age 60 _____

_____

_____

_____

Age 50 _____

_____

_____

_____

Age 40 _____

_____

_____

_____

Age 30 _____

_____

_____

_____

_____

Age 20 _____

_____

_____

_____

_____

Exercise 5.7 Roadblocks on the Human Path

If our experience on the human path is indeed the evolution of our soul-growth process, then roadblocks can metaphorically be used to describe a temporary halt to this evolutionary process. Roadblocks on the human path are not necessarily aspects in our lives that separate us from our divine source or mission—even though it may seem like this at times. Rather, roadblocks are *part of* the human path. Although initially they may seem to stifle or inhibit our spiritual growth, this only occurs if we give up or give in to them and do nothing. In the words of a Nazi Holocaust survivor, "Giving up is a final solution to a temporary problem."

Roadblocks take many forms, including unresolved anger or fear, greed, apathy, laziness, excessive judgment, and denial, just to name a few. More often than not, these obstacles manifest symbolically as problems, issues, and concerns (and sometimes people). Although the first thing we may want to do when coming upon a roadblock is retreat and do an about-face, avoidance only serves to postpone the inevitable. Miles down the road, we will encounter the same obstacles. Roadblocks must be dealt with.

First make a list of what you consider to be some of the major (tangible) obstacles on your human journey (e.g., the boss from hell, the ex-spouse from hell). Take a moment to identify each with a sentence or two.

1. _____

_____

2. _____

_____

3. _____

_____

4. _____

_____

5. _____

_____

Next, begin to ask yourself to identify what emotions are associated with each roadblock just listed. What emotions do they elicit, and why do you suppose these emotions surface for you as these obstacles come into view?

1. _____

_____

2. _____

_____

3. _____

_____

4. _____

_____

5. _____

_____

Exercise 5.8   Distractions on the Human Path

Distractions can best be described as those things that pull us off the spiritual path—indefinitely. Distractions begin as attractions, but the allure can often cast a spell of slumber over the soul-growth process. And although a respite on the human journey is desirable and even necessary at times, a prolonged distraction will ultimately weaken our spiritual resolve. The human spirit, like energy, must flow, never stagnate.

The lessons of distractions are quite common in fairy tales. Whether it is the story of Pinocchio or Hansel and Gretel, the warnings regarding distractions are as plentiful as the distractions themselves. The lessons of distractions are common in the great spiritual teachings as well. Here they are called *temptations*. Often, attractions that become distractions have an addictive quality to them as well.

What happens when we become distracted? Metaphorically speaking, we fall asleep on the human path. Like Dorothy and her friends on the way to Oz who stepped off the yellow brick road to smell the poppies and fell fast asleep, we lose our direction; our mission and our energy stagnates. The end result is never promising.

Unlike roadblocks, distractions are not so much meant to be circumvented, dismantled, or even transcended. Rather, they are meant to be appreciated—perhaps from afar, perhaps enjoyed briefly and then left behind. Fairy tales aside, what are contemporary distractions? Common examples of everyday distractions might include social contacts, alcohol, television, and the Internet.

Take a moment to reflect on what might be some distractions in your life. Make a list and describe each one in a sentence or two. Upon recognition of these, what steps can you take to "wake up" and get back on the path?

1. _____
   _____
   _____
   _____

2. _____
   _____
   _____
   _____

3. _____
   _____
   _____
   _____

4. _____
   _____
   _____
   _____

5. _____
   _____
   _____
   _____

Exercise 5.9 On Being a Good Mystic

In a recent Harris poll, over 70 percent of those questioned admitted to having a mystical experience. It's likely the number is even higher. There are many types of mystical experiences, many of which defy description, but by not attempting to articulate them into a comprehensible language, we begin to forget details of fragments that initially lingered in the mind. By writing them down we make the intangible slightly more tangible, the supernatural a little more natural, and the ordinary a little more extraordinary.

- Beyond the five senses: What experiences have you had that you consider to be of a mystical, divine nature? Please take a moment to describe two or three of the most memorable ones here.

_____

_____

_____

_____

_____

_____

- Carl Jung spent the better part of his professional career exploring the mystical nature of the mind. Much of his research involved dreams and dream analysis. He was of the opinion that we are not only capable of precognitive dreams and premonitions, but that these are common occurrences. Do you recall any dreams that foretold future events? Please explain them here.

_____

_____

_____

_____

_____

_____

- The word *synchronicity* was coined by Carl Jung as a means to describe two seemingly random events that come together with great significance. More than just a coincidence, synchronistic events are often thought to be divine messages, when we take the time to decode them. As the expression goes, "There is no such thing as a coincidence. It's God's way of remaining anonymous." What unusual coincidences have you had that are worth noting?

_____

_____

_____

_____

_____

_____

Exercise 5.9

- Abraham Maslow coined the term *peak experience* to convey a sense of oneness with the universe. People who experience this sensation describe it as touching the face of God. Although these experiences are often beyond description, describe as best you can (through metaphor, simile, or analogy) what this experience was like.

  _____

  _____

  _____

  _____

  _____

  _____

  _____

  _____

- To be a good mystic means to appreciate the mystery of life. M. Scott Peck, author of the acclaimed book *The Road Less Traveled,* stated that the highest stage of spiritual growth was to explore the mystery of life but never lose one's appreciation for it. To some, the mystical side of life—those things that cannot be explained rationally through the framework of Western science—is baffling. It leads to a sense of frustration rather than a sense of appreciation. Where do you fall on this continuum?

  _____

  _____

  _____

  _____

  _____

  _____

  _____

  _____

- If you have any other thoughts that you wish to share, please include them here.

  _____

  _____

  _____

  _____

  _____

  _____

  _____

  _____

  _____

Exercise 5.10 Seasons of the Soul

Centering, emptying, grounding, and connecting constitute the four seasons of the soul. Like the planet Earth, we can have many seasons occurring at the same time. There is a normal procession of these seasons; however, it is easy to get stuck in one particular season of the soul. The seasons are listed separately below. Based on the concepts explained earlier in this chapter, take a moment to identify where you feel you are in your life at this time. Please identify what you normally do in each season to get the most out of it.

The Centering Process (Autumn)

_____

_____

_____

_____

_____

_____

The Emptying Process (Winter)

_____

_____

_____

_____

_____

_____

The Grounding Process (Spring)

_____

_____

_____

_____

_____

_____

The Connecting Process (Summer)

_____

_____

_____

_____

_____

_____

Exercise 5.11 Muscles of the Soul

Giving up is the final solution to a temporary problem.
—Gerta Weizt, Nazi concentration camp survivor

Just as a circle is a universal symbol of wholeness, so the butterfly is a symbol of wholeness. Given the fact that butterflies, unlike the lowly caterpillar, have wings to fly, butterflies also are considered a symbol of transformation. They can rise above what was once considered a limiting existence. There is a story of a boy who, upon seeing a young butterfly trying to emerge from its chrysalis, tried to help by pulling apart the paper cocoon that housed the metamorphosis. The boy's mother, who saw what he was about to do, quickly stopped him by explaining that the butterfly strengthens its young wings by pushing through the walls of the cocoon. In doing so, the wings become strong enough to fly.

If you were to talk with people who have emerged gracefully from difficult situations, they would mostly likely tell you that the muscles they used to break through their barrier(s) included patience, humor, forgiveness, optimism, humbleness, creativity, persistence, courage, willpower, and love. Some people call these qualities *inner resources*. I call them *muscles of the soul*. These are the muscles we use to dismantle, circumnavigate, and transcend the roadblocks and obstacles in life. Like physical muscles, these muscles will never disappear; however, they will atrophy with disuse. We are given ample opportunity to exercise these muscles, yet not everyone does.

Using the butterfly illustration, write in the wings those attributes, inner resources, and muscles of the soul that you feel help you get through the tough times with grace and dignity, rather than feeling victimized. If there are traits you wish to include to augment the health of your human spirit, yet you feel aren't quite there, write those outside the wings and then draw an arrow into the wings, giving your soul a message that you wish to include (strengthen) these as well. Finally, if you have a box of crayons or pastels, color in your butterfly. Then hang it up on the fridge or bathroom mirror—some place where you can see it regularly—to remind yourself of your spiritual health and your innate ability to transcend life's problems, big and small.

Exercise 5.12 The Hero's Journey: Exploring the Wisdom of Joseph Campbell

An ancient proverb states, "It takes a brave soul to walk the planet Earth." In the eyes of God, we are all heroes. The role of a hero is not an easy one. To depart from home can promote feelings of insecurities and even abandonment. Initiations—and there are many in one lifetime—are demanding and arduous; the phrase "baptism by fire" comes to mind. Yet through it all we are assured a warm reception upon our return, no matter the outcome of our journey.

The hero's journey is a mythical quest. Myths are clues to the spiritual potential of human life. They offer meaning and significance as well as values. A myth is a source of truth, which often becomes exaggerated but still holds its own essence. According to Campbell, a myth does four things to assist us on this remarkable journey:

1. A myth brings us into communion with the transcendent realms and eternal forms.

2. A myth provides a revelation to waking consciousness of the power of its sustaining source.

3. A myth tell us that no matter the culture, the rituals of living and dying have spiritual and moral roots.

4. A myth fosters the centering and unfolding of the individual in integrity with the ultimate creative mystery that is both beyond and within oneself and all things.

Campbell was of the opinion that the greatest danger of the hero's journey is to fail to use the power of myth as a guide on the spiritual path. He was keenly aware that contemporary American culture has abandoned its association with myths, a clear and present danger to any society.

The Spiritual Quest: Your Mythical Journey

The plot of every myth includes a beginning, middle, and end. In this case, the beginning is a departure from the known and familiar, the middle is a set of trials (called *initiations*), and the end is the return back home. In truth, we engage in this process of the hero's journey many times in the course of our lives.

The Departure: Are you in the process of moving out of the familiar into the unknown? What are you departing from? Typically, there is a refusal of the call. Are you ignoring a call to move on?

The Initiation: The initiation is the threshold of adventure. Mythically speaking, the initiation is to slay a dragon or monster. In real life, initiations come in many forms, from rites of passage to issues, problems, and stressors. What is the single major life issue, concern, or problem that you are facing at the present moment?

_____

_____

_____

_____

_____

_____

_____

_____

_____

_____

_____

_____

The Return Home: The return is symbolized by coming home—home to the old life but with a fresh perspective. The return home bears a responsibility of sharing what you have learned on the journey. What have you learned from your most recent journey?

_____

_____

_____

_____

_____

_____

_____

_____

_____

_____

_____

_____

_____

A Working Myth: What myth (source of truth) do you hold as a compass on your spiritual quest? Where did you learn this myth and how has it helped you?

_____

_____

_____

_____

_____

_____

_____

_____

_____

_____

_____

_____

_____

_____

Any additional comments?

_____

_____

_____

_____

_____

_____

_____

_____

_____

_____

_____

_____

_____

Exercise 5.13   Health of the Human Spirit

Imagine, if you will, that there is a life force of divine energy that runs through your body. This life force is what we call the human spirit. We are a unique alchemy of humanity and divinity. Like a river, spirit runs through us with each breath. It is spirit that invigorates the soul. A lack of spirit can starve the soul, just as a lack of oxygen can starve each cell. The ways to nurture the soul are countless, yet each ensures a constant flow of this essential life force. Unresolved anger and fear are the two most common ways to choke the human spirit, yet whenever the ego dominates the soul, then the health of the human spirit is diminished. The following are just a few of the many ways to enhance the health of your human spirit. As you read through these ideas, write down, in the form of lists, some ideas of what you can do to engage in these activities and, in doing so, engage in the health of your human spirit.

The Art of Self-Renewal
Self-renewal is a practice of taking time to recharge your personal energy and reconnect to the divine source of life. List three ways in which you can find time to renew your personal energy—alone. Select the activity, the day, and the time of day.

1. _____

_____

2. _____

_____

3. _____

_____

The Practice of Sacred Rituals
Sacred rituals are traditions that we do to remind us of the sacredness of life. They include any habit we engage in to which we attribute a sense of the divine. List three rituals you partake in on a regular basis to remind you of the sacredness of life.

1. _____

_____

2. _____

_____

3. _____

_____

Embracing the Shadow
The shadow is a symbol of our dark side, when the ego rules our lives. The shadow appears in the behaviors of prejudice, arrogance, sarcasm, and other less than desirable attributes. To embrace the shadow doesn't mean to exploit these traits, but rather to acknowledge them and work to minimize them. List three aspects of yourself that you find less than flattering. How can you begin to come to peace with these aspects of yourself?

1. _____

_____

2. _____

_____

3. _____

_____

Acts of Forgiveness

Forgiveness is the antidote for unresolved anger. Every act of forgiveness is an act of unconditional love. When you forgive someone, don't expect an apology. Forgiveness is not the same thing as restitution. Forgiveness is a means of letting go and moving on with your life. A large component of forgiveness is learning to forgive yourself as well. List three people who currently have made it to the top of your "s" list. First write down why you feel violated, and then write down how you can let it go and move on with your life—forgive and start moving freely again.

1. _____

_____

2. _____

_____

3. _____

_____

Living Your Joy

Name your joy! What things in life give you pleasure—real unconditional happiness, without any sense of regret afterward? Name three things that make you happy and bring a smile to your face. Unresolved stress can inhibit the feelings of joy. List your top three pleasures. When was the last time you did each one of these? How soon can you do them again?

1. _____

_____

2. _____

_____

3. _____

_____

Compassion in Action

Compassion in action is pure altruism. It is doing for others without any expectation of reciprocation. Putting compassion into action is putting the work of the soul above the priorities of the ego. Compassion in action begins as random acts of kindness, but doesn't end there. List three things you can do to express your compassion in action. Is it a random act of kindness? Is it a generous gesture? Perhaps it is just being there—without feeling a sense of obligation. Next, set out to do all three of the things on your list.

1. _____

_____

2. _____

_____

3. _____

_____

PART II
Effective Coping Skills

6

Reframing: Creating a Positive Mind-Set

Attitude is the paintbrush with which we color the world.
—Ancient proverb

Ageless Wisdom of Positive Thinking

There are those who say the world is composed of two kinds of people: optimists and pessimists. Ageless wisdom reveals that within the mind of each person, there are at least two voices, a positive and a negative influence, suggesting that within each of us is the potential for both mind-sets. Since the days of Plato and perhaps much earlier, it has been observed that the direction of one's life, by and large, is a product of one's thoughts, beliefs, and attitudes. To be sure, we cannot avoid life's problems, nor should we. Our attitude about each situation, however, tends to forecast the outcome. Changing your attitude provides the impetus to change the direction of your life. As the old adage goes, "Attitude is the paintbrush with which we color the world."

In his critically acclaimed book *Man's Search for Meaning,* Viktor Frankl credited his survival in the most notorious Nazi concentration camp, Auschwitz, to his ability to find meaning in his suffering, a meaning that strengthened his willpower and choice of attitude. Frankl noted that despite the fact that prisoners were stripped of all their possessions and many essential human rights, the one thing concentration camp officials could not take away was their ability to choose their perceptions of their circumstances. To quote another adage, "Each situation has a good side and a bad side. Each moment, you decide."

The phrase "self-fulfilling prophecy" had been used long before Freud coined the word *ego.* Ageless wisdom confirms the idea that negative thoughts tend to create and often perpetuate negative circumstances. Likewise, positive thoughts attract positive outcomes. Current research regarding the power of intention upholds this timeless wisdom. Our thoughts, attitudes, perceptions, and beliefs unite as a powerful source of conscious energy. Therefore, it makes sense to use this energy for the best means possible.

The Influence of the Media

Current estimates suggest that the average person is bombarded with over 3,000 advertisements a day from television, radio, T-shirts, billboards, and the Internet—all of which constantly inundate us with messages that strike at our insecurities. In marketing circles, it is known as aggressive, in-your-face tactics. The desired result leaves one with an underlying sense of inadequacy, if not an inferiority complex. There is no doubt this method works; otherwise, marketers would move on to a different strategy.

Corporate marketing is only part of the fear-based media equation. As was so poignantly illustrated in the 2002 Academy Award–winning documentary *Bowling for Columbine,* both local and national news broadcasts have discovered that the addictive nature of fear sells. Even the Weather Channel has changed its focus recently to broadcast weather-related disasters between forecast updates just to keep viewers' attention. Moreover, the federal government is now accused of using the media to fan the flames of anxiety with hypervigilant color-coded terrorism alerts. One of the best ways to increase your tolerance to negative media is to reduce your exposure to it—limiting the time spent watching television, if not getting rid of it altogether.

Toxic Thoughts and Thought Stopping

You don't need negative marketing, depressing network news, or mudslinging political campaigning to bring you down in the dumps. Your ego can do a perfect job of this all by itself. Comments such as "I'm too fat," "I don't have any real friends," and "I'm too old to fall in love" are negative thoughts generated by the ego; the examples are nearly endless. In psychological circles this pattern of critical thinking has several names, including *toxic thoughts, irrational thoughts, fear-based thoughts,* and—a personal favorite—*stinking thinking.* Although everyone has negative thoughts generated by the ego every now and then, it becomes self-defeating to have nothing but these thoughts.

How do you keep the flood of toxic thoughts from contaminating your mind? One way is by *thought stopping,* in which you simply observe your thought processes and stop the negative thought in midsentence. Another technique, similar to thought stopping, involves the conscious process of making yourself aware of your thoughts, including the words coming out of your mouth. When you say something negative, follow that thought with a verbal statement such as "I erase that thought," and then counterbalance the negative thought with a neutral or positive thought. Negative thought stopping, in whatever form, is a practice of domesticating the ego. Meditation is a third way, where upon becoming relaxed, you step outside your thoughts, become the observer of your thoughts, and discard those that do not support your highest good.

An Attitude of Gratitude

Although it's true that it's difficult, if not impossible, to give sincere thanks for a crisis the moment it appears (that's called denial), continuously dwelling on a problem only tends to make things worse. A shift in consciousness toward those things that are blessings tends to balance the negative thoughts that persist from personal stressors. In doing so, an attitude of gratitude provides a perspective that helps resolve the problem at hand. In the midst of stress, regardless of the size of the problem, it is easy to take things for granted. The preferred option is to count your blessings by seeing even the smallest things as gifts.

One aspect of reframing suggests to do just that: Adopt an attitude of gratitude for all the things in life that are going right, rather than curse all the things that seem to be going wrong. What at first appears to be a curse may in hindsight actually be looked upon as a blessing. Many people caught in the midst of a crisis are heard to utter these words, "This is the worst thing that ever happened to me," only to reframe this perspective later to say, "This was the best thing that ever happened to me." In a society where only one day out of 365 is dedicated to giving thanks, the regular practice of an attitude of gratitude may not seem to be encouraged, but remember, this is the same society that promotes fear-based television programming. Buck the tide and make a habit of giving thanks regularly.

The Art of Acceptance

Clearly, there are some things in life we cannot change, nor can we change people's thoughts and behaviors involved with these situations. To do so becomes a series of control dramas that only perpetuate the cycles of stress. The ability to accept a situation for what it is, rather than exerting (and wasting) your energy to alter what you cannot change is a unique human resource, and a valuable component of reframing. Acceptance isn't a sense of resignation or defeat. Rather, it is a sense of liberation that allows you to release any emotional baggage and move on with your life. Acceptance may be an overnight epiphany for some, but for most people it's an attitude that takes several days, weeks, or months to adopt.

The Power of Positive Affirmations

If you were to eavesdrop on the continuous stream of your conscious thoughts, you might be surprised to hear whispers of sabotage. The overbearing voice of the ego is constantly striving to dominate the passionate voice of the soul. By the time most people reach their late teens, the ego has practically declared victory! Sometimes the voice of the ego sounds like background static. Other times it sounds like blaring headline news. The ego best communicates throughout the landscape of the mind by providing a steady stream of negative or fear-based thoughts, attitudes, beliefs, and perceptions that, over time, begin to cloud almost everything you see.

Renowned psychologist Carl Jung referred to the constant mental chatter of the ego as "psychic tension." Many people suffer from this type of stress; however, there is a way to break this cycle and redirect your thoughts toward a positive direction. Jung called this "psychic equilibrium." The balance of this mind-set is within the grasp of each individual, including you!

Using an apt metaphor, the negative voice of the ego that feeds subliminal (and perhaps obvious) messages of fear is similar to the broadcast of a local radio station. The good news is that there is a better choice of quality programming to listen to—primarily the optimistic voice that provides a clear message regarding your highest qualities, your inner resources (e.g., humor, creativity, faith) that enable you to reach your highest human potential.

If you were to talk to those people who have groomed themselves for success, from Olympic athletes and Billboard musicians to the countless untold heroes of every age, you would find that they have learned to switch the mind's radio dial from the nagging voice of the ego to the passionate, grounded voice of the soul. In doing so, they have become the masters of their destiny on the voyage of their highest human potential. You can do this too! People such as Lance Armstrong, Rosa Parks, and Google.com creator Sergey Brin have learned that confidence is not the same thing as arrogance. Affirmations become the mind's compass, leading the way toward humble success.

Developing Your Mastery of Reframing and Optimism

Grooming your mind's thoughts is a skill that takes practice, but it's not impossible. A quick study of elite athletes and Broadway actors reveals that they didn't get to the top by listening to the negative voices in their heads. They redirected their thoughts toward an optimistic belief system.

1. The first step of reframing a situation is an awareness of your thoughts and feelings. When you encounter a difficult situation, get in the habit of asking yourself how you feel, and why you feel this way. If you need validation of your perceptions, consider asking a friend for his or her honest opinion.

2. Once you have become familiar with the recurring pattern of your thoughts and feelings, the next step is to match each negative thought with a positive thought. In essence, find something positive in the negative situation. There is always something positive in a bad situation. Every situation—good, bad, and ugly—offers a valuable life lesson, and when this is acknowledged, something good can be gleaned from it.

3. Negative thoughts about a situation act like a mirror image to our own thoughts about ourselves, and they can have an immense negative impact on our self-esteem. Another step in the reframing process is to take an inventory of your personal strengths. By doing so, you begin to focus on your positive attributes rather than aspects that contribute to low self-esteem.

4. The last suggestion for adopting a positive mind frame includes the ageless wisdom to "count your blessings." Rather than focusing on what's not right, shift your attention to all that is right. There is a concept known as the self-fulfilling prophecy. Others call it the law of universal attraction. It states that the more you think about negative things, the more negative things come into your life to think about. The same is true for positive things. In essence, to a large extent, you attract into your life that which you think most about.

Remember, negativity and the repeated thought processes that produce it can become a downward spiral of consciousness.

Tips for Incorporating the Practice of Reframing

There are many ways to shift the focus of your attention from a negative mind-set to a neutral or positive frame of mind. Remember that reframing isn't a denial of the situation. Rather, it is a positive twist that acts to first recognize and then neutralize the sting of a potentially bad situation. Try these suggestions:

- When you find a situation to be stressful, ask yourself, What can be learned from this situation?

- When you find yourself in a stressful circumstance, take a moment to grieve the situation for what it is, and then (when ready) try to come up with between three to five things for which you are grateful.

- When things don't go as planned (unmet expectations), rather than focusing on your negative attributes, come up with three positive aspects about yourself that you know are your personal strengths. Then pick one and start to use it. Examples might include creativity, humor, and faith.

- To cultivate a positive mind frame in nonstressful times so that you have it to use during stressful times, place a short list of positive affirmations on your bathroom mirror or computer screen.

Tips for Incorporating the Practice of Making Positive Affirmation Statements

Effective positive affirmation statements have a few things in common:
- The use of the words "I am" to begin each statement (e.g., "I am a wonderful human being," or "I am confident of my abilities to succeed in this endeavor")

- Scripting the phrase in the affirmative (e.g., "I am going to make it" rather than "I am not going to make it")

- Scripting the phrase in the present tense (e.g., "I am succeeding in this endeavor" rather than "I am going to succeed in this endeavor")

The following are empowering affirmations to awaken the often-slumbering human spirit—suggestions offered for *your* internal radio station. The purpose is for you to consciously reprogram and incorporate these thoughts into the perpetually running tapes of your conscious and unconscious minds, so that you may achieve what Carl Jung called "psychic equilibrium," or mental homeostasis—the foundation for all success.

The ultimate goal in this process is to reclaim your mental and spiritual sovereignty, which in turn, allows you to transition from inertia to inspiration, from victim to victor on the path of what Joseph Campbell called "the hero's journey."

Please feel free to embellish, edit, and adapt any or all of these affirmations to best suit your needs. Keep in mind that, as with any new skill, listening to these might seem awkward at first, yet after a few sessions, it will become more normal—in fact, second nature. Soon you will notice that these thoughts, these affirmations, have become integrated into your normal thinking process, particularly in times of personal challenge, and brightly color everything you do with confidence and grace.

1. I seek balance in my life by bringing an optimistic perspective to everyday challenges, big and small.

2. I am grateful for all the many blessings in my life, even those that first appear to be less than desirable.

3. I am calm and relaxed.

Best Benefits of Reframing

The benefits of reframing and positive affirmations are amazing. With a new focus on life through an optimistic lens, your world will transform from black and white to full color. This is not to say that you are fooling yourself into thinking that life is a continual vacation at Disney World. Rather, reframing and positive affirmations become one of many resources to strengthen your resiliency during stressful times.

Additional Resources

There are many great books on the topics of positive affirmations and reframing, a selection of which is listed here. There are also many wonderful guided mental imagery CDs with tracks that include positive affirmations.

Books

Armstrong, L. *It's Not About the Bike*. New York: Putnam, 2000.
Dyer, W. *The Power of Intention*. Carlsbad, CA: Hay House, 2004.
Ornstein, R., and Sobel, D. *Healthy Pleasures*. Reading, MA: Addison-Wesley, 1989.
Peale, N.V. *The Power of Positive Thinking*. New York: Fawcett Columbine, 1996.
Ryan, M.J. *Attitude of Gratitude*. Berkeley, CA: Conari Press, 2000.
Seligman, M. *Learned Optimism*. New York: Knopf, 1991.

CDs

Naparstek, B. *Total Wellness*. New York: Time Warner Audiobooks, 1993. 800-800-8661.
Seaward, B.L. *Sweet Surrender*. Boulder, CO: Inspiration Unlimited, 2003. 303-678-9962.
Shamir, I. *A Thousand Things Went Right Today*. www.yourtruenature.com.

Exercise 6.1 Reframing: Seeing a Bigger, Clearer Perspective

Anger and fear that arise from encountering a stressful situation can narrow our focus of the bigger picture. Although the initial aspects of dealing with these situations involve some degree of grieving, the secret to coping with stress is to change the threatening perception to a nonthreatening perception. This worksheet invites you to identify one to three stressors and, if necessary, draft a reframed perspective (not a rationalization) that allows you to get out of the rut of a myopic view and start moving on with your life.

1. Situation: _____

_____

_____

_____

_____

Reframed Perspective: _____

_____

_____

_____

_____

2. Situation: _____

_____

_____

_____

_____

Reframed Perspective: _____

_____

_____

_____

_____

3. Situation: _____

_____

_____

_____

_____

Reframed Perspective: _____

_____

_____

_____

_____

Exercise 6.2

Exercise 6.2 1,000 Things Went Right Today!™

In a stress-filled world, it becomes easy to start focusing on the negative things in life. Pretty soon you begin to attract more negative things in your life. Breaking free from this thought process isn't easy, but neither is it impossible. There is an expression, coined by Ilan Shamir, that states, "A thousand things went right today."™ The concept behind this expression suggests that by beginning to look for the positive things in life, you will start attracting these as well—and let's face it, we can all use more positive things in our lives.

Rather than taxing your mind to come up with 1,000 things, or even 100, try starting with 10 things that went right today, and then see if you can begin to include this frame of mind at the midpoint of each day to keep you on course. Remember, in a world of negativity, it takes work to be happy!

1. _____

2. _____

3. _____

4. _____

5. _____

6. _____

7. _____

8. _____

9. _____

10. _____

After having written down these things, is there any lesson that comes to mind that you can learn from this experience? _____

_____

_____

CHAPTER

7

Comic Relief: The Healing Power of Humor

Against the assault of laughter, nothing can stand.
—Mark Twain

Ageless Wisdom of Comic Relief and Humor Therapy

There is a cute three-panel cartoon of a cave man. In the first panel he is walking along holding his club on his shoulder. In the second panel, he stops and laughs. The third panel shows him walking again. The caption below reads, "the first private joke!"

Humor has been very much a part of the human landscape as a means to cope with the most grueling problems, even before recorded history. Although there were no cartoons or jokes written on the walls of Neanderthal caves in southern Europe, it's safe to assume that, indeed, these guys could produce a good belly laugh. Ancient Greek theater balanced tragedies with comedies. One of the most quoted passages from the Old Testament comes from the book of Proverbs (17:22): "A merry heart does good like medicine, but a broken spirit drieth the bones." It seems that no sooner were radio and television invented than comedy hours were broadcast over the airwaves. Families would huddle around the new Zenith radio listening to George Burns and Amos and Andy, and 60 years after the first *I Love Lucy* show was broadcast, the show can still be seen in syndication—all over the planet. Humor has been and always will be a tool of the mind to combat stress.

Despite the intuitive sense that humor is good for both body and soul, it wasn't until Norman Cousins used humor to heal himself from a debilitating chronic disease that the medical establishment stood up and took notice. By creating his own laughter prescription by watching several comedies, from Charlie Chaplin to the best of *Candid Camera,* Cousins was able to lessen his pain, reverse his condition, and eventually restore himself to health. Cousins planted a seed of wisdom that took root to become the foundation of the field of psychoneuroimmunology: Our thoughts and feelings greatly affect our state of health, for better or worse.

The word *humor* comes from a Latin word of the same spelling that means "fluid" or "moisture." Today that definition is translated to mean "go with the flow." Given the chance, humor eases the pain of life to do just that. Humor is a human magnet. People love to listen to jokes, just as much as they like to share them, particularly over the Internet.

Humorful Insights

As a psychological phenomenon, humor is a little more complicated than simply telling a joke. There are many different types of humor, and there is more than one reason why we laugh and smile. Just as two people can hear the same joke and only one person laughs, so too two people can hear the same joke and laugh for different reasons. Moreover, there are humor styles that reduce stress, just as there are a few types of humor that actually promote it. By first understanding some of the nuances of humor, the healing power of humor takes on a more profound effect.

Reasons Why We Laugh and Smile

There is a small group of academics who spend their time studying and writing on the topic of the psychology of humor. Sadly, their work is devoid of humor, but a synthesis of this information reveals that there seem to be four distinct reasons why people laugh and smile. Perhaps by no coincidence, each mirrors one of the four components of holistic wellness.

Superiority Theory.   In Ancient Greece, it was Plato who first suggested that people laugh and smile at the expense of other's misfortune. When people put themselves above others, it gives them a sense of superiority—hence the name *superiority theory*. Plato noted that the higher the position of authority, the greater the laugh. The superiority theory is an emotion-based theory, and examples abound everywhere in contemporary culture, from poking fun at politicians such as George W. Bush to snickering at the foibles of Martha Stewart.

Release/Relief Theory.   Sigmund Freud is credited with this theory. Freud was of the opinion that all thoughts and behaviors are instinctual. He also proposed that all thoughts and behaviors have a hidden sexual component to them. So perhaps it should come as no surprise that Freud believed that humor was not only a defense mechanism, but that the reason why we laugh and smile is as a physical means to release sexual tension. This may be the reason why sexual jokes never fade in popularity.

Incongruity Theory.   The incongruity theory is a cognitive-based theory, suggesting that laughter and smiles result from the mind's inability to make rational sense of something. In the failure to find the logic of a situation, one either thinks huh? or ha, ha. Much of the humor described as irony and quick-witted humor serves as examples for this theory.

Divinity Theory.   Could humor be a gift from God? Some scholars think so. A strong component of human spirituality is the aspect of connection, and when two people laugh at the same joke, a connection is made, no matter how brief. Chaucer, the author of the *Canterbury Tales,* once said that many a truth has been told in jest, suggesting that there is a divine quality in the ability to use humor to make a point. In some cultures tribal shamans (witch doctors, healers) were not only healers but also jokesters of a sense. The original derivation of a clown was as a personification of the divine, and if the make-up is right, one shouldn't be able to tell if the clown is male or female.

Types of Humor

There are many different types of humor, just as there are many different venues in which humor can be staged. Sometimes these styles can be combined to add even greater depth to the field.

Parody.   Parody is best defined as making fun of something. An example is *Saturday Night Live,* in which the cast performs skits that parody everything, and nothing is sacred. Self-parody is the unique ability to make fun of yourself without compromising your self-esteem. For this reason, parody is ranked at the top of the list.

Satire.   Satire is often defined as a written form of humor with a strong aspect of parody running through it. American satirists are highly esteemed through newspaper columns and Web pages, including Dave Barry, Molly Ivans, and P.J. O'Rourke. *Shrek, The Princess Bride,* and *South Park* also qualify as examples of satire.

Slapstick.   Pies in the face, slipping on banana peels, and slaps across the face are just a few of the examples of slapstick. Slapstick humor is based on early 20th-century vaudeville. The word *slapstick* conveys a sense of physical farce, where it looks like someone is getting hurt, but really isn't (that's the farce). Slapstick humor may seem to have an aggressive nature to it, but it's really a way to diffuse anger, like a pie in the face.

Black Humor.   Black humor isn't ethnic humor, as some people think. Black humor, also called gallows humor, is morbid humor that relieves the stress of death and dying. It's the most common type of humor among nurses, physicians, police officers, emergency medical technicians, and anyone who works on the front lines of death. The popular show *M*A*S*H* was based on black humor, as was the cult classic movie *Harold and Maude.*

Absurd/Nonsense Humor.   Absurd humor dates back to medieval times, and perhaps much earlier. This is the kind of humor that is very creative, but leaves many people scratching their heads. When cartoonist Gary Larson introduced his single-panel *Far Side* cartoon decades ago, he set a new standard for absurd humor. Although Larson has officially retired, he has spurred a new generation of cartoonists to carry the absurd humor torch. About the time that *The Far Side* was making waves in the newspapers across the country, comedian Steven Wright brought absurd humor to a whole new level in his stand-up acts.

Double Entendre.   When a joke has two meanings, it is called a *double entendre.* Many sexual jokes fall in this category, but not all double entendres are sexual in nature. Many of the early Disney cartoons were written with both child and adult humor and thus were loaded with double entrendres. More often than not, so is the dialogue in James Bond movies (e.g., "Sometimes I wake up grumpy, and sometimes I let him sleep in").

Quick-Witted Humor.   Clever humor that makes you stop and think falls under the domain of quick-witted humor (e.g., it takes many nails to build a crib—but only one screw to fill it). NPR's show *Car Talk* is an example of this type of humor, as is the humor of Jerry Seinfeld.

Dry Humor and Puns.   Mark Twain used dry humor. Garrison Keillor of *Prairie Home Companion* also uses it, and there are people who really like this style of humor. Puns are simple word-play jokes. An example is a sign on a music shop door: "Bach in a minuet!" Some people call this style of humor the lowest form of humor, but there are two styles even lower.

Bathroom Humor.   Body functions performed behind closed doors have always been the subject of jokes, including farts, burps, and things that cannot be mentioned here. This topic was once considered taboo, but with the threshold dropped to the ground by Hollywood with movies such as *Dumb and Dumber, Something About Mary, American Pie,* and *Along Came Polly,* bathroom humor has become a fixture of American culture.

Sarcasm.   If you were to look up the word *sarcasm* in any dictionary, you will see the expression "to tear flesh." Sarcasm is often called biting humor, and there is a good reason. Sarcastic comments that hit the intended target hurt. The use of sarcasm represents one or more underlying unresolved anger issues. It doesn't resolve stress; it promotes it. This style of humor should be avoided at all costs.

How to Incorporate Humor Therapy into Your Life Routine

Here's a short list of tips that people have found helpful as a means to provide emotional balance to a stress-filled life. Whether you have a headache, cancer, or a lousy day at the office, these are some ideas to boost your laughter quota to a healthy level.

- **Learn not to take yourself too seriously.** Have you ever had a bad day and said to yourself, "A year from now, this is going to be funny, but right now, it's not funny!" Why wait a whole year and miss out on the fun? Whether it's the Puritan curse or just plain human ego, we tend to take ourselves way too seriously. This bit of sage advice reminds us to loosen up. Remember, the word *humor* actually means "moisture," as in going with the flow. Try doing one thing a day to prove you really can take yourself lightly. Exercise 7.1 challenges you to give this a try.

- **Look for one humorous thing a day.** Humor is like a magnet. The more you pull in, the more you attract. So set out to find one humorous thing a day and you will be amazed and surprised what comes your way. Now, be prepared for the fact that what you find funny may be completely "geographic jokes," as in "you had to be there." But don't let this stop you. If you're looking for a place to start, try the greeting card section of the grocery store. Move on to *Calvin and Hobbes* or *Bizzaro* cartoon books or the *National Enquirer,* and round out the day with Internet sites such as www.jokes.com, www.jokesgallery.com, or www.ahajokes.com. When you're driving, look for funny bumper stickers (but don't rear-end somebody) like these: "My son is inmate of the month at the state penitentiary" "Clean up the earth, it's not Uranus!" or "My other car is a Nimbus 2000." Pretty soon, you will find that you don't have to look too hard. Humorous moments are everywhere.

- **Work to improve your imagination and creativity.** Humor and creativity go hand in hand like peanut butter and jelly. You don't have to be a heavyweight like Walt Disney to be creative. Anything will do. Write a funny poem or limerick. Take candid snapshots of people picking their noses at the nearest mall—anything! Create funny captions for your photo scrapbook so that anyone who reads it will be entertained.

- **Seek and find a host of humorous venues.** You can find humor in books, movies, plays, magazines, television shows, and comedy clubs. Make a list of places you can go to get a good laugh. Then start going to them. The more venues you have at your disposal, the stronger your funny bone will become.

- **Learn to exaggerate when describing a story.** Many people think that to have a good sense of humor you have to be good at telling jokes. Not true! Having a good sense of humor means you appreciate funny jokes. Telling jokes, however, doesn't hurt either. Exaggeration brings out the ironic and incongruous aspects of life—and there are many! Comedians have perfected the exaggeration theme to the fullest. For example, Rodney Dangerfield tells this joke: "Boy, did I have it rough. A rough childhood, even a rough infancy. My mother was Jewish, my father was Japanese. I was circumcised at Benihana's."

- **Build a humor (tickler) notebook.** Rather than have my students write a term paper, I had them make a scrapbook. And not just any scrapbook! It was called a *tickler notebook* (Exercise 7.2). They were instructed to collect cartoons, photos, birthday cards, funny Dear Abby columns, email jokes, JPGs, and photocopies of anything that brought a smile to their face. To this day I still get students and workshop participants contacting me to tell me they are on their fourth tickler notebook. Give it a try! It will become one of your best friends. Speaking of friends . . .

- **Call on a good friend or friends to lift your spirits.** We all have days when we are down in the dumps. That's when you use the secret weapon: a good friend. Norman Cousins had Alan Funt, the producer of *Candid Camera,* who spliced together the best of *Candid Camera* for his sick buddy. We all have friends. The people to call on are the former class clowns, who, to be honest, are still looking for an audience. Don't deny them this opportunity. Call them today.

Humor is not only a muscle of the soul, but also nutrition for the spirit. It may not cure cancer or solve world hunger, but it certainly makes every life challenge more bearable.

Best Benefits of Comic Relief

If chronic emotional stress is considered to be a preponderance of negative thoughts and feelings, then humor is the means to break up the continuity of this negativity. Humor has the ability to decrease fear and diffuse anger. Although humor isn't an emotion, it certainly elicits positive emotions that are sorely needed in times of chronic stress. Humor serves to diminish the ill effects of stress in two ways. First, humor acts as a mental diversion from the cares and worries that plague the mind. Second, the physical effects of humor appear to have a number of physiological benefits, from reducing muscle tension to promoting the release of beta endorphins that create a sense of euphoria and block pain. In short, humor decreases pain and increases pleasure.

Additional Resources

Cousins, N. *Anatomy of an Illness*. New York: Norton, 1969.
Funny Times. *The Best of the Best American Humor*. New York: Three Rivers Press, 2002.
Funny Times (monthly journal). 888-386-6984.
The Humor Project. Saratoga Springs, New York. 518-587-8770. www.humorproject.com.
   (Joel Goodman, director of the Humor Project, puts on one of the best conferences you'll ever attend!)
Klein, A. *The Healing Power of Humor*. Los Angeles: Tarcher Books, 1989.
LaRoche, L. *Life Is Short—Wear Your Party Pants*. Carlsbad, CA: Hay House, 2003.
LaRoche, L. *Relax—You May Only Have a Few Minutes Left*. New York: Villard, 1998.

Exercise 7.1 Working the Funny Bone

1. It's time to create a new answering machine message. Most likely your answering machine message is the same as everyone else's. Here is an example of a winning voice mail message. See if you can come up with something equally funny:

    Hi, you've reached the home of Bob and Jill. We can't come to the phone right now, because we are doing something we really enjoy. Jill likes doing it up and down. I like doing it sideways. Just as soon as we get done brushing our teeth, we'll call you right back.

    Your new voice mail message:

    _____

    _____

    _____

2. *Humor* means "fluid" or "moisture," so let the juice flow. Complete the following sentence by filling in the blank. Combine your talents of creativity and exaggeration to come up with something funny.

    You know you're having a bad day when _____

    _____

    _____

    _____

3. You (or a good friend) are new in town and are looking for a new romantic relationship. The problem is shyness, so the solution is a personal ad. Remember that a sense of humor is one of the first things people look for in a mate.

    _____

    _____

    _____

4. You are a vaudevillian songwriter who has been asked to write some new lyrics for the chorus of one of these commonly known songs. Parody a topic (e.g., health care problems, political characters, environmental problems, any news headline).
    a. "Home on the Range"
    b. "Our House"
    c. "Cabaret"
    d. "My Favorite Things"
    e. A rap song
    f. Your choice

    _____

    _____

    _____

Make a list of your top five movie comedies (with the intention of seeing them again):

1. _____

2. _____

3. _____

4. _____

5. _____

Exercise 7.2 Making a Tickler Notebook

Consider this: The average child laughs or giggles about 300 times a day. The typical adult laughs about 15 times a day (less if they're Republicans). Research reveals that the average hospital patient never laughs at all. This assignment invites you to begin to make a tickler notebook (three-ring notebooks work best), comprising favorite jokes, photographs, JPGs, birthday cards, love letters, Dear Abby columns, poems, or anything else that brings a smile to your face. Keep the tickler notebook on hand, so if you are having a bad day, you can pull it out to help you regain some emotional balance. And, if you ever find yourself in the hospital for whatever reason, be sure to bring it along so that you can at least get your quota of 15 laughs a day. The following are some jokes to help you form a critical mass of funny things to include in your notebook.

Joke Collection

The Slacker A company, feeling it is time for a shake-up, hires a new CEO. This new boss is determined to rid the company of all slackers. On a tour of the facilities, the CEO notices a guy leaning on a wall. The room is full of workers and he wants to let them know he means business! The CEO walks up to the guy and asks, "And how much money do you make a week?" Undaunted, the young fellow looks at him and replies, "I make $200 a week. Why?"

The CEO hands the guy $1,000 in cash and screams, "Here's a month's pay, now *get out* and don't come back!" Surprisingly, the guy takes the cash with a smile, says "Yes sir! Thank you, sir!" and leaves.

Feeling pretty good about his first firing, the CEO looks around the room and asks, "Does anyone want to tell me what that slacker did here?" With a sheepish grin, one of the other workers mutters, "Pizza delivery guy from Domino's."

The Bell Curve of Life

At age 4, success is . . . not peeing in your pants.

At age 12, success is . . . having friends.

At age 16, success is . . . having a driver's license.

At age 20, success is . . . having sex.

At age 30, success is . . . having money.

At age 50, success is . . . having money.

At age 60, success is . . . having sex.

At age 70, success is . . . having a driver's license.

At age 75, success is . . . having friends.

At age 80, success is . . . not peeing in your pants!

Final Exam An eccentric philosophy professor gave a one-question final exam after a semester dealing with a broad array of topics. The class was already seated and ready to go when the professor picked up his chair, plopped it on his desk, and wrote on the board: "Using everything we have learned this semester, prove that this chair does not exist."

Fingers flew, erasers erased, notebooks were filled in furious fashion. Some students wrote over 30 pages in one hour attempting to refute the existence of the chair. One member of the class, however, was up and finished in less than a minute. Weeks later when the grades were posted, the rest of the group wondered how the first student to leave could have gotten an A when he had barely written anything at all. His answer consisted of two words: What chair?

CHAPTER

8

Simple Assertiveness and Healthy Boundaries

Even if you're on the right track, you'll get run over if you just sit there.
—Will Rogers

Ageless Wisdom of Assertiveness

Within the paradigm of wellness lies a paradox. On one hand, there is no separation between mind, body, spirit, and emotions. They all combine to form one dynamic package. All efforts to separate them are done purely for academic and theoretical purposes. Ageless wisdom acknowledges that separation of anything is, in fact, an illusion. At some level everything is connected. Quantum physics supports this fact. On the other hand, borders between subjects and objects are necessary to clearly identify one thing from another. Moreover, boundaries are important to ensure that everything doesn't merge together as one big mess. This is particularly true with people. On one level, boundaries lead to confusion; on another level, they provide security. It is a wise person who knows the difference.

Setting clear boundaries in one's life is a part of the great learning process of the human journey. Knowing when to say yes versus when to say no can mean the difference between inner peace and emotional anguish. In terms of day-to-day situations, boundaries are structures of the mind, based on a set of values, that provide a sense of security and guidance in which to live a balanced life. In today's world, personal boundaries include everything from how many hours of television you watch per day to keeping your checkbook balanced by spending within your financial means. Relationships certainly involve boundaries, just as the use of technology (e.g., cell phones and laptops) does. It's fair to say that just as all life connects, so too all aspects of life necessitate personal boundaries.

Boundaries have become *the* issue of the first decade of the 21st century. At no time in the history of humanity has the permeability of boundaries become so weak or nonexistent. In a 24-7 society where everything and practically everyone is accessible, there is a very strong correlation between poor boundaries and high stress levels. Moreover, poor boundaries pave the path toward inappropriate behaviors, which then further erode one's boundaries.

Sociologists, those people who keep their fingers on the pulse of humanity, are quite concerned if not alarmed regarding the many factors affecting the integrity of the human condition. Consider these facts:

- Not long ago retail stores were closed Sundays (and often on Mondays). Now most stores are open seven days a week and many stores are open 24 hours a day.

- There was a time when television programming was scheduled from 6 A.M. to 12 midnight. This too, is now running on a 24-7 schedule.

- Less than two decades ago, most homes only had one or two TVs in the house. Now there are often more televisions than there are people living in each house, with each child having a TV in his or her bedroom.

- Less than a decade ago, most homes had one phone number. Today many people have several phone numbers and make themselves accessible 24-7 as well.

- Years ago most people had one job (and many wives stayed home to raise the children). Today wives work outside the home and many husbands and wives work more than one job—just to make ends meet.

- Less than a decade ago, the nightly news was information based. Now it's hard to distinguish between news and commercials or news and entertainment, because both are sensationalized to acquire the highest ratings.

- Eating out at restaurants used to be considered an infrequent treat, yet with the advent of fast food restaurants people now cook less at home. Super-sized meals and beverages are just one of the many reasons cited for an obese population, but consuming mass amounts of calories falls under the domain of poor eating habits, which is a boundary issue.

- Although loans have been a stable practice in banking, credit cards are a new creation. The danger of buying on credit is that it gives one the illusion of wealth—until the bills come in. Americans are renowned for huge amounts of credit card debt, suggesting very poor financial boundaries.

It's no exaggeration to say that trends in society, including corporate stock expectations and the rapid advances in technology (e.g., cell phones, email) have undermined many values, which in turn sets the stage for personal boundaries to be less stable. One of the most important issues facing Americans today—and some sociologists feel it is *the* most important issue concerning balance—is the issue of healthy boundaries or the lack thereof. Today there is no shortage of poor boundary issues between home and work, eating habits, personal finances (credit card debt), alcohol use, and personal relationships (infidelity, sexual abuse, etc.). The consequence of poor boundaries is mental, emotional, and spiritual stress through feelings of victimization.

The Art of Healthy Boundaries

Healthy boundaries are nothing more than rules and guidelines that you establish as the defense for a preferred lifestyle. Based on a set of values that you have adopted (consciously or unconsciously), healthy boundaries provide structure and integrity so that you don't feel victimized by the invading forces of life's situations and other people's inappropriate behaviors. Setting clear, healthy boundaries and enforcing them is empowering.

There is a cautionary note about healthy boundaries. Just as poor boundaries can lead to feelings of victimization and stress, rigid boundaries can cause stress as well. Healthy boundaries are organic, meaning that they grow and change based on present conditions. Healthy boundaries can become unhealthy when there is no flexibility, so that the established boundaries become a prison of sorts. Moreover, just as friends, family members, colleagues, and strangers can certainly approach the edge of our personal boundaries and even cross the line at times, so too can we ignore our own personal boundaries and victimize ourselves. Without a doubt, establishing and maintaining healthy boundaries is essential for optimal health and well-being.

Developing a Mastery of Healthy Boundaries

The first step to creating healthy boundaries involves an awareness of your values and personal goals. As an example, if one of your values is privacy yet you answer your phone every time it goes off, then a conflict arises and boundary violations run rampant. Employing steady but humble assertiveness is essential to maintaining healthy boundaries. Exercise 8.1 invites you to take a closer look at your personal boundaries to determine which, if any, need attention and reinforcement. Exercise 8.2 addresses the topic of personal values. By completing this exercise, you no doubt will have a better idea of the relationship between values and boundaries.

Best Benefits of Healthy Boundaries

The benefits of solid, yet flexible boundaries are immeasurable. First, they provide structure and stability to your life. In times of uncertainty, which we are certainly living in, structure and stability are assets worth striving for and maintaining. Healthy boundaries also provide a sense of empowerment over potential feelings of victimization; in essence, you don't allow yourself to be walked over all the time. Additionally, high self-esteem is a critical factor in maintaining healthy boundaries, yet the maintenance of healthy boundaries can, in turn, promote a greater sense of high self-esteem as well. The two go hand in hand for optimal wellness.

The Anatomy of High Self-Esteem

Self-esteem plays a critical role in how we handle day-to-day stress. Low self-esteem becomes a bull's-eye for problems and issues to target, whereas high self-esteem allows small problems to roll off our backs and bigger problems to be divided and conquered. The secrets of high self-esteem have been studied for ages and no longer are deemed secrets. Moreover, as odd as this may seem, the ego is essential to high self-esteem, for without it, one's sense of self-worth would be nothing. Conversely, too strong of an ego tips the scales of high self-esteem out of balance, from confidence to cockiness.

Although there are many things that compose the totality of self-esteem, five key aspects seem to be regarded as the components of this essential human attribute necessary to successfully navigate the shoals of life's waters. These five characteristics are (1) uniqueness, (2) role models, (3) connectedness, (4) the ability to take calculated risks, and (5) empowerment. Let's take a closer look at each.

- **Uniqueness:** This aspect of high self-esteem is based on the concept of specific attributes that we see in ourselves that we deem unique or special and which distinguish us from others. These attributes are both tangible and intangible and include everything from the color of one's hair to one's sense of humor. Uniqueness also includes the individual's combination of inner resources (the muscles of the soul mentioned in Chapter 5).

- **Role models:** Heroes, mentors, and role models include those people whom we greatly admire. They have certain characteristics that we wish to emulate and incorporate as aspects of our own personality.

- **Connectedness:** Having a sense of connectedness and belonging is essential for health and well-being. Friends, family members, peers, and colleagues constitute what is now called a personal "support group." Not only do friends make us feel accepted, but they also tend to buffer the effects of stress when we are feeling low.

- **Calculated risks:** Fear is an immobilizing emotion that holds one back from a multitude of life's experiences and adventures. Taking a calculated risk involves a number of inner resources, not the least of which is courage, a unique alchemy of confidence and faith that allows you to move through the barriers of fear to enjoy the rewards of life's best moments. Calculated risks allow you to be an active participant in life, rather than a passive victim of it.

- **Empowerment:** Empowerment is best described as a sense of personal energy or vitality. Some even call it inspiration. Empowerment is a sense of keeping one's personal power rather than giving it away to one's job, significant other, possessions, sports teams, therapist, or even celebrities. Giving away personal power is a drain of personal energy, which can ultimately lead to disease and illness.

The Importance of Empowerment

From a holistic perspective, empowerment is not only vital to one's self-esteem, it's essential to one's life force or energy. A quick survey of our society suggests that it's human nature to give our power away. In some cases it is given in exchange for something, such as restored health from a team of physicians. In other cases there is no exchange or benefit whatsoever! Healers who observe the human energy field around their clients explain that a loss of power is an energy leak, analogous to a water tank with a crack at the bottom.

People tend to confuse empowerment with control, yet these are two entirely different concepts. At its best, *empowerment* is the exhibition of one's highest potential exhibited as grace. *Control* is an attempt to manipulate oneself, others, or both. Control has an addictive quality to it, in that no matter how much one has, it never seems to be enough. Empowerment is the realization that control is an illusion, at which point the leak is fixed and the tank becomes filled up again. Exercise 8.3, "Giving Your Self-Esteem a Healthy Boost," helps you integrates these ideas in your life.

The Anatomy of Assertiveness

To be walked over, taken advantage of, or not appreciated for one's talents and abilities is the first stage of victimization. Conversely, to be arrogant, rude, manipulative, and self-centered constitutes the hallmark of aggressiveness. Like so many aspects of holistic stress management, where balance is the key to inner peace, assertiveness resides between passivity and aggressiveness. Assertiveness means standing up for your rights, yet not controlling or manipulating others. To be assertive means to act with a conscience. It means to balance freedom with responsibility by taking what is yours without taking away from anyone else. The epitome of assertiveness is the display of a well-balanced ego.

Acts of assertiveness require a fair amount of diplomacy, humbleness, and grace, because anything less will come across as aggressive behavior and will immediately draw a defensive reaction from others. Examples of assertiveness range from asking the waiter for a better table to requesting someone to turn off his or her cell phone at the cinema. Assertiveness is also essential for establishing healthy boundaries, because without the means to make your intentions or preferences known and honored, feelings of victimization may ensue.

One final note about empowerment: It's best to know the subtle difference between rights and entitlements. *Rights* fall under the domain of being treated with respect. *Entitlements* are privileges that may or may not be extended to everyone. Confusion between these two constructs can promote stress, particularly when one has expectations of receiving entitlements when there may be none to be had. As our vast world becomes a small global village, many expectations go unmet, and tempers flare as a result. The anatomy of assertiveness includes humbleness.

How to Incorporate Assertiveness into Your Life Routine

Developing a mastery of assertiveness lies in the wisdom of knowing when to say yes (advocating for your rights) and knowing when to say no (knowing your limitations so as not to feel victimized with too many responsibilities). This mastery also includes fine-tuning the inherent balance between freedom and responsibility. As a rule, people tend to take on too many responsibilities.

Here are some time-honored tips for simple assertiveness:

- **Learn to say no.** When others ask for your time, learn to say no if you really don't have the time. Even if you say yes initially, you can always come back and say no as long as you are diplomatic.

- **Use "I" statements.** By using the word *I*, you claim ownership of your thoughts and feelings (e.g., I am angry that you did this!).

- **Use direct eye contact.** When speaking to people, look them directly in the eye to make your point.

- **Use assertive body language.** How you stand and position your arms can come across as defensive, weak, or strong. Stand on two feet and use your hands to express your point.

Best Benefits of Assertiveness

The best benefit of engaging in acts of assertive behavior is restoring and maintaining a sense of self-worth and self-esteem. As mentioned in Chapter 6, self-worth is easily defeated by negative self-talk. Incorporating an attitude of assertiveness and taking proactive steps to make assertiveness a key inner resource allays the feelings of victimization and helplessness so that you can live your life in balance.

Additional Resources

Branden, N. *The Six Pillars of Self-Esteem*. New York: Bantam Books, 1994.
Burns, D. *The Feeling Good Handbook*. New York: Plume, 1999.
McKay, M., and Fanning, P. *Self-Esteem*, 3rd ed. Oakland, CA: New Harbinger, 2000.
Shiraldi, G. *The Self-Esteem Workbook*. Oakland, CA: New Harbinger, 2001.

Exercise 8.1 Healthy Boundaries

We are living in an age in which the average person has very poor boundaries in his or her life. Technology may be a factor, but it's not the only reason. People bring their work home, while at the same time problems from home invade their professional lives. It seems that almost everyone has poor financial boundaries, with the average person carrying well over $5,000 annually in credit card debt. People think nothing of bringing their cell phones into restaurants and movie theaters, and what begins as just an hour in front of the television ends up being a whole evening. Poor personal boundaries result in feelings of being overwhelmed, annoyed, and victimized—all of which contribute to a critical mass of stress.

First, healthy boundaries require an insight about what's appropriate in each and every setting in which you find yourself—in essence, creating the boundaries you need and want to maintain a sense of personal balance. Next, healthy boundaries require courage to assert your boundaries so that they are not violated. Finally, healthy boundaries require willpower and discipline to honor what you yourself have established in order to give you better structure and stability in your life.

I. List four areas in your life that you feel have weak boundaries (or perhaps no boundaries). Examples might include finances, alcohol, technology, eating habits, or television watching.

1. _____

_____

2. _____

_____

3. _____

_____

4. _____

_____

II. Now, please list four boundaries that you would like to create in your life to bring about a sense of balance. Then add a few words about what you can do to have these boundaries honored.

1. _____

_____

2. _____

_____

3. _____

_____

4. _____

_____

Exercise 8.2 Value Assessment and Clarification

Values—those abstract ideals that shape our lives—are constructs of importance. They give the conscious mind structure. They can also give countries and governments structure. The U.S. Declaration of Independence is all about values, including "life, liberty, and the pursuit of happiness." Although values are intangible, they are often symbolized by material objects or possessions, which can make values very real. Some everyday examples of values are love, peace, privacy, education, freedom, happiness, creativity, fame, integrity, faith, friendship, morals, health, justice, loyalty, honesty, and independence.

Where do values come from? We adopt values at a very early age, unconsciously, from people whom we admire, love, or desire acceptance from, like our parents, brothers and sisters, school teachers, and clergy. Values are often categorized into two groups: *basic* values, a collection of three to five instrumental values that are the cornerstones of the foundation of our personalities, and *supporting* values, which augment our basic values. Throughout our development we construct a *value system,* a collection of values that influences our attitudes and behaviors, all of which make up our personality.

As we mature, our value systems also change because we become accountable for the way we think and behave. Like the earth's tectonic plates, our values shift in importance, causing our own earth to quake. These shifts are called *value conflicts* and can cause a lot of stress. Classic examples of value conflicts include love versus religious faith or social class (e.g., Romeo and Juliet), freedom versus responsibility, and work versus leisure (e.g., the American Dream). Conflicts in values can be helpful in our own maturing process if we work though the conflict to a full resolution. Problems arise when we ignore the conflict and avoid clarifying our value system.

The purpose of this exercise is for you to take an honest look at your value system, assess its current status, and clarify unresolved issues associated with values in conflict. The following are some questions to help you in the process of value assessment and clarification.

1. Make a list of the core values you hold (values come from things that give your life meaning and importance, yet they are abstract in nature).

2. See if you can identify which of these values are *basic,* or instrumental, at this point in your life and which *support* or augment your basic values.

3. How are your values represented in your possessions? (For example, a BMW may represent wealth or freedom.)

4. Describe how your values influence your dominant thoughts, attitudes, and beliefs.

5. Do you have any values that compete for priority with one another? If so, what are they, and why is there a conflict?

6. What do you see as the best way to begin to resolve this conflict in values? Ask yourself if it is time to change the priority of your values or perhaps discard values that no longer give importance to your life.

_____

_____

_____

_____

_____

_____

_____

_____

_____

_____

_____

_____

_____

_____

_____

_____

_____

_____

_____

_____

_____

_____

_____

_____

_____

_____

_____

_____

_____

_____

_____

_____

_____

_____

_____

_____

Exercise 8.3 Giving Your Self-Esteem a Healthy Boost

Self-esteem is thought to be composed of five components: uniqueness, role models, empowerment, connectedness, and calculated risk taking. With this in mind, let's take a look at your level of self-esteem with respect to these five areas. Try to answer the following questions as best you can.

Uniqueness
List five characteristics or personal attributes that make you feel special and unique (e.g., sense of humor, being a good cook, a passion for travel).

1. _____
2. _____
3. _____
4. _____
5. _____

Empowerment
List five areas or aspects of your life in which you feel you are empowered.

1. _____
2. _____
3. _____
4. _____
5. _____

Mentors and Role Models
Name five people (heroes, mentors, or role models) who have one or more characteristics that you admire and wish to emulate or enhance as a part of your own personality. Please describe the person and the trait or traits.

1. _____
2. _____
3. _____
4. _____
5. _____

Social Support Groups
Friends and family are now thought to be crucial to one's health status. To have a sense of belonging is very important in one's life. Who (or what) gives you a sense of belonging? Please describe each in a sentence.

1. _____
2. _____
3. _____
4. _____
5. _____

Exercise 8.3

Calculated Risk Taking

List five good risks that you have taken in the past year that you feel have augmented your sense of self-worth and courage.

1. _____

2. _____

3. _____

4. _____

5. _____

Exercise 8.3

CHAPTER
9

Effective Time Management: Living with Time to Spare

Time is a way of preventing everything from happening all at once!
—Anonymous

Ageless Wisdom of Time Management

One of the biggest complaints heard over the ages is simply not having enough time to do what needs to get done in the course of any given day. Perhaps since time began, humankind has done everything in their power to manipulate time, from tinkering with daylight savings to numerous revisions of the yearly calendar. Did you ever wonder why the annual lunar cycle is 13 months, yet the typical calendar only has 12 months?

Nearly everyone wishes they had more time for leisure and less hours of the day devoted to earning a paycheck. Ironically, the promise made decades ago that technology would allow more leisure time never materialized. Although technology has provided a plethora of wonderful gadgets (e.g., cell phones, answering machines, laptop computers, microwave ovens, washers, dryers, dishwashers, and word processors), few if any people are sitting back comfortably with hours upon hours of leisure time on their hands these days. If anything, people seem to have less leisure time, not more, than a decade ago. For this reason, people are continually seeking out ideas and suggestions to better organize their time as well as enjoy the time they have. Day planners and Palm Pilots are nice, but there are literally hundreds of ways to streamline your day for higher efficiency, productivity, and relaxation without compromising your integrity. Exercise 9.1 is a worksheet that can be used in group situations to help brainstorm new ideas to manage time. Remember that if you get one good idea that you can use, it's worth it.

Time management is best defined as the prioritization, scheduling, and execution of responsibilities to one's personal satisfaction. Let's take a closer look at each of these aspects so that you can begin to manage your time even better.

Prioritization

Prioritization first requires one to identify specific tasks and responsibilities that you need to accomplish. To prioritize one's to-do list means knowing the difference between what's essential and what's not. In the business model, it's imperative to know the difference between what's urgent and what's not, and what's important and what's not. Human nature tends to want to gravitate toward things that are of high interest and low priority, leaving the things of high urgency and low interest until last.

There are several ways to identify the urgency of responsibilities. The first includes the ABC rank-order method (A = highest priority, B = moderate priority, and C = low priority). The second, based on the work of Steven Covey, is the Important vs. Urgent grid, where you gain clarity regarding what needs to get done first by writing down tasks into one of four grid boxes. Exercise 9.2 includes both of these methods.

Scheduling

Once tasks and responsibilities are identified comes the need to set each task a time schedule to get it accomplished. Scheduling involves the skills of organization to know when is the best time to get things done and what are the best means to do so.

Experts in the field of time management suggest various techniques for the most efficient means of scheduling tasks and responsibilities. *Clustering* is the name given to grouping tasks together. Examples include clustering errands together (e.g., post office, dry cleaners, and video store) so that time is not wasted driving all over the place. *Boxing* is the term given to designating large segments of the day when big chunks of uninterrupted time are needed for big projects. *Dismantling* is the name given to breaking down large projects into smaller, more manageable tasks. Examples might include doing year-end taxes, term papers, wedding plans, or backyard landscaping. *Time mapping* is a technique used to designate specific parts of each hour for scheduling purposes. It's also a good tool to see where your time robbers are hiding. Exercise 9.3 is an example of time mapping.

Execution (Action Plan)

To be able to prioritize responsibilities and schedule them into your day is good, but it's not enough to get the job done! Rolling up your sleeves and actually doing the work is the lion's share (85 percent) of effective time management. Execution is the act of carrying out, completing, or finishing each and every task you set out to accomplish and doing it well. A large part of time management's execution is sheer willpower—the drive to get things done and done to one's personal satisfaction.

One way to add some inspiration to your willpower is to consider assigning a reward for each large task looming on your horizon. Whether the reward is large (a weekend getaway) or small (a piece of chocolate), tangible (a Hawaiian vacation) or intangible (sheer happiness), having an incentive is often helpful. It's important to remember in this age of instant gratification, however, that the reward comes *after*, not before, the task is completed. Exercise 9.4 provides a template for matching various personal tasks with possible rewards that may serve as a motivation to get each task accomplished. Although rewards don't work for everyone, they might be an idea worth considering. One caution about any carrying out of an action plan: Avoid multitasking!

The Art of Subtraction

It may be human nature to accumulate things, but as anyone knows, too much of anything is not good. By and large, Americans are very good at honoring the art of addition. Just look inside anyone's overflowing garage! Not all stuff carries with it endless responsibilities, but most possessions do. Effective time management honors the inherent concept of balance. To achieve balance, you must occasionally let go of things that you have accumulated.

Technology, consumerism, and many American values promote a lifestyle of addition. Holistic stress management requires living a life in balance, meaning that the art of subtraction must be practiced as well. How does one engage in the art of subtraction? Ideas include but are not limited to bringing clothes to Good Will, recycling newspapers and bottles, and watching less television. The overriding premise of the art of subtraction is making life simpler by having less things and people in your life that waste time. Exercise 9.5 invites you to make a list of things and people that either clutter your life or pull badly needed energy from you and ultimately serve as a distraction to getting things done.

Time Robbers

Have you ever spent hours cleaning the house, garage, or car when you really should have been finishing a project or paying bills? If so, know that you're in good company! You are also in the company of one of life's many time robbers (also known as avoidance). *Time robbers* are behaviors that steal your valuable time away from responsibilities that really need attention. Time robbers can also be things that literally suck the energy right out of your life. Although procrastination, in all its many forms, constitutes a large number of time robbers, that which steals minutes or hours out of your life includes more than just the little things you do to avoid necessary responsibilities. People can be time robbers too! For this reason, having healthy boundaries is essential when setting out to start and complete things on your to-do list.

If you think that you waste time in the course of each day or feel that, like sand slipping through an hourglass, valuable time is slipping away, consider using Exercise 9.3 (time mapping) to chronicle the time robbers in your life.

Time-Honored Time Management Tips

- **Be assertive.** Learn to say no when others ask you to do work for them or activities with them that impede the progress of your own work schedule. By not being assertive, you may begin to feel victimized, which leads to feelings of anger.

- **Delegate.** Whenever possible, assign tasks to others rather than controlling the situation by doing everything yourself.

- **Schedule personal time each day and use it.** Your health is essential to ensure the best quality of life. If you neglect personal time for exercise, healthy eating, and nurturing relationships, then your health will become compromised, thus adding more stress to your life.

- **Cultivate your networking skills.** Many tasks can be done by yourself, but others require help. Make a practice of cultivating relationships with friends, neighbors, family members, and professional colleagues who can assist you by offering anything from sound advice to a helping hand when needed.

- **Get a good night's sleep.** People have the odd belief that shaving off hours of sleep on either end of the day will allow them to get more work done. Poor sleep compromises mental acuity, thus compromising your quality of work. Get a good night's sleep every night.

- **Do one activity at a time (no multitasking).** There are few people who can do two things at once and do them well. The best the rest of us can do is accept mediocrity, which does not support the premise of holistic stress management. Multitasking may be the in thing, but it rarely results in a quality job.

- **Let technology serve you, rather than you serving it.** Cell phones, laptops, and Palm Pilots are wonderful tools to increase efficiency, yet they are not meant to be used every hour of the day. There is a strong addictive quality to technology (constantly checking email, voice mail, etc.) that soon reverses the relationship so that people become slaves to the very things that are supposed to serve them. Good boundaries are essential with the ever-changing face of high technology. This fact cannot be overstated!

- **Watch less television.** The average person watches between 20 and 30 hours of television a week. This is nearly a full-time job! Although there are a few good programs on television these days, most people agree that the rest is mindless junk. For most people, television is human kryptonite! It sucks your power away. Establish a healthy boundary with television and consider eliminating TV altogether.

How to Incorporate Time Management into Your Life Routine

The first step in incorporating effective time management skills into your life routine is to observe where your time robbers are. The second step is to do a quick survey and determine how to apply the art of subtraction. Determine what things you can delete from your life that are taking up valuable time or that drain your personal energy.

The third step is to identify and prioritize daily responsibilities (your to-do list) into larger goals and personal goals (e.g., buying a house, taking a vacation, writing a book). Remember to include in your daily responsibilities time for exercise, meditation, adequate sleep, healthy meals, social time, and even a few unscheduled interruptions.

Next, clear all distractions and sit down and get to work on the things of highest priority and urgency. Remember that big projects need to be broken down into smaller pieces, so that the end result can be accomplished successfully.

At the end of each day, take a quick inventory to see what got done, and what needs to roll over into the next day. Before you call it a day, consider spending a few minutes doing some organizational prep work so that you can start the next day without a huge adrenaline rush.

Effective time management requires moment-to-moment corrections of your personal daily schedule because life is dynamic, not static, and changes can and will occur. Perhaps the biggest obstacle to effective time management is the ego, which has a tendency to want to step in and control everything. Remember, there are many people who could work 20 hours a day and still not get everything done. At some point you have to resign yourself to the fact that the quality of work must be balanced with the quantity of tasks and responsibilities.

How to Develop Your Mastery of Time Management

Effective time management skills involve both a sense of discipline and flexibility. Discipline is essential with regard to healthy boundaries so that you know when not to take on additional responsibilities, thus feeling overwhelmed and possibly victimized. Flexibility is critical in terms of moving through the course of each day and shifting with new priorities without feeling stressed about other things that also need to be accomplished. Developing your mastery of effective time management is a skill that must be continually refined because the dynamics of one's life constantly change.

Ultimately, time management becomes the most important coping skill for holistic stress management, because if one doesn't make the time for the other coping and relaxation techniques to fully integrate, balance, and harmonize mind, body, spirit, and emotions, then even the best efforts for inner peace will be ultimately compromised, if not abandoned altogether.

Best Benefits of Time Management

The benefits of effective time management are numerous. Rather than running around in a state of frenzy, you feel a sense of empowerment from getting things done and having the time to enjoy life's simple pleasures. A large part of effective time management includes setting healthy boundaries and having the willpower to enforce these boundaries. There is simply no way to add more time to a 24-hour day, which means that spending your time wisely is the greatest benefit of all.

Additional Resources

Allen, D. *Getting Things Done*. New York: Penguin Books, 2003.

Jasper, J. *Take Back Your Time: How to Regain Control of Work, Information and Technology*. New York: St. Martin, 1999.

Knaus, W. *The Procrastination Workbook*. Oakland, CA: New Harbinger Publications, 2002.

Koch, R. *The 80/20 Principle: The Secret of Achieving More with Less*. New York: Bantam Doubleday Dell, 1998.

Morgenstern, J. *Time Management from the Inside Out*. New York: Henry Holt, 2000.

Exercise 9.1 Time Management Idea Exchange

Read through the following questions and list the best answers that come to mind.

1. List five reasons why people don't manage their time effectively. Which ones apply to your current lifestyle?

    a. _____

    b. _____

    c. _____

    d. _____

    e. _____

2. Explain your feelings of stress when your time isn't managed as well as you'd like it to be.

    a. _____

    b. _____

    c. _____

    d. _____

    e. _____

3. List the most beneficial time management techniques that you find helpful to effectively manage your time and keep on schedule, and then explain why.

    a. _____

    b. _____

    c. _____

    d. _____

    e. _____

4. Think up five new ways to manage your time more effectively (consider including ways to deal with the flood of technology).

    a. _____

    b. _____

    c. _____

    d. _____

    e. _____

5. Select one idea from question 3 or 4 that you like and outline the steps you can take to implement this technique.

    a. _____

    b. _____

    c. _____

    d. _____

    e. _____

Exercise 9.2 The Importance of Prioritization

The following are two methods of improving your organizational skills for effective prioritization and time management skills.

ABC Rank-Order Method

A	B	C
Highest Priority	**Moderate Priority**	**Low Priority**
1. _____	1. _____	1. _____
2. _____	2. _____	2. _____
3. _____	3. _____	3. _____

Important vs. Urgent Method

	High Importance	Low Importance
High Urgency	I: a. b. c.	III: a. b. c.
Low Urgency	II: a. b. c.	IV: a. b. c.

Exercise 9.3 Time Mapping

The following exercise invites you to chart out your day by clearly identifying how each 15-minute block of time is spent. You can also simply record your daily activities to observe how to best utilize and schedule your time and where time robbers are stealing your time in the course of each day.

7:00 A.M. _____

7:15 A.M. _____

7:30 A.M. _____

7:45 A.M. _____

8:00 A.M. _____

8:15 A.M. _____

8:30 A.M. _____

8:45 A.M. _____

9:00 A.M. _____

9:15 A.M. _____

9:30 A.M. _____

9:45 A.M. _____

10:00 A.M. _____

10:15 A.M. _____

10:30 A.M. _____

10:45 A.M. _____

11:00 A.M. _____

11:15 A.M. _____

11:30 A.M. _____

11:45 A.M. _____

12:00 Noon _____

12:15 P.M. _____

12:30 P.M. _____

12:45 P.M. _____

1:00 P.M. _____

1:15 P.M. _____

1:30 P.M. _____

1:45 P.M. _____

2:00 P.M. _____

2:15 P.M. _____

2:30 P.M. _____

2:45 P.M. _____

3:00 P.M. _____

3:15 P.M. _____

3:30 P.M. _____

3:45 P.M. _____

4:00 P.M. _____

4:15 P.M. _____

4:30 P.M. _____

4:45 P.M. _____

5:00 P.M. _____

5:15 P.M. _____

5:30 P.M. _____

5:45 P.M. _____

6:00 P.M. _____

6:15 P.M. _____

6:30 P.M. _____

6:45 P.M. _____

7:00 P.M. _____

7:15 P.M. _____

7:30 P.M. _____

7:45 P.M. _____

8:00 P.M. _____

8:15 P.M. _____

8:30 P.M. _____

8:45 P.M. _____

9:00 P.M. _____

9:15 P.M. _____

9:30 P.M. _____

9:45 P.M. _____

10:00 P.M. _____

After you have written down the events or plans in the course of your day, what observations can you make from this exercise?

_____

_____

_____

Exercise 9.3

Exercise 9.4 Getting Things Done: The Execution of Tasks

Lacking motivation to get some things done? One way to fan the fires of inspiration is to provide some incentives to accomplish big or arduous tasks by giving yourself a reward. Although the real reward is the accomplishment of the deed, a little incentive may be just the thing needed to get it done on time. Remember, not all rewards have to be material possessions. A phone call to a close friend at the end of the day can be as rewarding as a vacation to Tahiti in some cases. Remember, rewards are meant to decrease stress, not increase it.

Goal to Accomplish   Incentive/Reward

1. _____

2. _____

3. _____

4. _____

5. _____

6. _____

7. _____

8. _____

9. _____

10. _____

Exercise 9.5 Practicing the Art of Subtraction

Does your life feel cluttered with too much stuff? Are your garage and basement filled with stuff that you haven't used (or seen) in years? Are there people in your life who are so emotionally needy that when you see them, you want to run and hide? Are there things in your life that at first seemed to simplify things and now seem to be complicating things? If so, you might want to consider engaging in the art of subtraction (also known as "editing your life").

Clutter

Walk through your house or apartment and make a list of five things that fall into the category of personal clutter (this can include equipment, clothes, books, or anything lying on the floor). Once you have made this list, collect the things and consider giving them away to Good Will or some other charitable organization.

1. _____

_____

2. _____

_____

3. _____

_____

4. _____

_____

5. _____

_____

People

Are there people in your life who take up time rather than contribute to your quality of life? Take inventory if you have any "friends" who seem to be a drain of your emotional energy. The next question to ask yourself is this: Do you drain other people's energy? Do you give as well as take in your relationships and friendships?

a. _____

b. _____

c. _____

Simplicity vs. Complexity

We tend to bring things into our lives out of both interest and fear. What things are in your life right now that may have been begun out of interest, but now you are ready to let go of? Another way to phrase this question is to ask yourself: What things in your life tend to add complexity rather than simplicity? Once you have identified three things, begin to ask yourself what you can do to subtract these things to bring your life back into balance.

1. _____

_____

2. _____

_____

3. _____

_____

CHAPTER 10

Creative Problem Solving

If your only tool is a hammer, you'll see every problem as a nail.
—Abraham Maslow

Ageless Wisdom of Creativity

Invention, innovation, imagination, incubation, adaptation, and inspiration. These are but a few of the many words that come to mind when one begins to articulate the revered concept known as creativity and the creative process in which these seeds of creativity take root. One cannot help but stand in awe of such creations as da Vinci's Mona Lisa, Beethoven's Fifth Symphony, or Peter Jackson's film adaptation of J.R.R. Tolkien's *The Lord of the Rings*. Less venerated, but no less important, are inventions such as the weaving loom, automobile, jet airplane, and laptop computer. It has been said that it is the creative mind of the human species that separates us from all other species.

Necessity, it is said, is the mother of invention. Although necessity is not the same thing as stress, pushed to the limits, it can elicit the stress response very quickly. It's no secret that many creative moments come under duress, which is a means to make the unworkable work, and the immovable move. Stress can prove to be a force of inspiration, which in turn results in some rather amazing inventions, and works of art. If necessity is the mother of invention, then play certainly commands a paternal role in this unique process. Many of the world's finest creations, inventions, and innovations didn't occur in stressful episodes but rather from relaxed moments of tinkering (playing) in the garage.

By most accounts human beings are the only species on the planet Earth that employ the dynamics of creativity. Architecture, songs, drawings, and mechanical devices are just some of the many things that humankind, for better or worse, leaves as a legacy to the rest of the world. Ironically, in a country known for its "American ingenuity," creativity is not cultivated as a human resource skill in the U.S. education system. Instead, critical thinking is encouraged and highly praised. Interestingly, today American business leaders are in search of creative talent in other parts of the world. Given the rapid rate of change today in our personal lives, as well as the changes (both large and small) in the global village, it's no secret that creative problem solving will become one of the most sought-after coping skills in all levels of human endeavors. Creativity is also considered to be one of the essential traits in the stress-resistant personality profile. For this reason, a review of these skills is essential in the paradigm of holistic stress management.

The Creative Process Revealed

The creative process has been inspected, dissected, and analyzed in the hopes of revealing the secrets to coming up with such inventions as the lightbulb, the telephone, and the Internet. Those who have cut open the proverbial goose to see how the golden egg is formed have all come to the same conclusion: Creativity is a multifaceted process combining imagination with organization, intuition with collaboration, and, more recently, the right-brain functions with the left-brain skills.

In his effort to understand the creative process, scholar and author Roger von Oech identified, in a creative way, four distinct aspects that reveal a more thorough understanding of the often elusive, yet always in demand, creative process. Von Oech described four aspects or roles of the creative process, including the explorer, the artist, the judge, and the warrior. Let's take a closer look at these components.

- **The explorer:** The first stage of the creative process begins with a search for new ideas! To find ideas, you have to leave the known and venture into the unknown. In other words, you have to venture off the beaten path! The explorer begins to look for ideas anywhere and everywhere. The farther you go off the beaten path, the more likely you are to come up with many original ideas. In new environments, our sensory receptors are more open to new stimuli. Where do people go to explore new ideas? Art museums, hardware stores, greenhouses, travel magazines, and late-night talk radio are some possibilities. Thomas Alva Edison was a big advocate of the exploration process: "Make a practice to keep on the lookout for novel and interesting ideas that others have used successfully. Your idea only has to be original in the adaptation to the problem you are working on." Nobel Prize laureate Linus Pauling put it this way: "The best way to get a good idea is to get a lot of ideas." New ideas become raw materials for the next stage of the creative process, so you need lots of raw materials. How does one sharpen his or her exploration skills? Creative experts suggest the following: Be curious, leave your own turf, break out of your routine, and don't overlook the obvious.

- **The artist:** Once the explorer returns home with lots of raw materials with which to work, the artist grabs the relay baton and continues the creative process by incubating, manipulating, adapting, parodying, and connecting ideas until one idea surfaces as the best idea. In the role of the artist, you play with ideas. In the words of Pablo Picasso, "Every act of creation is first an act of destruction." An artist sheds all inhibitions to get his or her hands dirty by turning ideas upside down. The artist asks questions like, What if . . . ? After a given amount of time, the artist comes to a natural conclusion that one idea definitely stands out above the rest and then presents this idea to be judged.

- **The judge:** The judge plays a very crucial, yet delicate role in the creative process. One must be flexible enough to validate the artistic abilities, but critical enough to make the best selection possible. As one shifts from the artist to the judge, one shifts from the right (imaginative) brain to the left (analytical) brain. The biggest hazard in the creative process is a reshuffling of these roles, so that the judge begins the process. In every attempt where the mental processing begins with judgment, creativity is stifled or, worse, killed. The role of the judge is to select the best idea of all the ideas gathered and then pass this idea to the warrior so the idea can take flight.

- **The warrior:** A good idea that has no backing will sink like a rock! The role of the warrior is to champion the cause of the idea and make it a reality. To be a good warrior, you have to believe in yourself. Courage is a must, but so is tough skin, because not everyone is going to be as crazy about your idea as you are. The warrior must overcome the fear of failure, the fear of rejection, and the fear of the unknown. But the warrior must be brave. Should it be realized that the idea turned out to be less than ideal, then the creative team must reconvene to either overhaul the first idea or scrap it entirely and select a new one.

Within you reside all four members of the creativity team: explorer, artist, judge, and warrior. Exercise 10.1, "The Roles of Creativity," highlights these roles as four aspects of your creative process by encouraging you to wear each of these hats in the right order. Exercise 10.2 entices you to shift from a left-brain analytical mind-set to a right-brain focus and get the creative juices flowing in preparation for your next creative endeavor. Exercise 10.3 is your next creative endeavor.

Unlocking Your Creative Powers

Everybody is creative, but not everyone chooses to use this inherent skill. Nine times out of ten, fear is the force immobilizing people and inhibiting their creative skills. In their efforts to understand the creative process, leaders in this field have come to understand that they must also address roadblocks that obstruct the creative process. The following, as outlined in Roger von Oech's best-selling book *A Whack on the Side of the Head,* are a few of the more common creative roadblocks that must be dismantled before these valuable coping skills can allow us to reach our highest potential.

Me? Creative?

The biggest block to the creative process is the belief that you are not creative. The roots of this belief typically sprout early in childhood, when creative efforts are met by others with scorn rather than enthusiasm. This sends a message of inadequacy or, worse, failure. So, rather than looking inept, most people simply forgo their creative skills and let this muscle atrophy.

The truth is that everyone is creative but that creativity, like any other skill, takes practice to develop. If you think you are not creative, you will fulfill your limitations. Here's an idea: Learn to see yourself as the creative genius that you really are. Start with small projects, such as cooking a fine meal or writing a poem, and then work up to bigger projects.

No Time for Play

Remember that play is a critical factor in the creative process. Kids love to play. Adults soon forget the freedom of play as more and more responsibilities invade our lives. Play is critical in the role of the artist, and play is always more fun when it includes others. So, consider inviting some friends to join you in playtime. Playtime can include anything from a mental health day of downhill skiing to wandering the aisles of Home Depot. For play to be effective, keep your ego at home when you venture out!

Perfection Is Stifling

Nobody likes to make a mistake, and certainly not in front of an audience. Rest assured that embarrassment and humiliation are forms of fear-based stress. Ironically, the truth is that the creative process involves mistakes and failures. In the words of Woody Allen, "If you are not failing every now and then, it's a sign that you are not trying anything very innovative." And in the words of IBM founder Thomas J. Watson, "The way to success is to double your rate of failure." Edison failed with over 1,000 types of filaments for the lightbulb before he found one that worked. We might still be in the dark if he gave up on number 900. Follow Edison's advice: Learn to focus on the positive, not the negative, and then keep going.

But There's Only One Way

The ego loves to be right and will do all it can to prove it is right. Ironically, in the creative process, there are many right answers. On occasion, there may be a best answer, but there are always many right answers. Looking for the right answer means stepping out of the box, exploring the unknown, and finding many answers from which to choose. In the words of French philosopher Emile Chartier, "Nothing is more dangerous than an idea when it is the only one you have." Learn to become comfortable with many right answers and many solutions to a problem.

Fear of the Unknown

Creativity is certainly stifled in an age of specialization where professionals are kings of minutiae and the jack of trades is nowhere in sight. Once again, in an effort not to look stupid, fear overrides the mental thought processes by claiming either ignorance or territorial turf issues and refusing to get involved. Learn to make every area your area by embracing the wonder of all aspects of life.

Are your creative efforts blocked by the fear that whatever you might do might not be good enough? Exercise 10.3, "My Creativity Project," is an exercise to break through these blocks by delving into the creative process and coming out a victor. Enjoy!

From Creativity to Creative Problem Solving

The creative process is not a linear process with a direct route from problem to solution. If it were that easy, everyone would claim to be creative! Although the creative process isn't hard, it's not direct either. To use von Oech's metaphor of the four roles of creativity, most likely you will be switching hats often, from explorer to warrior, until it becomes obvious that the problem is solved with complete satisfaction. The following is a tried-and-true method of creative problem solving. Once you have read through this process, Exercise 10.4 provides this same template to be used for any current problems you are facing that demand a creative solution.

1. **Describe the problem.** Take time to identify and describe the problem. Sometimes the answer can be found in how the problem is identified or defined. Consider being playful in this first step, such as describing the problem as a child might see it or as an alien might view it. In the method of divide and conquer, try breaking the problem down into smaller pieces.

2. **Generate ideas.** What to cook for dinner tonight? Come up with five selections. Where to take your next vacation? Come up with five possible ideas. How to pay for your college education? Come up with five viable solutions. Generating ideas is the fun stage of the creative problem-solving process. To do a good job generating ideas, learn to get comfortable stepping out of your comfort zone (the box) and venture out to search for great ideas.

3. **Idea selection and refinement.** Once you have several ideas, you can begin to narrow the selection down to the "best" idea. To pick the best idea, consider playing the game What If? Try to imagine the idea already implemented and see how it works. Visualize it. Think the idea through to its desired result. Ask yourself what the pros and cons are. Although you won't know till you try, selection involves both intuition and imagination as well as good judgment skills.

4. **Idea implementation.** Putting an idea into play can take minutes or weeks, depending on the problem begging to be solved. The implementation of every idea requires some risk as well as some faith that it will work. Implementation means taking the first step back into the unknown. It may mean making a phone call or getting in your car and driving somewhere. It may mean sitting down and talking with someone, and most likely it may mean a collaborative effort to pull it off. Fear inhibits this stage of the creative process, but don't let it! Remember, face your fear and it will disappear.

5. **Evaluation and analysis of the idea.** When ideas work and the crisis is over, people tend to forget the magic that made it happen. But success begs to be highlighted by taking a good look so that the lessons can be learned should they be needed again. It's a good habit to study successes as well as unmet expectations: Valuable lessons can be learned from both ends of the creative process.

How to Incorporate Creative Problem Solving into Your Life Routine

The best way to incorporate creative problem skills into your life routine is to follow the template in Exercise 10.4 for any and all problems. Reading books on creativity can help (and is strongly encouraged), but reading about doing something and actually doing it are two different things. Be on the lookout for how others solve their problems (this is a coping skill called *information seeking*). Adaptation of ideas to your unique situation can prove to be very empowering!

The best way to enhance your creative skills is to practice them, even in areas that are totally unrelated to problems begging for resolution. There is a wonderful transfer effect from the creative processes of music, photography, cooking, or writing to the problems and dilemmas that face us each day. Engaging in small acts of creativity gives one the courage to try bigger things. When looking to initiate the creative problem-solving process, start small (e.g., what should I prepare for dinner tonight?).

Best Benefits of Creative Problem Solving

Everyone holds the keys to creativity; however, there are those who refuse to believe they are holding the keys in their hands. There are two kinds of people in this world: Those who think they are creative and those who don't. The people who believe they are creative are, indeed, very creative. Perhaps as no surprise, the people who don't believe they are creative are not creative. Creativity is a very empowering inner resource, and for this reason is coveted as an essential personality trait to successfully cope with stress. Tackling a problem through ingenuity makes you feel like you can conquer the world. By engaging fully in the creative process, one learns to let go of fears and anxieties that tend to hold one back and sails ahead on the river of life.

Additional Resources

Gelb, M. *How to Think Like Leonardo da Vinci*. New York: Dell/Random House, 1998.
McMeekin, G. *The 12 Secrets of Highly Creative Women*. Berkeley, CA: Conari Press, 2000.
Michalko, M. *Cracking Creativity*. Berkeley, CA: Ten Speed Press, 2001.
Tharp, T. *The Creative Habit*. New York: Simon and Schuster, 2003.
von Oech, R. *Creative Whack Pack*. New York: Warner Books, 1988.
von Oech, R. *A Whack on the Side of the Head*. New York: Warner Books, 1988.
von Oech, R. *A Kick in the Seat of the Pants*. New York: Perennial Books, 1986.

Exercise 10.1 The Roles of Creativity

Roger von Oech is right when he states that many hats are worn in the creative process! Reviewing these four specific roles, take some time to examine how you can integrate these creative aspects into your repertoire of skills. If you are like most people, you tend to see yourself as wearing only one of these hats, rather than all four. This is OK when projects or problems require more than one person to contribute their talents. For now, let's assume that you can wear all four hats.

The Explorer
To help you think outside the box, make a list of ten new places you can explore to find new ideas for any creative project. Next, make a list of five new resources to explore for any creative project.

_____

_____

_____

_____

_____

The Artist
Inside each and every one of us is an artist begging to play. Make a list of five new ways to engage in the art of play to enhance your creative skills.

1. _____

2. _____

3. _____

4. _____

5. _____

The Judge
How good are your judgmental skills? Are they too good? Are you the kind of person who judges first and asks questions later?

_____

_____

_____

_____

_____

The Warrior
The warrior is the "legman" in the creative process. A great idea without someone to market it and implement it is not really a great idea. How good are your warrior skills? What can you do to improve them?

_____

_____

_____

_____

_____

Exercise 10.2 Getting the Creative Juices Flowing

Living in our left-brain culture tends to inhibit the creative process. The following exercises are provided to help you whack your way of thinking (from left brain to right brain) so that the creative problem-solving process may become just a bit easier.

I. Create two metaphors/definitions for an optimist and a pessimist.

A. Optimist is someone who . . .

1. _____

2. _____

B. Pessimist is someone who . . .

1. _____

2. _____

II. Describe two things that a cat and a refrigerator have in common.

_____

_____

III. Describe the following colors to a person who has been blind from birth.

a. Red _____

b. White _____

c. Blue _____

d. Green _____

e. Yellow _____

IV. Mind games. In the following line of letters, cross out six letters so that the remaining letters, without altering their sequence, will spell a familiar English word.

BSAINXLEATNTEARS _____

V. Create a metaphor for the meaning of life. Finish this sentence:

Life is like a _____

Exercise 10.3 My Creativity Project

This exercise is geared to help inspire you to take some initiative in starting and completing a project that requires some creative license. Initially, this assignment was developed for a holistic health class to fully engage students in the creative process. Many people found this project to be the ticket to a new job. The purpose of this exercise is to challenge you to extend your creative talents to your highest limits. This project involves three aspects:

Part I: First, play the roles of the *explorer, artist, judge,* and *warrior* respectively, to come up with a very creative idea and then bring it to reality. If you wish, you can use the template in Exercise 10.1 for this exercise.

Part II: Next, write up the experience describing what you did (describe your experience in each of the four stages of creativity) and how you accomplished it.

Part III: Finally, explain what you learned from this experience.

The area and magnitude of creativity is entirely up to you. It is suggested, however, that you pick an area that is somewhat familiar (in other words, don't try to build the Brooklyn Bridge if you have never played with Legos), but not one in which you have a five-star command. Challenge yourself! Select a project, which can range from art, poetry, cooking, composing, photography, designing fashions, writing a screenplay, choreographing a dance, to anything! Start with an interest, passion, or a craving desire. Build from this a dream. Consult your intuition and then come up with a finished product. Remember that the creative process cannot be rushed or demanded. This assignment will take some time, so plan accordingly.

Make the project manageable. In other words, do not—repeat, do not—try to build a re-creation of the Eiffel Tower in your back yard or compose the sequel to Handel's *Messiah* in two days. On the other hand, simply putting a new message on your answering machine is not the best way to go either. Make the project a quality job and one of which you will be proud. The following are examples from previous students and workshop participants:

- Producing a music video presentation
- Writing a family/neighborhood cookbook
- Producing a multimedia slide presentation
- Creating a holistic cancer treatment plan

- Recording/producing a musical CD
- Planning a vacation around the world
- Designing/planning a rose garden
- Writing a nonfiction book proposal

My creativity project: _____

_____

How I did it: _____

_____

_____

_____

_____

_____

_____

_____

_____

_____

What I learned: _____

_____

_____

_____

Exercise 10.4 Creative Problem Solving

There are many good ways to solve a problem! All you need do is spend some time working at it from different directions until a number of viable solutions surface, and then choose the best one. The following is a time-tested strategic plan for creatively trying to solve problems and come to a sense of resolution.

1. **Define/describe the problem.** Please be as specific as you can.

    _____

    _____

    _____

2. **Generate great ideas.** Come up with at least four viable ideas and one zany one (x) to bring out the play factor.

    a. _____

    b. _____

    c. _____

    d. _____

    (x). _____

3. **Idea selection and refinement.** Pick the best idea from above and explain why you think this is the best idea.

    _____

    _____

    _____

    _____

    _____

4. **Idea implementation.** Explain how you will put this idea into action. Make a brief outline—four specific points of an action plan to make this happen.

    a. _____

    b. _____

    c. _____

    d. _____

5. **Evaluation and analysis of "action plan."** How did the idea work? What, if any, are some ways to improve on this idea should you decide to use it again?

    _____

    _____

    _____

    _____

    _____

CHAPTER

11

Art Therapy

The mind is a place of living images, and our hearts are the organs that tell us so.
—Anonymous

Ageless Wisdom of Art Therapy

If we used only words to share our thoughts and emotions, we would find this means of communication to be extremely limiting. There is a world of thoughts, feelings, and emotions that simply cannot be expressed in words, all of which beg for another outlet. With the realization that holistic stress management is the collaboration, not separation, of the conscious and unconscious minds, one must remember to utilize the powerful nonverbal aspects of the unconscious mind when looking for answers to resolving issues of stress. As has been mentioned many times in this book, the unconscious mind holds a wealth of information, with insights begging to be shared through a powerful combination of colors, symbols, and images.

Art therapy is a powerful coping technique that not only taps into this wealth of information from the unconscious mind but also, when given the chance, becomes integrated with the verbal aspect of the conscious mind to work toward a peaceful resolution of problems, challenges, concerns, and issues.

It's uncertain how long mankind has used art as a form of expression, but if the prehistoric artwork found in the caves of Lascaux, France, is any indication, then art as a form of self-expression may indeed be one of the oldest methods of therapy.

The roots of art as a recognized form of therapy date back to the work of both Freud and Jung. After World War II, art therapy became respected as a viable modality of healing, as both a means of catharsis and a window into the unconscious mind. Today, art therapy is used in a number of settings as a tool to help people unlock the means of expression that cannot be found in words alone. War veterans, anorexics, rape victims, prisoners, abused children, college students, corporate executives, and senior citizens have all engaged in the practice of art therapy as a means to resolve stress. Like a key that unlocks a door to a whole new world, the results, in many cases, have been nothing less than astounding.

You don't have to be Picasso, Rembrandt, or Georgia O'Keeffe to engage in the practice of art therapy. It's not how good you draw, paint, or sculpt. Talent has nothing to do with the message of the work. Instead, the power of art therapy is based on the nature of what is drawn, the colors used, and the symbols represented pictorially. Everything has meaning! Figures 11.1 and 11.2 are examples of emotional expression through art therapy.

Figure 11.1

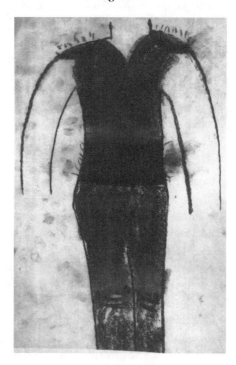

Figure 11.2

The Interpretation of Art in Art Therapy

Exercises 11.1 ("The Human Butterfly") and 11.2 ("Beyond Words") offer you several artistic themes for this technique. Drawing, painting, sculpting, or any other artistic means to reveal the secrets of the unconscious mind is only part of the art therapy process. Taking the time to verbally interpret the artwork is as important as composing the piece of artwork itself. Just as dreams are best left to the dreamer to fully comprehend the meaning, the artist (with a little bit of training) is the best qualified to uncover the meaning of what was expressed and represented artistically because the artist knows his or her mind better than anyone else.

Perhaps because pastels and colored pencils or crayons are the most accessible, this has become the most common medium of art therapy. As such, each color used in an art therapy session holds significance. Based on the initial work of Jung and his many followers who went on to develop the field of art therapy, a key of archetypal colors is now available to help interpret one's drawing (see page 122).

Art Therapy and Chronic Illness

One of the most recognized benefits of art therapy made itself known over 30 years ago with the work of Carl Simonton. He used art therapy (along with other coping modalities) as an integrated approach to treating cancer patients. Patients began to draw themselves, their tumors, and other aspects of their lives, which often gave insight into the disease and in many cases the best way to treat it. Today art therapy is used as an integrative healing modality for several types of chronic diseases, including hypertension, irritable bowel syndrome, lupus, migraine headaches, coronary heart disease, and rheumatoid arthritis.

How to Incorporate Art Therapy into Your Life Routine

It has often been said that there is no wrong way to do art therapy. Although this may be true, there are certain steps that you can take to enhance the process so that you gain as much from the experience as possible. The following are some tips that may augment your art therapy experience.

- Drop all inhibitions about your artistic abilities. Art therapy is not about being an artist, but about simply drawing, as best you can, your thoughts and feelings.

- Consider having on hand a good selection of art supplies, including pastels, crayons, colored pencils, and large sheets of white paper.

- Give yourself about 20 to 30 minutes to draw one or more themes (see Exercise 11.2). Sometimes having some quiet instrumental music playing in the background helps to engage the right (creative) side of the brain.

- It's important to remember to use whatever colors you wish. If you are doing these exercises in a large group and you need a blue pastel and cannot find it, call out for it. Laziness is not a good excuse for a mediocre art therapy experience.

- Working alone on a picture may lessen one's inhibitions, but doing this activity together with a small group of friends can really add to the experience, particularly when it comes time to articulate your interpretation. In the process of explaining to others what you have drawn, you help yourself process this experience as well.

- Consider hanging your artwork on the refrigerator, bathroom mirror, or your home office corkboard for several weeks so that you can see it regularly. Often a deeper meaning may surface several days after creating your art piece.

Best Benefits of Art Therapy

Art therapy appears to hold both immediate and long-term benefits as a tool for holistic stress management. The immediate effects can be summed up in the word *catharsis,* which means an emotional release.

The long-term effects are more subtle than the short-term cathartic release, yet equally powerful. When art therapy participants elect to post their pieces of artwork where they can be seen regularly (e.g., the refrigerator), then the unconscious mind continues its work to reveal more messages. It is not uncommon for people to say that after looking at their art therapy work for several days they begin to see new meaning in each piece. With new meaning and deeper interpretation comes a shift in consciousness allowing either greater insight into problems (a means toward a faster resolution) or simply a different perspective.

Additional Resources

Edwards, B. *The New Drawing on the Right Side of the Brain,* 2nd ed. New York: J.P. Tarcher, 1999.
Farrelly-Hansen, M. *Spirituality and Art Therapy.* Philadelphia: Jessica Kingsley Publishers, 2001.
Malchiodi, C. *The Soul's Palette.* Boston: Shambhala Books, 2002.
Malchiodi, C. *The Art Therapy Sourcebook.* New York: McGraw Hill, 1998.

Exercise 11.1 The Human Butterfly

Theme

The butterfly is a symbol of transformation—of rising above life's issues and problems and moving on. The word *butterfly* and *soul* are also synonymous in Greek.

Activity

Spread out some colored crayons or pastels on a table or floor area where you can easily access them. If you are doing this with others, please remember to share! Allocate about 10 to 15 minutes to color in the wings of your butterfly (see the accompanying figure).

As an additional phase of the human butterfly exercise, consider writing in the butterfly wings those inner resources or muscles of the soul (e.g., humor, patience, forgiveness, creativity, optimism) that you use to effectively cope with problems. If there are inner resources that you feel you would like to have be a stronger part of who you are (to enhance your coping skills), then write those attributes on the outside of the butterfly and draw an arrow from the word into the wing of the butterfly. By doing so, you send a direct message to your unconscious mind to begin to utilize these inner resources more often.

Interpretation

If you do this exercise in a small group, take turns showing your butterfly illustration and explain to the group your best interpretation from an archetypal perspective (see page 122). When viewing others' work, you cannot help but be impressed—if for no other reason than from seeing how different and unique each butterfly is when colored.

Outside Assignments

Consider hanging your butterfly on the fridge or office wall as a means to remind you (both consciously and unconsciously) of your inner resources.

Exercise 11.2 Beyond Words: Drawing for Emotional Relief

Art Therapy Themes

There are several themes to choose from when trying this exercise in art therapy. The following is a list of popular themes in the field of art therapy from which to choose.

1. Draw an expression of how you feel when you are either angry or afraid.

2. Draw a sketch of yourself (how you see yourself).

3. Closing your eyes, draw a line on the paper. Then open your eyes and slowly rotate the paper around until an image appears from which to continue and finish the sketch.

4. In the theme of healing, draw an actual or representational illustration of a part of your body that is not whole (e.g., from disease or illness). Then draw a second image in which healing has occurred.

5. Draw a mandala (a circular personal coat of arms with four quadrants depicting four aspects of your life that are important to you).

6. Draw your favorite animal.

7. Draw a house (either one you live in or perhaps wish to live in).

8. Draw whatever you wish!

Instructions

Please read through the list of eight themes and then select one and begin to create your piece of artwork, spending about 15 to 20 minutes for this exercise. If time permits, you might consider selecting a second theme, which then allows you to choose which to share when done as a group activity.

Interpretation

If you do this exercise in a small group, take turns showing your illustration and explain to the group your best interpretation, including the interpretation of colors selected (see page 122). Remember that the best person qualified to interpret his or her drawing is the person who drew it. If you do this as a group activity, it's strongly recommended not to interpret other people's work.

Outside Assignments

Consider hanging your art piece on the fridge or office wall, because often more subtle aspects of interpretation take a while to surface toward conscious recognition.

Art Therapy Color Code

Although there are exceptions, there is a consensus among art therapists (and even psychologists) that regardless of gender, nationality, or ethnic upbringing, each color used in art therapy represents an archetypal meaning. Typically, the color selection, as well as the objects drawn (house, tree, etc.) parallel emotional expressions of one's mental/emotional health. The absence of a color does not mean a lack of something; rather, the colors used express that which the unconscious mind wishes to convey at the time of the drawing. The following list suggests associations between colors and their archetypal meanings.

Red: Passionate emotional peaks (from pleasure to pain). It can represent either compassion or anger.

Orange: Suggests a life change (big or small, often more positive than negative).

Yellow: Represents energy (usually a positive message).

Green and blue: Suggest happiness and joy (blue may even mean creativity). These colors also suggest a strong sense or desire of groundedness and stability in your environment.

Purple/Violet: Suggests a highly spiritual nature, unconditional love.

Brown (and earth-tone colors): A sense of groundedness and stability.

Black: Can either represent grief, despair, fear, or a sense of personal empowerment.

White: Can either mean fear, avoidance, cover-up, or hope.

Gray: Typically represents a sense of ambiguity or uncertainty about some issue you are working on.

CHAPTER
12
Additional Coping Skills

God gave us two ends. One to sit on and one to think with.
Success depends on which end you use. Heads, you win. Tails, you lose.
—Anonymous

There are literally dozens of effective coping techniques in the field of holistic stress management. To be effective, though, each technique must help increase awareness of the cause of the problem and assist you in the efforts to work toward a peaceful resolution. The following are some additional coping techniques that merit attention and might prove to be quite useful to you as you augment your repertoire of effective coping skills for the duration of your life journey.

Journaling: The Art of Soul Searching

The mind can quickly become a flurry of thoughts and feelings that, like a tempest wind, rush around the inside of your head at dizzying speeds. Without a release, the pressure can build up dramatically to a point that eventually clouds your vision and ultimately inhibits clear thinking. One way to release this pressure is to get your thoughts and feelings down on paper, and that's the purpose of journal writing.

As a coping technique, journaling serves several purposes. First, it provides the means for a healthy catharsis—a way to release pent-up thoughts and feelings from the head and onto paper. It has long been believed that thoughts and frustrations can eventually become toxic if they are not allowed to flow freely out of your system. In fact, research now shows that people who keep a regular journal actually have a healthier immune system. Not only is there a cathartic effect to journaling, but writing your thoughts and feelings down on paper (or perhaps in a computer document) seems to provide insights regarding possible solutions to a host of various problems.

Aside from a healthier immune system, journaling has some long-term benefits as well. By rereading journal entries, you can begin to see certain behavior patterns emerge that you might not notice with an occasional journal entry. In its simplest form, journal writing is nothing less than soul searching. There are many themes that can be used as vehicles for self-exploration, including writing poetry (making order out of the chaos of your mind), composing letters (a message of resolution), or simply making lists to organize your thoughts. Exercise 12.1 is a journal theme that actually helps to provide insights that help you work toward a resolution of a personal relationship in your life.

Support Groups: Friends in Need

In 1989 a landmark study was conducted to show that support groups did nothing to promote the longevity of cancer patients. When it came time to analyze the data, Dr. David Spiegel was stunned. The message was clear: Support groups definitely enhanced the quality and quantity of lives. Without a doubt, those patients who partook in support group activities significantly outlived those who did not.

By and large, human beings are social animals. We need the companionship and company of others, if not for physical survival then at least for moral and spiritual support on our own human journey. Having a few close friends or colleagues with whom to share time and common interests provides a sense of belonging, a factor long thought to be critical for health and longevity. Sociologists call this the *buffer theory,* suggesting that friends, family, and peers help minimize stress by simply being there to lend a helping hand or an ear to listen when needed. In many cases friends can offer objective insights or opinions that can widen your perspective of the problem at hand.

In this age of high technology, our society has become increasingly fragmented. People spend more time in front of a computer screen or television and less quality time spent with friends and family. Research based on the tend-and-befriend theory underscores the importance of support groups for women; however, men certainly benefit from this coping skill as well. Connectedness is essential for health and well-being. Exercise 12.2 challenges you to build stronger support groups as a buffer to stress.

Social Engineering: Taking the Path of Least Resistance

Avoidance is the number one coping skill for dealing with stress. Avoidance is also the number one *ineffective* coping skill for dealing with stress. For this reason, avoidance is never advocated unless your life is in physical danger.

Social engineering is often called the path of least resistance—sidestepping potential obstacles that might later create more stress. Social engineering is not the same thing as avoidance. Social engineering is a coping skill that enables you to organize and reorganize various responsibilities and events in your day or week to decrease feelings of being overwhelmed. Although aspects of social engineering such as prioritizing and scheduling fall under the umbrella of time management, many give this coping skill a place of its own on the spectrum of effective coping techniques because it's that important.

One of the hazards of social engineering is constantly rearranging your social contacts with friends, shortchanging both yourself and others. Be careful not to take advantage of your friends, or the foundation of your support group may start to crumble.

Hobbies and Outside Interests: Following Your Bliss

What do stamp collecting, golfing, and Akebono have to do with stress relief? When used as a diversion from the pressures of work, hobbies can provide a wonderful respite from the hassles of the 9-to-5 job. First and foremost, hobbies offer an escape, a diversion from life's boredom or craziness. Hobbies and outside interests not only provide balance to the mind, but also in many cases help you cope with problems in other aspects of your life by transferring the creative juices back to your job or career.

By and large, the challenge of hobbies is to make order out of some controlled sense of chaos, such as through gardening, photography, music, or mountain climbing. The conventional wisdom suggests that by mastering the skills necessary to generate a sense of organization and creativity, these same skills will then transfer to other aspects of your life where chaos looms. Exercise 12.3 challenges you to explore this coping style further.

Dream Therapy: The Royal Road of the Unconscious Mind

Deep in the recesses of the unconscious mind lies a wealth of wisdom there simply for the asking—wisdom and guidance that offer keen insights and the means of resolution to a host of issues and problems that surface in the course of your daily life. Unlike the conscious mind that shuts down while we are asleep, the unconscious mind is active and aware every hour of the day. There is a small catch to obtaining these nuggets of wisdom: They come in a coded language that has to be decoded before they can be utilized. Actually, the unconscious mind is multilingual through the language of dreams, symbols, Freudian slips, and a series of cognitive functions that are clearly associated with the right hemisphere of the brain (e.g., irrational thinking, nonlinear thinking, imaginative thinking, global thinking, intuitive thinking). It is the job of the conscious mind to decode the message of dream symbols. Unfortunately, most people never take the time to learn this language. Consequently, they wander aimlessly through a maze of personal problems and issues, unable to read the map provided by the unconscious mind, and hence stress is perpetuated.

Dream therapy is a process of taking the time to learn the symbolic language of the unconscious mind as presented in the dream state. Before dream interpretation can be done, one must first make a habit of remembering one's dreams. This can be done by programming your conscious mind to remember your dreams or dream fragments when you awake each morning. Upon waking, call to mind these dream passages. The next step is to take pen and paper to hand and record them as best you can. Analyzing your dreams is a process whereby the code of the dream symbols is broken. This can be done in a number of ways, including playing with the dream symbol and providing many interpretations until some tangible insight reveals itself.

Of great interest is the topic of recurring dreams, which are a message from the unconscious mind that, indeed, there is some problem begging for resolution. This avenue of dream therapy utilizes the power of lucid dreaming (similar to visualization, where you are awake and programming your mind to view a series of scenes). You then finish the dream by visualizing and writing the script for a logical and peaceful conclusion. Exercise 12.4 takes you through this healing process, if you choose to do so.

Forgiveness: The Art of Moving on with Your Life

Anger is a survival emotion to be used long enough to get out of harm's way. Anger held longer than this brief moment in time turns toxic and becomes a control issue. You may tend to resent those by whom you feel you have been violated or victimized, perhaps first as a protection but then as a type of revenge. As discussed in Chapter 3, revenge is an unhealthy style of mismanaged anger.

If anger becomes a toxin, then forgiveness is an antidote. The last thing people want to hear about in the face of violation is forgiveness, because it feels as if one receives another slap across the face or kick in the butt. Certainly, there must be adequate time for grieving. However, prolonged grieving can perpetuate mismanaged anger. Forgiveness is both the last stage of grieving and the first stage of celebration.

Here are some quick tips about engaging the art of forgiveness:

- **Forgiveness means moving on.** Realize that by forgiving someone of a misdeed, you are not doing him or her a favor. Rather, you are releasing yourself from the chains of anger so you can move on with your life. If unresolved anger is giving your power away, then forgiveness means reclaiming your personal power.

- **Forgiveness does not mean the same thing as restitution.** Do not expect an apology because of your act of forgiveness—you could be waiting a very long time. Most likely you will never receive one.

- **Forgiveness starts within.** Forgiving someone his or her misdeed requires that you first learn to forgive yourself for those things you have done that have been less than stellar. Only by realizing your own faults can you extend a sense of compassion to others, and true forgiveness (without any conditions) is compassion in action.

If you feel there is someone toward whom you have been carrying a grudge or whose name you have kept on the top of your "s" list, now is the time to resolve this stressor, make peace in your heart, and move on. Exercise 12.5 challenges you to engage in the act of forgiveness so that you can carry on with your life without carrying undue baggage.

The Healing Power of Prayer: Divine Connections

In times of stress it is not uncommon to turn to others for help. Sometimes we turn to friends and family. Other times we turn to a greater source or higher power. If stress is indeed a perception of being cut off from the divine, then prayer is one means to reestablish this connection. Prayers come in many forms, from words of gratitude to calls for help (also known as *intercessory prayer*). Over the past decade, the topic of prayer has been of great interest, particularly intercessory prayer when used as a modality of healing in the field of complementary and alternative medicine. Regardless of one's spiritual background, religious upbringing, or lack thereof, the underlying premise of prayer appears to be the quality of intention put forth with the request for help and assistance.

To gain the greatest benefit from the healing power of prayer, it's best to understand how to coordinate the efforts of both conscious and unconscious minds. Based on the wisdom of luminary Sophy Burnham, the following are some aspects (nearly identical in nature to the template for visualization) to consider when using this modality as a coping technique.

- **Present tense:** To the universal mind or divine consciousness, there is only one time zone: the present moment. Past memories and events as well as future events and aspects are all considered to be included in the present moment. Simply stated, divine consciousness appears not to understand events as anything other than *now!* Therefore, as you state your prayer, think in terms of bringing the image into the present moment as if you were experiencing it now.

- **Focused concentration:** Prayer requires a clear transmission of intention. Maintaining a clear focus of your attention allows this to occur. Under duress, feelings of fear or anger act like static and tend to garble the message so that it is not heard clearly. Take time to quiet the mind and clear the static for a clear transmission of your request and intention.

- **Positive thoughts and intentions:** Just as the unconscious mind only understands one time zone, it also only understands positive thoughts. Words expressed negatively are translated into a positive framework. Therefore, to coordinate both the conscious and unconscious minds toward a unified goal, construct your prayer in a positive mind frame.

- **Emotional vibration:** New research on visualization and prayer indicates that thoughts alone produce no lasting effect. What really galvanizes the power of prayer is the emotion (compassion) behind your intention. So as you begin to articulate your intention, generate a feeling of compassion with your request or expression of gratitude.

- **Detached outcomes:** Placing an expected outcome on the desired intention of each prayer is analogous to throwing down an anchor on a boat that is about to set sail. It halts any progress. Although it's human nature to place expectations on dreams, this too becomes an emotional vibration that negates the intended outcome. The ego projects strong expectations. For prayer to have the greatest effect, you must detach the ego from the outcome and simply let what happens, happen.

- **Attitude of gratitude:** Upon the completion of your prayer, offer an expression of gratitude for the experience. An honest expression of gratitude fills the sails of every prayer with wind to transport it to the intended destination, wherever that may be.

Times of stress can certainly elicit feelings of fear and anxiety, yet these same feelings can be counterproductive when the call for divine assistance is summoned. When fear enters the heart in the prayer process, there is no doubt that the message can be compromised. Exercise 12.6 guides you through this template to cultivate your prayer style for the best possible outcome. Remember that whatever the outcome, there is a bigger game plan than we can ever imagine, and answers to prayers come in their own time and way, in accordance with this bigger picture.

Additional Resources

Burnham, S. *The Path of Prayer*. New York: Compass Books, 2002.
Delaney, G. *Living Your Dreams*. San Francisco: Harper SanFrancisco, 1996.
Dossey, L. *Prayer Is Good Medicine*. New York: HarperCollins, 1996.
Luskin, F. *Forgive for Good*. San Francisco: Harper SanFrancisco, 2002.
Pennebaker, J. *Opening Up*. New York: William Morrow, 1990.
Seaward, B.L. *Managing Stress: A Creative Journal,* 3rd ed. Sudbury, MA: Jones and Bartlett, 2004.

Exercise 12.1 Journal Writing: Unwritten Letters

Many times we wish to communicate with someone we love, like, or just know well, but for one reason or another—whether it be anger, procrastination, or not finding the right words at the right time—we part ways without fully resolving those special feelings. There was once a college student whose former boyfriend took his life. In the note left behind, he specifically mentioned her, and the words haunted her for what seemed like an eternity. As a result of counseling, she decided to write him a letter to express her feelings of anger, sorrow, loneliness, and love. Through her words, her letter began the resolution process and ultimately her path toward inner peace.

This theme of resolution through letter writing has been the subject of many books, plays, and movies. In a movie made for television entitled *Message to My Daughter,* a young mother with a newborn baby discovers she has terminal cancer. As a part of her resolution process, she records several cassette tapes with personal messages to her daughter. Many father–son relationships also fall into this category when emotional distance becomes a nearly impassable abyss. Years later, a movie titled *My Life,* starring Michael Keaton, had a similar plot. It is a common theme.

It has been said that with recent advances in technology, from the cell phone to the microchip, Americans are writing fewer and fewer personal letters. Sociologists worry that future generations will look back on this time period, the information high-tech age, and never really know what individuals were actually feeling and thinking because there will be few, if any, written entries to trace these perceptions. Moreover, psychologists agree that many of today's patients are troubled and unable to articulate their thoughts and feelings completely, which leaves them with feelings of unresolved stress.

This journal entry concerns the theme of resolution. The following are some suggestions that might inspire you to draft a letter to someone you have been meaning to write. Now is your chance.

1. Compose a letter to someone you were close to who has passed away or someone you haven't been in contact with for a long time. Tell that person what you have been up to, perhaps any major changes in your life, or changes that you foresee occurring in the months or years ahead. If you have any unresolved feelings toward this person, try expressing them in appropriately crafted words so that you can resolve these feelings and come to a sense of lasting peace.

2. Write a letter to yourself. Imagine that you have one month to live. What would you do in these last thirty days? Assume that there are no limitations. Who would you see? Where would you visit? What would you do? Why?

3. Pretend that you now have a baby. What would you like to share with your son or daughter now, should, for some reason, you not have the opportunity to do so later in life? What would you like your child to know about you? For example, perhaps you would share things that you wanted to know about your parents or grandparents, which now are pieces missing in your life.

4. Write a letter to anyone you wish for whatever reason.

Exercise 12.2 Defining Your Support Group

Support groups are vital to the quality and length of our lives. Support groups are composed of friends, colleagues, peers, neighbors, and, perhaps most of all, family members. Your support group is made up of those people to whom you feel closest, who are there to socialize with, to give you a helping hand, or to provide a shoulder to cry on when you feel like doing so. The following exercise is to help you reinforce the foundations of your support group.

1. As best as you can, create what you think is the best definition of a friend. A friend is:

   _____

   _____

2. Make a list of those people who you feel constitute your support group.

   a. My closest males friends are:

   _____

   My closest females friends are:

   _____

   b. The friends I know I can share any problem with at any time include:

   _____

   _____

   c. The friends I can call to go play or go shopping include:

   _____

   _____

   d. These friends energize me; they don't drain my energy:

   _____

   _____

   e. Friends on whom I know I can call for a favor at any time include:

   _____

   _____

   f. Friends who are mentors include:

   _____

   _____

   g. Friends who expand my personal horizons with new ideas or activities are:

   _____

   _____

3. How has your support group changed over the past five years?

   _____

   _____

4. Some people in our support groups tend to drain our energy rather than replenishing it.

   Do you have friends like this? _____

   If so, how do you cope with them? _____

5. What factors in your life detract from your ability to "be there" for others in your support group? _____

   _____

   _____

6. It has often been said that we can never have enough friends. Although this may be true, you cannot spend repeated quality time with everyone, because this weakens the integrity of true friends. What do you do to nurture the connections between you and your friends? In other words, how are you a good friend to others?

   _____

   _____

7. For a variety of reasons, friends tend to come and go in our lives. New friends can become a breath of fresh air in our lives. New friends are harder to make and keep as we age. It helps to continually foster new interests and hobbies. Make a list of three new places where you can begin to meet new people to add as possible members of your support group.

   _____

   _____

   _____

   _____

   _____

   _____

   _____

   _____

   _____

   _____

   _____

   _____

   _____

   _____

   _____

   _____

   _____

Exercise 12.2

Exercise 12.3 Hobbies and Outside Interests

Here is a question to consider: What would you do for a living if your career didn't exist? Here is another question: If money wasn't a factor in sustaining your desired lifestyle, how would you spend the rest of your life? Hobbies and outside interests provide a sense of balance to the long hours of work that tend to define who we are in this world. The truth is that you are not your job, your career, or even your paycheck. Yet, without claiming some outside interests as a significant part of your life, it becomes easy to see yourself as a passive victim in a rapidly changing world.

1. What are your current outside interests? Name three things or activities that you partake in on a regular (weekly) basis.

   a. _____

   b. _____

   c. _____

2. If you had a hard time coming up with three specific outside interests that qualify as true hobbies, or perhaps you are looking for some new interest to enter your life, consider examples of things you have always wanted to do or to get involved with. What groups or organizations have you wanted to become a member of that can help get you started in this direction?

   a. _____

   b. _____

   c. _____

3. Playing the guitar, knitting a sweater, or making plans to remodel the kitchen are great things to do, but they require time. Making time for hobbies and outside interests requires some discipline. What steps do you take to ensure that you have the time to fulfill the passions of your personal outside interests?

   _____

   _____

   _____

   _____

   _____

   _____

   _____

4. Would you say that your involvement in one or more of your hobbies has a transfer effect in other aspects of your life? If so, how? Please explain:

   _____

   _____

   _____

   _____

   _____

   _____

   _____

Exercise 12.4   Dreams Revisited

Although we all have dreams, remembering them is not always easy. But there are occasions when a certain dream is replayed in our mind over the course of months, perhaps even years. These recurring dreams may only have a short run on the mind's silver screen, or they may last throughout the course of our lifetime. These dreams, perhaps foggy in detail, surface occasionally in the conscious state, and the story they tell is all too familiar.

It is commonly believed that recurring dreams symbolize a hidden insecurity or a stressful event that has yet to be resolved. They don't have resolved endings. Although there is much about the dream state that is still unknown, it is believed that dreams are images that the unconscious mind creates to communicate to the conscious mind in a language all its own. This form of communication is not a one-way street. Messages can be sent to the unconscious mind in a normal waking state as well.

Through the use of mental imagery, you can script the final scenes of a recurring dream to give it a happy ending. What seems to be the final scene of the dream is actually the beginning of the resolution process. The following is a true story: Once there was a young boy who had an afternoon paper route. One day while the boy was delivering papers, a large black German shepherd jumped out of the bushes and attacked him. The owner called the dog back, but not before the dog drew blood. As the boy grew into adulthood, his love for dogs never diminished, but several times a year he awoke in a sweat from a recurring dream he had had once too often.

The dream: It is dark and I am walking through the woods at night. Out from behind one of the trees comes this huge black dog. All I can see are his teeth, and all I can hear is his bark. I try to yell for help, but nothing comes out of my throat. Just as he lunges for me, I awake in a panic.

With a little thought and imagination, a final scene was drafted to bring closure to this dream story. **Final scene:** I am walking through the woods at night with a flashlight, a bone, and a can of mace. This time when the dog lunges at me, I shine the light in his eyes and spray mace in his face. He whines and whines, and then I tell him to sit. He obeys. I put the bone by his nose and he looks at me inquisitively. Then he licks the bone and starts to bite into it. I begin to walk away and the dog gets up to follow, bone in mouth. I stop and look back and he stops. He wags his tail. The sky grows light as the sun begins to rise, and the black night fades into pink and orange clouds. As I walk back to my house, I see the dog take his new find down the street. I open the door and walk upstairs and crawl back into bed.

It has been five years, and this man has never had this dream again.

Ultimately, we are the creators of our dreams. We are the writers, directors, producers, and actors of our dreams. Although drafting a final scene is no guarantee that the issues that produce recurring dreams will be resolved, it is a great starting point in the resolution process, a time for reflection that may open up the channels of communication between the conscious and unconscious minds. Do you have a recurring dream that needs a final scene to be complete? Write out your recurring dream and give it a final scene.

_____

_____

_____

_____

_____

_____

_____

_____

_____

_____

_____

Exercise 12.5   Sweet Forgiveness

You cannot shake hands with a clenched fist.
—Indira Ghandi

Every act of forgiveness is an act of unconditional love. If unresolved anger is a toxin to the spirit, forgiveness is the antidote, and where anger is a roadblock, forgiveness is a ladder to climb above and transcend the experience. For forgiveness to be complete and unconditional, you must be willing to let go of all feelings of anger, resentment, and animosity. Sweet forgiveness cannot hold any taste of bitterness, because they are mutually exclusive.

Victimization is a common feeling when one encounters stressors in the form of another person's behaviors. When we sense that our human rights have been violated, feelings of rage can quickly turn into feelings of resentment. Left unresolved, these toxic thoughts can taint the way we treat others and ourselves. To forgive those who we feel have wronged us is not an easy task. Often it's a process, and at times, a very long process. Yet turning the other cheek does not mean that you have to let people walk all over you. Forgiveness is not a surrender of your self-esteem, nor is it a compromise of your integrity. When you can truly forgive the behavior of those by whom you feel violated, you let go of the feelings of control and become free to move on with your life.

Resentment and grudges can become roadblocks on the human path. Forgiveness turns a hardened heart into an open passageway to progress on life's journey. Think for a moment of someone who might have violated your humanness. Is it time to let go of some toxic thoughts and initiate a sense of forgiveness?

To begin this journal entry, write the name of that person or those persons toward whom you feel some level of resentment. Beside each name write down what action or behavior it was that offended you and why you feel so violated. What feelings arise in you when you see this person, or even hear his or her name? Next, make a note of how long you have felt this way toward this person. Finally, search your soul for a way to forgive the people on your list, even if it means just to acknowledge their human spirit. Then practice the act of forgiveness as best you can, and let the feelings of resentment go.

Exercise 12.6   The Healing Power of Prayer

Regardless of one's religious background or lack thereof, prayer is a common coping technique that is used in times of duress. To seek help in times of need is considered a savvy strategy for overcoming problems, no matter what size. Although prayer can be a very personal behavior, we now know that there are certain steps to ensure a clear transmission for divine intercession. Based on the information on page 126, consider using the following outline as a personal template to refine the healing power of prayer.

Intention: _____

1.   **Present tense.** State your prayerful intention in the present tense below.

_____

_____

_____

2.   **Focused concentration.** Clear your mind by using the space below to write down any distracting negative thoughts as a means of releasing them.

_____

_____

_____

3.   **Positive thoughts and intentions.** State your intention in the most positive way below.

_____

_____

_____

4.   **Emotional vibration.** Call to mind the most favorable emotions you can feel. If it helps, write down the experience and feeling to help re-create this feeling now.

_____

_____

_____

5.   **Detached outcomes.** Below, write any fears, anxieties, or desires that need to be released to make the prayer fly.

_____

_____

_____

6.   **Attitude of gratitude.** Take a moment to write a few words of thanks here for what you are grateful for as this happens.

_____

_____

_____

Exercise 12.6

PART III

Effective Relaxation Techniques

CHAPTER

13

The Art of Calm: Relaxation Through the Five Senses

If you are looking for fast acting relief, try slowing down.
—Lily Tomlin

Ageless Wisdom of Physical Relaxation

A quick study of ancient Greece reveals that hot baths, muscle massage, aromatic fragrances, melodic music, and scrumptious food were only a few of the many ways that were used to achieve balance from the cares and worries of the day. The Greeks weren't alone in their efforts to promote relaxation. Similar means to seek balance between mind, body, and spirit can be found in the cultures of ancient civilizations around the world, from Egypt to Polynesia. Ageless wisdom emphasizes the importance of achieving balance between hard physical work and relaxation.

In their wildest dreams, citizens of ancient civilizations could never have conceived the high-tech, fast-paced global village we live in today. Laptop computers, airplanes, iPods, and microwave ovens never even entered their imagination. Yet, in many ways, their lives were no different than ours today. Stress has always been and always will be a part of the human landscape. What citizens of previous generations did know was the importance of taking time to relax, something that we often fail to remember. Indeed, there is an art to relaxation, an art to the mastery of calmness and tranquility in a stress-filled world. Ironically, like the basis of most stress, this mastery is cultivated through the perceptions of the five senses. The art of calm is derived from knowing how to turn off the negative input and replace it with positive sensations.

Sight. Sound. Smell. Taste. Touch. These five senses are the portals through which information enters the brain so the mind can determine threat from nonthreat, friend from foe. Just as information comes into these five senses to detect danger, so too these same portals of sensory information are receptive to any and all information that calms the mind and body. Massage therapy, aromatherapy, music therapy, and hydrotherapy are but a few of the contemporary examples of ageless wisdom employed to return to a sense of calm through one or more of the five senses.

As the planet spins faster and faster into a world of rapid change and high technology, the human spirit yearns for a sense of stability garnered through the wisdom of time-proven methods of rest and relaxation. Muscle massage, aromatherapy, hydrotherapy, good food, good music, deep breathing, and peaceful images to seduce the mind into a state of tranquility are more than fads or popular trends. By all accounts, these are time-honored practices. So it's no secret that references to all of these modalities of healing can be found in the texts and lifestyles of ancient Greece, Egypt, Polynesia, Australia, and the Mayan peninsula. These ancient traditions remind us what we so often forget: to take time to balance the rush of life with frequent rest-filled pauses. The art of calm reminds us that we are human *beings,* not human *doings,* and as such, we need to take frequent breaks to simply be.

An often-asked question about relaxation techniques is this: Isn't sleeping as good or better than meditation, yoga, or any other relaxation technique? The simple answer is NO! Sleeping does not produce the same effects, because during sleep the unconscious mind is continuously working to resolve issues of the previous day. Stress-based emotions that were suppressed or left unresolved tend to show up in a variety of ways while sleeping, including high blood pressure, muscle tension, and TMJD, to name a few. What makes every effective relaxation technique unique when compared with nocturnal sleep (where the conscious mind is inactive) is the "conscious intention" to relax. The act of sleep is involuntary, whereas these techniques are voluntary, meaning that there is a conscious effort to achieve homeostasis. By doing so, rather than acting as adversaries, both the conscious and unconscious minds work in unison for the integration, balance, and harmony of mind, body, spirits, and emotions.

Sense of Sight

As humans we are, above all else, visual animals. Approximately 70 percent of our sensory information is processed through our eyes. Another 20 percent is garnered by the ears, and the remaining 10 percent is taken in by the other three senses. As such, it makes sense to believe that if we were to close our eyes, if only momentarily, then our stress levels should drop dramatically. Perhaps this is why, when people choose to relax by using diaphragmatic breathing, listening to music, or receiving a massage, they close their eyes rather than keep them open.

Using the sense of sight to relax may be an oxymoron, because in many cases, the sense of sight is quite literally turned off. In other cases, however, a calming image or photograph is used to replace a stressful scene. When asked to name a calming image, most, if not all, people turn their eye toward nature: mountain vistas, ocean beaches, lush primeval forests. The grandeur of nature brings all problems into perspective. Using the sense of sight to promote relaxation does all these things.

Sense of Sound

Sounds can either rile one's nerves or tame the wildest of beasts. Like all information that is processed through the five senses, one's perception makes the difference between tranquility and annoyance—in this case, between melody and noise. Sounds that promote a sense of calm are endless and can include soft rippling waterfalls, rhythmic ocean waves caressing a sandy beach, and chimes moving in the wind. Music therapy is the name given to the use of music to promote a sense of deep relaxation through the principle of entrainment (see Chapter 17). Classical, jazz, new age, and scores of other types of music, some of which include ocean waves, dolphin songs, and rain storms, are just a few of the many soothing sounds employed to calm one's nerves.

Sense of Smell

Fragrances have long been held in esteem by people the world over as a means to lift one's spirits and calm one's mind. There appears to be a universal agreement that flower scents (e.g., roses, star lilies, and orchids) as well as many herbs (e.g., peppermint, rosemary, and allspice) can diffuse the meanest temper. For some, pine trees hold the same accolades, as can the smell of the ocean—and, of course, almost everyone's attention is swayed by a wide selection of food smells.

Sense of Taste

It's been said that 80 percent of taste is smell. Those who have experienced a cold might tell you that food simply doesn't taste as good when they are sick. The tongue's taste buds are divided into four specific regions: sweet, bitter, salty, and sour. (Japanese culture includes a fifth region: astringent.) For some, taste also includes the feel of the morsels of food as they pass over the tongue, roof of the mouth, and down the throat. It would be fair to say that taste involves a little bit of touch as well.

Sense of Touch

Humans not only crave touch, but research now reveals that without it, our health diminishes greatly. Human contact through touch is critical to the health of each newborn baby. Without it, babies die. Skin is the largest organ of your body, and with so many neural endings at the periphery of muscle and skin, the sense of touch is by far the most delicate sense. Muscle massage in all its many forms (see Chapter 19) is not the only means to relax through the power of touch. Hot baths, saunas, petting furry cats and dogs, kneading bread, holding hands, walking barefoot on cool grass, hot showers, and making love are just a few of the many ways that touch exalts the human spirit to deeper levels of relaxation.

The Divine Sense

There are some experiences that cannot simply be summed up by one of the five senses. In fact, many experiences involve a synergistic effect of two or more sensory cues that tip the scales toward utter delight. Then there are some events or experiences that rise above the five senses to simply delight the human spirit at the soul level—the feeling that you have touched the face of God. Each of these experiences will vary from person to person, but the one quality they share is that they bring the individual out of his or her personal experience to become one with something greater than the self.

How to Incorporate Relaxation Techniques into Your Life Routine

Every technique for relaxation is a skill, and skills require not only practice but the discipline to practice. Just like learning to type on a computer keyboard, shoot baskets, hit a golf ball, or speak a foreign language, so too every relaxation technique has a learning curve, meaning that the more you practice, the more efficient you become at it.

Although the end result of each technique is the same—homeostasis—every technique has its own nuances and amount of time necessary to achieve the best effect. For example, diaphragmatic breathing can be done in as little as 5 minutes a day, whereas a full body massage requires about 90 minutes. Regardless of which technique you employ, the ideal approach is to do something every day to unwind and return to homeostasis.

By and large, relaxation techniques are simple and cost effective (free). It doesn't take much time or money to sit quietly, close your eyes, and breathe. Yet in this fast-paced life, some techniques are better suited to a classroom setting, such as yoga, Tai Chi, and cardiovascular exercise. Massage therapy is in a category all by itself (although massaging your own muscles feels good, nothing beats a full body massage by a certified massage therapist). If you are the kind of person who needs some encouragement, discipline, or perhaps just camaraderie, then you might consider choosing a relaxation technique in which coaching is encouraged and there is an added sense of community. Exercises 13.1 and 13.2 guide you through the awareness of relaxation through the senses.

Developing Your Mastery of Relaxation Techniques

There is no one way to calm the mind, body, and spirit; there are many ways! How you choose to return to homeostasis is entirely up to you. Regardless of which technique you choose, it will involve one or more of the five senses. Some techniques will prove their effectiveness immediately (e.g., muscle massage), whereas others (e.g., meditation) may take repeated exposure to sense the profound impact they can truly have.

Perhaps it's human nature to be a creature of habit, but most people tend to gravitate toward one or maybe two relaxation techniques. In the holistic approach, it is suggested to cultivate the power of all your senses. As such, it's to everyone's advantage to have a repertoire of at least five personal favorites, ideally one from each sense. If that seems overwhelming, consider simply becoming adept at one or two techniques initially. The rest of this book highlights many tried and true relaxation skills.

Stress Relief and Chronic Pain

Nearly every relaxation technique is useful in the effort to decrease chronic pain. Physical relaxation is the perfect antidote for all stress: mental burnout, physical exhaustion, emotional distress, and the absence of inner peace. Most, if not all, techniques for physical relaxation help to minimize the symptoms of chronic pain; this use will be addressed in each subsequent chapter.

Best Benefits of Physical Relaxation

When the body is aroused for fight or flight, even at low intensities during periods of chronic stress, every organ in the body is at risk for becoming a target of neural or hormonal activity or both. Our muscles are the most frequently hit target organ. Muscle tension is the number one symptom of stress. Although muscle tension doesn't necessarily place people in the hospital, other organs targeted for stress surely will. The heart, the stomach, the skin, the adrenal glands, and the ovaries all become at risk for what Hans Selye called the General Adaptation Syndrome: excessive wear and tear on the body due to a lack of homeostasis.

Each technique for relaxation has one aim: to return the body to a state of homeostasis. In our current 24-7 society in which fast food lifestyles and virtual relationships are the norm, the body not only craves homeostasis, it requires it on a daily basis. Although most, if not all, of these techniques are used as a preventive measure against disease and illness, it is not uncommon to see people who, caught in the grips of chronic disease, use one or more of these techniques for relief from chronic pain. In many cases, various techniques have been known to reverse the damage caused by the disease and the symptoms of stress associated with it.

The cost of not returning to a state of homeostasis is potentially lethal. Remember that the body is the battlefield for the war games of the mind. Simply stated: Stress kills! When the body is not given the chance to return to a baseline level of rest, organs targeted by the emotional consequences of stress will certainly be affected. This fact cannot be understated. Therefore, it stands to reason that the need to relax is as important as taking a daily shower or brushing your teeth. It's that important!

What are the specific benefits of habitual periods of rest and relaxation? They include but are not limited to the following:

Decreased resting heart rate

Increased sleep quality

Decreased resting blood pressure

Increased integrity of immune system

Decreased respiration cycles

Increased digestion

Decreased stress hormone activity

Increased mental concentration and attention span

Decreased fatigue levels

Increased sense of self-esteem

Decreased sense of anxiety

Increased sense of well-being

Decreased muscle tension

Additional Resources

Matthews, A.M. *The Seven Keys to Calm*. New York: Pocket Books, 1997.
Seaward, B.L. *The Art of Calm*. Deerfield Beach, FL: Health Communications, 1999.

Exercise 13.1 The Art of Calm: Relaxation Through the Five Senses

Please list ten ideas for relaxation for each of the five senses. Note that a sixth category, the divine sense, was added for any ideas that might be a combination of these or perhaps something beyond the five senses (e.g., watching a child being born). Describe each in a few words to a sentence. Be as specific as possible, and be creative!

The Sense of Sight

1.
2.
3.
4.
5.
6.
7.
8.
9.
10.

The Sense of Taste

1.
2.
3.
4.
5.
6.
7.
8.
9.
10.

The Sense of Sound

1.
2.
3.
4.
5.
6.
7.
8.
9.
10.

The Sense of Touch

1.
2.
3.
4.
5.
6.
7.
8.
9.
10.

The Sense of Smell

1.
2.
3.
4.
5.
6.
7.
8.
9.
10.

The "Divine" Sense

1.
2.
3.
4.
5.
6.
7.
8.
9.
10.

Exercise 13.2 Relaxation Survival Kit

A relaxation survival kit is like your personal first-aid kit for stress. Keep it well stocked with things that nurture or sustain your personal sense of homeostasis—in this case, homeostasis that comes from pleasing one or all of the five senses. Just like a first-aid kit, please be sure to replace any items that have been used—such as chocolate (taste)—so that in the event of another personal disaster or day from hell, you can pull out your kit and put yourself back on the path toward inner peace. To start this process, begin by making a list of the items you wish to include in your relaxation kit, and then use this list as a means of keeping inventory.

Sight

1. _____

2. _____

Sound

1. _____

2. _____

Taste

1. _____

2. _____

Touch

1. _____

2. _____

Smell

1. _____

2. _____

Additional Items

1. _____

2. _____

CHAPTER
14

The Art of Breathing

There are over forty different ways to breathe.
—Ancient Chinese proverb

Ageless Wisdom of Breathing

There is an ancient proverb that is often cited to students learning the art of self-discipline. It states: There are over forty ways to breathe. If you are like most people, you might smirk or perhaps even laugh at this notion. After all, most people think there is only one way to breathe—a combination of inhaling and exhaling. The ageless wisdom of this proverb, however, suggests that the art of breathing opens the mind and body to a profound sense of relaxation. If you look closely at the plethora of relaxation techniques, from hatha yoga and Tai Chi to autogenics and meditation, you will see that diaphragmatic breathing is used in all of these practices. Indeed, there are many ways to breathe that promote relaxation, most of which place the emphasis of the breath on the lower stomach.

Although there is no one-size-fits-all relaxation technique that works for everyone, there is one that comes close. It's called *diaphragmatic breathing,* and the beauty of this technique is that it can be done anywhere and at any time.

By and large, Americans are thoracic breathers, meaning that we tend to breathe with our upper chest. Diaphragmatic breathing, also known as *belly breathing,* places the emphasis of each breath on the lower stomach area. If you were to watch anyone breathing while they sleep, you would notice that this is the only way they breathe. You breathe like this when you sleep because in a resting state, the body tries to maintain the greatest level of homeostasis.

How to Incorporate the Art of Conscious Breathing into Your Life

Exercises 14.1 ("Breathing Clouds Meditation") and 14.2 ("Dolphin Breath Meditation") guide you through steps of diaphragmatic breathing. The best way to incorporate breathing as a relaxation technique is to practice belly breathing every day, even if it's only for five minutes each day. We all have five minutes. Here are some suggestions:

- When you wake up in the morning, before you get out of bed, take five comfortably slow, deep breaths.

- While in the shower, with your hands at your side, take five comfortably deep breaths.

- While driving to work, turn off the radio for five minutes and consciously breathe.

- Close the office door for five minutes and sit quietly and simply breathe.

- Take five deep sighs on the way home from work.

- Take five deep sighs waiting in line at the grocery store, post office, or bank.
- As you close your eyes to fall asleep, take five comfortable, slow, deep breaths.

Developing Your Mastery of Diaphragmatic Breathing

Believe it or not, this is one technique you have nearly already mastered. At this point all you need to do is practice what you already know. Simply place the emphasis of each breath on your lower stomach. This sensation may feel awkward at first, but soon it will feel quite comfortable and normal. Breathing Clouds and the Dolphin Breath Meditation are just two of the forty techniques available by which to help you develop your mastery of diaphragmatic breathing.

Stress Relief and Chronic Pain

Breathing can become quite short and shallow under high-pressure situations, which is why body wisdom generates a long, deep sigh every now and then. Long, deep breaths begin to reverse the physical effects of a stressful moment. Many pain centers incorporate breathing techniques as a complementary modality for chronic pain. Moreover, one technique specifically invites the individual to imagine breathing into the area where there is pain as a means to reduce the tension in this area, often with great results.

Best Benefits of Diaphragmatic Breathing

If you were to sit in the presence of a meditating yogi and count the number of his breath cycles per minute, you might find that he can comfortably breathe one breath cycle (inhaling and exhaling) per minute, perhaps less. If you were to count the number of breaths you take per minute in the course of any given day, most likely you would count between 14 and 16 breath cycles per minute. When people get stressed, they tend to breathe more frequently per minute, with each breath being more shallow. The benefits of diaphragmatic breathing may seem simple, but they have a profound influence on other aspects of human physiology, including decreasing the resting heart rate, the resting blood pressure, and muscle tension.

Stop reading this for a moment and take a long, deep sigh. Notice how you feel when you exhale. Relief! The breathing cycle is actually a cycle of slight tension or expansion (inhalation) followed by a phase of complete relaxation (exhalation). This is why the exhalation phase is considered to be the most relaxing phase of the breathing cycle. Diaphragmatic breathing works the same way as a deep sigh—only better!

Additional Resources

Farhi, D. *The Breathing Book*. New York: Owl Books, 1996.
Hendricks, G. *Conscious Breathing*. New York: Bantam Books, 1995.
Iyengar, B.K. *Light on Pranayama*. New York: Crossroad, 1981.
Rosen, R. *The Yoga of Breathing: A Step by Step Guide to Pranayama*. Boston: Shambhala Books, 2002.

Exercise 14.1 Breathing Clouds Meditation

Introduction

The words *spirit* and *breath* are synonymous in virtually all cultures and languages. So important is the breath as a means to achieve inner peace, that it is *the* hallmark of nearly every meditation practice. Breath is the life force of energy. If you have ever been aware of your own normal breathing style, you may have noticed that under stress, your breathing becomes more shallow. You may also realize *just how good* a deep sigh really feels. *This* is the underlying message of the Breathing Clouds Meditation: to instill a wonderful sense of inspiration with each inhalation, and total relaxation with each exhalation.

Ancient mystics have said that there are over forty different ways to breathe. What they mean by this is that the breath serves as a powerful metaphor for releasing thoughts and feelings and cleansing the mind, thus promoting a deeper level of contemplation as well as achieving a profound sense of inner wisdom. Although there are many ways to achieve this goal, conscious breathing—that which unites mind, body, and spirit— offers a direct and unencumbered path toward inner peace.

This meditation/visualization exercise is deeply rooted in Eastern culture, a world rich in metaphor. The implied message here is to release, detach, and let go of any and all thoughts and feelings that no longer serve your highest good. This powerful image of breathing clouds is a vehicle to do just this.

As with any type of visualization exercise, please feel free to augment, edit, and embellish the suggestions in this session, to make them the most vivid and empowering for you.

There are two primary images in this meditation. The first is white clouds, which represent the inhalation phase of the breathing cycle. The second is dark clouds, which symbolize the exhalation phase. The white clouds symbolize clean, fresh air. The dark clouds represent stressful thoughts, lingering anxieties, nagging problems, issues, or concerns that trouble you or simply add weight to an already busy mind.

The goal of this meditation is to clear any and all pressing issues, those unresolved feelings, those negative thoughts, or perhaps even excess energy, so that your mind becomes clear of thought and your body becomes completely relaxed.

This breathing exercise includes 12 breathing cycles, with each cycle composed of one inhalation (breathing in through your nose) and one exhalation phase (breathing out through your mouth). As you come to the 11th and 12th cycles—with your mind cleared of mental chatter—you may notice that the air you exhale has become as clean and clear as the air you inhale. This is the goal: homeostasis!

Once again, remember that as you follow the suggestions of this meditation, please follow a breathing cycle that is the most comfortable for you, even if it varies from the pace of this exercise. And, as with all of the exercises, take from this what you need and leave the rest.

Instructions

To begin, find a comfortable place to sit or lie down where there are no interruptions—a time and place for you, and for you alone. Take a moment to adjust any clothing to enhance your own comfort level.

Then close your eyes and take a comfortably slow, deep breath. Breathe in slowly, and as you exhale, feel a sense of calm throughout your *entire* body. Please repeat this casual, normal breathing cycle about four more times, making each breath comfortably slow and comfortably deep. And should your mind wander, know that this is OK, but gently guide it back to the attention of your breath. As you do this, feel your abdominal area expand as you inhale, and then contract as you exhale.

1. After several comfortable breath cycles, when you feel ready, imagine that the next breath that you take in (inhaling through your nose) is drawn from a beautiful cloud of pure white air—clean, fresh air! As you slowly breathe in this cloud of clean air through your nose, feel it circulate up to the top of your head and down the back of your spine, to where it resides at the *base* of your spine.

   Then, when you are ready to exhale, feel the air move up from your stomach area, into your lungs, and out through your mouth. As you *slowly* exhale, visualize that the air you breathe out is a dark cloud of dirty air—this symbolizes any stress and tension you may be feeling. As you begin to exhale, call to mind a problem or issue that has occupied your thoughts for the past several days. Then, allow this thought or feeling to leave as you exhale through your mouth.

2. Once again, using your mind's eye to focus on a beautiful white cloud, breathe in clean, fresh air through your nose, and feel it circulate throughout your body.

   When you are ready to exhale, breathe slowly out through your mouth, and as you do, once again visualize a cloud of dark air leaving your body, symbolic of any thoughts and feelings that at one time may have served you but now no longer do so. To hang on to these thoughts and feelings only weighs you down and holds back your highest potential.

3. On the next inhalation, slowly breathe in a white cloud of clean, fresh air through your nose, and again feel it circulate throughout your body, and this time, cleanse every cell in your body.

    When you are ready to exhale, breathe slowly out through your mouth, and once again as you do, visualize a cloud of dark air leaving your body, Again, this represents any frustrations, anxieties, or anything that needs to be released.

4. Slowly now, inhale clean, fresh air through your nose. When you're ready, slowly exhale dark, dirty air through your mouth.

5. Inhale . . .   Exhale . . .

6. Inhale . . .   Exhale . . .

7. Inhale . . .   Exhale . . .

8. Inhale . . .   Exhale . . .

9. Inhale . . .   Exhale . . .

10. Inhale . . .   Exhale . . .

11. Slowly inhale clean, fresh air though your nose, and as you do, feel the air slowly circulate up to the top of your head. As it begins to move down the back of your spine, feel this clean, pristine air move into every cell in your body to cleanse and invigorate the entire cell, clear down to the structure of your DNA.

    As you begin to exhale, once again breathe out slowly through your mouth, and as you do this, you notice now that the air you breathe out is nowhere near as dark as the air you first exhaled moments ago. Continue exhaling through your mouth, and observe the air you exhale.

12. Inhale clean, fresh air through your nose once more, and as you do, feel the air slowly circulate up to the top of your head. As it begins to move down the back of your spine, feel this clean, pristine air move into every cell in your body. Allow it to cleanse and invigorate the entire cell, including the strands of your DNA.

    As you slowly begin to exhale, breathe out, once again, through your mouth, and as you do this, notice that the air you breathe out has become as clear as the air you have been breathing in. This symbolizes a deep sense of inner peace. Continue to exhale through your mouth and observe the air you breathe out.

    Now begin to notice that as you become more and more relaxed, more calm and more energized by the clean, fresh air circulating through your body, your body is completely relaxed, and your mind is wonderfully calm and clear. As you return to normal breathing, think to yourself as you begin to exhale: "I *am* calm and relaxed." (Repeat!)

With your next breathe, slowly bring yourself back to the awareness of the room you are in. Become aware of the time of day, the day of the week, and what you have planned after you have completed this relaxation session.

When you feel ready, slowly open your eyes to a soft gaze in front of you. If you'd like, go ahead and stretch your arms and shoulders. Notice that although you feel very relaxed, you don't feel tired or sleepy. You feel fully energized and ready to accomplish whatever goals you have planned, fully realizing that now you are renewed and refreshed to once again feel the power of relaxation, as it energizes your whole being.

Exercise 14.1

Exercise 14.2   Dolphin Breath Meditation

Introduction

Breathing is perhaps the most common way to promote relaxation. Taking a few moments to focus on your breathing to the exclusion of all other thoughts helps to calm mind, body, and spirit. By focusing solely on your breathing, you allow distracting thoughts to leave the conscious mind. In essence, clearing the mind of thoughts is very similar to deleting unwanted emails, thus allowing more room to concentrate on what is really important in your life—that which really deserves attention.

In a normal resting state, the average person breathes about 14 to 18 breath cycles per minute. Under stress, this can increase to nearly 30 breath cycles per minute. Yet in a deep relaxed state, it is not uncommon to have as few as 4 to 6 breath cycles in this same time period. The breathing style that produces the greatest relaxation response is that which allows the stomach to expand, rather than the upper chest (this is actually how you breathe when you are comfortably asleep). Take a few moments to breathe, specifically focusing your attention on your abdominal area. And, if any distracting thoughts come to your attention, simply allow these to fade away as you exhale.

Sometimes, combining visualization with breathing can augment the relaxation response. The Dolphin Breath Meditation is one such visualization.

Instructions

Imagine, if you will, that, like a dolphin, you have a hole in the crown of your head with which to breathe. Although you will still breathe through your nose or mouth, imagine that you are now taking in slow, deep breaths through the opening at the top of your head. As you do this, feel the air or energy come in through the top of your head, down past your neck and shoulders, and reside momentarily at the base of your spine.

Then, when you feel ready, very slowly exhale, allowing the air to move back out through the dolphin spout, the opening situated at the top of your head. As you slowly exhale, feel a deep sense of inner peace reside throughout your body.

Once again, using all your concentration, focus your attention on the opening at the top of your head. Now, slowly breathe air in through this opening—comfortably slow, comfortably deep. As you inhale, feel the air move down into your lungs, yet allow it to continue further down, deep into your abdominal region. When you feel ready, slowly exhale, allowing the air to move comfortably from your abdominal region up through the top of your head.

Now, take three slow, deep dolphin breaths, and each time you exhale, feel a deep sense of relaxation all throughout your body.

1. Pause . . . Inhale . . . Exhale

2. Pause . . . Inhale . . . Exhale

3. Pause . . . Inhale . . . Exhale

Just as you imagined a hole in the top of your head, now imagine that in the sole of each foot there is also a hole through which to breathe. As you create this image, take a slow, deep breath and through your mind's eye visualize air coming in through the soles of each foot. Visualize the air moving in from your feet, up through your legs, past your knees and waist, to where it resides in your abdominal region. When you feel ready, begin to exhale slowly, and allow the air to move back out the way it came, out through the soles of your feet.

Using all your concentration, again focus your attention on the openings at the bottom of your feet and once again breathe in air through these openings—comfortably slow, comfortably deep. As before, feel the air move up your legs and into your abdominal region as your lungs fill with air. Then, when you feel ready, exhale, allowing the air to move slowly from your abdominal region back through your legs and out the soles of your feet.

Once again, please take three slow, deep breaths, this time through the soles of your feet, and each time you exhale, feel a deep sense of relaxation all throughout your body.

1. Pause . . . Inhale . . . Exhale

2. Pause . . . Inhale . . . Exhale

3. Pause . . . Inhale . . . Exhale

Now, with your concentration skills fully attentive, with your mind focused on the openings of *both* the top of your head and the soles of your feet, use your imagination to inhale air through both head and feet.

As you do this, slowly allow the passage of air entering from both head and feet to move toward the center of your body, where it resides in the abdominal region, until you exhale. Then, when you feel ready, slowly exhale and direct the air that came in through the top of your head to exit through the dolphin hole, while at the same time directing the air that entered through the soles of your feet to leave from this point of entry as well. Once you have tried this, repeat this combined breath again three times. With each exhalation, notice how relaxed your body feels.

1. Pause . . . Inhale . . . Exhale

2. Pause . . . Inhale . . . Exhale

3. Pause . . . Inhale . . . Exhale

When you're done, allow this image to fade from your mind, but retain the sense of deep relaxation this experience has instilled throughout your mind, body, and spirit. Then take one final slow, deep breath, feeling the air come into your nose or mouth and down into your lungs, and allow your stomach to extend out and then deflate as you begin to exhale. Again, feel a deep sense of calm as you exhale.

When you feel ready, allow your eyes to slowly open to a soft gaze in front of you, and bring your awareness back to the room where you now find yourself. As you bring yourself back to the awareness of the room you are now in, you feel fully energized, recharged, revitalized, and ready to accomplish whatever tasks await you ahead.

Exercise 14.2

CHAPTER

15

The Art of Meditation

Meditation—It's not what you think!
—Anonymous

Ageless Wisdom of Centering

So important is the practice of meditation that every culture since the beginning of time has included it as a fundamental practice of living. Historically, credit is given to the Asian continent as the birthplace of meditation. A closer look, however, reveals that the practice of centering or "quieting the mind" is known the world over as a time-honored practice to achieve inner peace.

The premise of meditation is simple: By quieting the mind from both external noise and internal chattering, you begin to gain greater clarity regarding important aspects of your life. In 2003, *Time* magazine's cover story on meditation revealed that over 25 million Americans meditate regularly. What was once considered to be a passing fad, promoted by the Beatles after an exposure to Maharishi Mahesh Yogi (the founder of Transcendental Meditation) in India, has now become a mainstay of the American culture. Moreover, magnetic resonance imaging (MRI) technology has been used to research the activation of various brain tissue during meditation to reveal that, much as the wisdom keepers spoke of eons ago, the practice of meditation rewires the neural circuitry to promote calmness throughout the brain and body.

Although Freud coined the term *ego* about a hundred years ago, the concept of the conscious mind's censor is ageless. In many Eastern cultures, the ego, as we understand it, is referred to as "the self" or "false self." The purpose of meditation is to quiet the voice of the *false self* so that the inherent wisdom from the higher self or the true self can be accessed. Perhaps this is best explained in the ancient Chinese proverb that states "When the pupil is ready, the teacher will come." We are both the pupil and teacher. This inherent wisdom suggests that when we take the time to quiet the mind of the mental chatter that tends to distort clear thinking, we become receptive to insights (simple and profound) that give clarity and direction on the human path. For this reason, the fruits of meditation are often described as enlightenment.

You don't have to be watching CNN to know that the information age has taken off with a vengeance. Cell phones, laptops, micro-computer chips, and the Internet all spew bits and bytes of information incessantly in a 24-7 world. Everyone and everything seems to have instant accessibility. What this means is that there is very little down time to simply sit and relax without being bombarded with information. Even if you turn off the computer, TV, or other distractions, your mind, under the control of the ego, picks up the slack and continues the babble. Because the mind is such an abstract concept, it and the practice of meditation are often explained in terms of metaphors. Before the introduction of computers, meditation was described as being like a broom that sweeps away the dust of the mind, or an ocean wave that washes away footprints in the sand.

In the high-tech information age, a newer, perhaps more apt metaphor, explains meditation as a process similar to deleting old, unwanted emails.

Types of Meditation

Although there are many hundreds of ways to meditate, all varieties of centering tend to fall into one of three categories: exclusive meditation, inclusive meditation, and mindfulness (which some people consider a form of inclusive meditation). Let's take a closer look at these various forms of centering, as well as examples of each.

Exclusive Meditation

To hold one thought in the focus of your concentration, to the exclusion of all other thoughts, is the premise of exclusive meditation. A busy mind can race from thought to thought in milliseconds and become easily distracted. The consequence of a distracted mind is mental distortion, which is the antithesis of increased awareness. In the East this is called "clouded thinking."

Various means to promote a focused concentration include sensory cues such as a verbal mantra (e.g., repeating the word *om*), a visual object (e.g., looking at a mandala), an audio mantra (e.g., ocean waves), or a tactile object (e.g., rosary beads). The premise behind exclusive meditation (also called *restrictive meditation*) is that by training the mind to focus on one thought, all other thoughts are compelled to evaporate from the conscious mind, thus allowing for increased awareness. The various forms of mental cleansing (e.g., mantras) act like a metaphorical wind that blows away the clouds—distractions produced by the ego. Transcendental Meditation, Deepak Chopra's Primordial Sound Meditation, and Herbert Benson's Relaxation Response are all examples of exclusive meditation.

The most common mantra for the use of exclusive meditation is to focus on your breathing. To do this you sit quietly with your eyes closed and, through your mind's eye, observe the continuous inhalation and exhalation of each breath. If distracting thoughts appear to divert your attention, they are metaphorically exhaled on the out breath. So common is the breath as a mantra and so symbolic is breathing as a tool for cleansing that it is used in conjunction with nearly every known relaxation technique. Exercise 14.1, "Breathing Clouds Meditation" (Chapter 14), is a variation on the theme of using the breath as a means to cleanse the mind. Exercise 15.1, "Rainbow Meditation," is an exclusive meditation exercise that uses a series of affirmations and visualizations with breathing to allow a clearing of the body's major energy centers (chakras).

Inclusive Meditation

Imagine that you are observing yourself, watching yourself engaged in the thinking process. Inclusive meditation is the ability to step outside your thoughts and detach yourself from your stream of consciousness by looking and observing, but not judging, your thoughts and emotions. Rather than excluding thoughts, inclusive meditation invites the practitioner to observe all thoughts, but not cast judgment on any thoughts or emotions. By commanding a practice of inclusive meditation, you begin to honor the discipline of detaching your ego's desires and the expectations that you hold of others and yourself.

Some practices of inclusive meditation include the contemplation of an imponderable puzzle, also known as a *koan* (e.g., How many angels can dance on the head of a pin? or What is the sound of one hand clapping?). Zen meditation, various forms of Buddhist meditation, contemplative meditation, and centering prayer all serve as examples of inclusive meditation in which the higher states of consciousness are attained from the observed becoming the observer.

Mindfulness Meditation

To be fully present with each and every activity that you do is the hallmark of mindfulness meditation. Rather than multitasking and having your mind ricocheting all over the place at every moment of each waking day, mindfulness meditation invites the practitioner to be fully present with each and every activity he or she does. For example, when washing the dishes, one would focus one's attention by feeling the water and soap over one's hands, then feel the shape of the dish as it is handled and cleaned. Similarly, when walking outside, be mindful of the air temperature, the position of the sun, the smell of the earth, and so forth. Mindfulness also includes maintaining a sense of gratitude for all the many blessings in life, rather than ego-driven thoughts of feeling victimized by a series of personal injustices. A classic exercise in mindfulness is to pick up an apple, smell it, feel it, look at its color and texture, and feel the weight in the palm of your hand. Be mindful of where it was grown and how it nourishes the body when eaten, and then take a bite to savor the taste of the apple, being mindful with each bite of all of these aspects. Exercise 15.2, "Healing Water Meditation," is an example of mindfulness meditation.

Insightful Meditation

Insightful meditation isn't so much a type of meditation as it is an effect of cleansing the mind to unveil new thoughts, intuitive thoughts, insights, or what some people call enlightenment. All types of meditation can offer insight. Theoretically speaking, once the mind is still, it begins to reflect a deep-seated wisdom contained in the depths of the unconscious mind or, as Carl Jung suggested, "the collective unconscious."

As the expression goes, you cannot demand enlightenment. One must trust that insights will, indeed, come when the pupil is truly ready. Insights shouldn't be considered the goal of any meditation practice, for goals are accompanied by desires, and desires are, for the most part, deeply rooted in ego. The primary goal of meditation is to calm the mind, even if nothing shows up once this state is reached. In other words, it's nice if it happens, but it doesn't always happen. There are ways, however, to encourage the ego to be still long enough so that, given the chance, deep insights may appear. Exercises 15.3, "Crystal Cave Meditation," and 15.4, "Celestial Heavens," are examples of insight meditation/visualization exercises that augment the process of clarity by removing mental and emotional obstructions to allow a greater sense of insight regarding personal issues and one's human potential.

Meditation and Cognitive Function

It has long been held that the practice of meditation increases awareness by helping to access regions of the unconscious mind that are often deemed inaccessible because of the ego's censorship. Although the unconscious mind and the right hemisphere of the brain are not the same thing, it appears that the cognitive functions of the unconscious mind are very similar to the functions associated with the right hemisphere of the brain. In fact, the right side of the brain may be the specific organ of choice for the unconscious mind to do its work. The overall effect of meditation appears to allow both hemispheres of the brain to work in unison. Under stress, left-brain skills tend to dominate our thinking patterns, thus promoting a less than holistic approach to mental, emotional, and spiritual well-being. The following is a short list of recognized right- and left-brain cognitive functions.

Left-Brain Thought Processes	Right-Brain Thought Processes
Analytical skills	Synthesis skills
Judgmental skills	Accepting, receptive nature
Time conscious	Non-time conscious
Verbal acuity	Symbolic thought processes
Linear thought progression	Nonlinear thought processes
Math acuity	Irrational thought processes
Logical thought processes	Highly intuitive nature
Sequential thought processes	Highly imaginative
Literal	Humor/playfulness

Concrete/fact oriented	Metaphorical thought processes
Skeptical	Spontaneous
Cautious	Music appreciation
Works well with things	Works well with people

Meditation and Attention Deficit Disorder

It's no secret that attention deficit disorder (ADD) has become a national epidemic in America. The inability to focus one's attention on anything for a specific period of time has become a societal norm. There are many reasons for this, ranging from poor diet (lack of omega-3 fatty acids and an abundance of aspartame) to the oscillations of repeated television broadcast signals (not to mention commercial camera shots and angles). Add to this the obsession with voice mails, emails, instant messages, and the newest technology device about to hit the market, and it's a wonder that anybody gets anything done at all with the proliferation of technological distractions. Despite the push for medications, we can safely assume that people do not have a Ritalin deficiency.

Zen masters laugh at the notion of ADD. Not because it's funny, but because they are of the opinion that *everybody* with an ego has ADD. They hold the conventional wisdom that meditation is the means to train the mind to focus. More specifically, meditation is the way to domesticate the ego from wandering all over the conscious map. Meditation is the age-old tool of consciousness to increase attention and sharpen one's focus.

There are many people who claim that because they have been diagnosed with ADD, they cannot (and perhaps never will be able to) meditate. Nothing could be further from the truth! Although it may be hard at first (and to be honest, initially it is hard for everyone to learn to meditate), stay with it. It will get easier. It would be a good idea to learn to minimize distractions such as cell phone use and to eat healthier too by avoiding foods that negatively affect brain chemistry.

How to Incorporate Meditation into Your Daily Routine

The best way to begin and maintain a practice of meditation is to dedicate time to sit (or lie) quietly for a short period of time each day. Like taking a shower or brushing your teeth, meditation is best adopted as a daily practice or ritual, not merely as a casual leisure activity when time permits. Most people claim not to have enough time in the day to sit quietly, yet the practice of meditation, or centering, need only take five minutes a day to start.

Select a time of day. Morning is often suggested as the best time to ground you for the rest of the day, but any time will work. Next, select a specific quiet place (either home or work) that is designated as your meditation place—a corner of the bedroom or den. By designating a place to do this (as you do with eating or brushing your teeth), you create a healthy boundary for this purpose. The next step is to minimize all distractions. The purpose of meditation is to minimize distractions generated from the ego to gain insight from the depths of your unconscious mind. Because the ego is so easily distracted by external stimuli, it defeats the purpose of meditation (particularly when you are starting this practice) to have external distractions, such as blaring televisions, stereos, and radios, or cell phones going off in the midst of deep concentration. Exercises 15.1 to 15.4 guide you through several meditation experiences.

Additional Suggestions

- It is highly recommended not to meditate on a full stomach. This tends to promote drowsiness or sleep, which does not lend itself to full awareness.

- Select a time in the day (mornings are thought to be best, before breakfast, or evenings well after dinner). Keep this time as a regular part of your daily schedule.

- Keeping your spine straight is the optimal position for meditation because it not only produces minimal neural discharge but also offers a clear and unobstructed path for the energy of the spine (known as Kundalini energy) to move to the crown of the head.

- If you prefer, consider playing some soft music (as white noise) to promote a deeper sense of awareness. Some people also prefer to burn a candle or incense. The use of relaxing sensory stimuli really helps to create a calm environment conducive for a sound meditative practice.

- Boredom is a common experience in the initial stages of a meditative practice, and some say a necessary stage in reaching the realms of higher consciousness. Obsession with boredom is the ego's way of manipulating the mind to abandon meditation as a practice. Rather than giving in, it's best to sit through this phase until the ego is fully domesticated. Having said that, some meditative practices tend to lose their appeal after a prolonged period (for some, months; others, years). Should you find that your meditative practice has become flat and predictable and no longer allows you to cross the threshold of insight, consider varying your practice by using different music, a different mantra, or perhaps shifting entirely from exclusive to inclusive meditation (or vice versa).

- Meditation CDs can serve as a means to either enhance or provide variety to one's meditative practice. There are many different types of meditation CDs with a host of different meditation themes. If you find that it is really difficult to minimize distractions (e.g., intrusive family members), you may wish to consider listening to a selection from a meditation CD with headphones on to help strengthen the mind.

- As a variation to your meditation practice, consider inviting like-minded friends or colleagues to do a group meditation (e.g., for world peace). Additionally, meditation groups meet regularly in community and church settings; this might offer a means to enhance your meditation practice or add some variety to it.

- Sometimes it's nice to begin a meditation session by reading a short passage from a daily meditation book. There are many books to choose from, including *356 Tao, Promise of a New Day,* and, of course, the Bible.

Developing Your Mastery of Meditation

If you have an interest in starting a meditation practice, you don't need to travel miles away to an Indian ashram or Buddhist temple. The practice of meditation can be done anywhere you can find or make a quiet space. Like all other techniques in this book, meditation is a skill that serves you best with regular practice—in this case, every day. Developing a mastery of meditation does not mean that you will be able to levitate, bi-locate, or become psychic. What a mastery in meditation does allow for is the ability to stay centered and grounded in the midst of change, to hold a place of inner peace in the heart, which ultimately is what centering means.

Stress Relief and Chronic Pain

Ageless wisdom reminds us that meditation is essential for stress relief. Mindfulness meditation is perhaps the most common form of meditation used with those suffering from chronic pain, as revealed by the work of Jon Kabat-Zinn. Focusing on your pain might seem like the last thing you wish to do; however, the practice of mindfulness meditation often allows for deeper insights into the mind-body connection, which, in turn, minimize and may even heal the pain.

Best Benefits of Meditation

By all accounts, the benefits of meditation for both mind and body are quite impressive. A short list includes but is not limited to the following:

- Increased attention span
- Increased imagination and creativity
- Increased patience
- Increased tolerance
- Increased intuitive awareness
- Decreased resting heart rate
- Decreased resting blood pressure
- Increased immune system
- Increased quality of sleep
- Combined brain hemispheric lateralization

Additional Resources

Benson, H. *The Relaxation Response*. New York: Morrow Press, 1975.

Dyer, W. *Getting into the Gap* [with CD]. Carlsbad, CA: Hay House, 2003.

Kabat-Zinn, J. *Wherever You Go, There You Are: Mindfulness Living in Everyday Life*. New York: Hyperion Books, 1994.

Seaward, B.L. *Quiet Mind, Fearless Heart*. New York: John Wiley & Sons, 2005.

Tolle, E. *The Power of Now*. Novato, CA: New World Library, 1999.

Weiss, B.L. *Meditations* [with CD]. Carlsbad, CA: Hay House, 2002.

Meditation CDs

Miller, E. *Letting Go of Stress*. www.DrMiller.com. 1-800-528-2737.

Seaward, B.L. *A Wing and a Prayer*. Inspiration Unlimited, 2003. 303-678-9962.

Seaward, B.L. *A Change of Heart*. Inspiration Unlimited, 2002. 303-678-9962.

Seaward, B.L. *Sweet Surrender*. Inspiration Unlimited, 2002. 303-678-9962.

Exercise 15.1   Rainbow Meditation

From a metaphysical perspective, there are seven regions of the body that need to be constantly revitalized with universal energy to maintain optimal wellness. These same seven areas also correspond to seven major endocrine glands. Perhaps by no coincidence, there are seven notes to the harmonic scale and seven colors to the rainbow. This mental imagery exercise brings to mind these seven areas and the colors associated with them. Each area is represented as a circular window through which energy passes. This window goes by the name of *chakra,* a Sanskrit word to describe a spinning wheel. With each color, there is a series of meditational phrases that can be repeated to yourself as you visualize this image.

When first learning this exercise, it is best to try this lying down, if possible. And, as with any guided mental imagery exercise, feel free to modify these suggestions to augment the strength of the image for you. For example, glasses filled with different-colored water, different-colored flowers, or even fruit offer variety to this theme.

The Base of the Spine: Red

Imagine a beam of light emanating from the base of your spine: a laser beam of red light. This area and color are metaphorical symbols representing your being grounded to the earth. To be grounded means to feel stable and securely rooted in your environment, both physically and emotionally. Take a slow, deep breath and as you exhale, see this beam of red light and say this phrase to yourself: "I feel grounded." Take one more deep breath and repeat this phrase again.

Two Inches Below the Belly Button: Orange

Now, focus your attention to the center of your body. If you are like most people, this point is approximately two inches below your belly button. Imagine that from this point emanates an orange beam of light outward toward infinity. This area of your body represents both the literal and figurative center of your body. To become centered means to focus inward and to maintain a personal balance. To be centered also means to feel self-confident and worthy of high self-esteem. Think what it is like to have a strong sense of self-confidence and self-esteem. Now, take a slow, deep breath and as you exhale see this beam of orange light and say this phrase to yourself: "I feel centered." or "I have confidence." Take one more deep breath and repeat the phrase again.

The Upper Stomach: Yellow

Bring your attention to your upper stomach. This area is often referred to as the *solar plexus.* From this area imagine a beam of brilliant yellow light emanating outward toward infinity. This area and color are symbolic of several factors, including self-empowerment and the ability to receive love—love from family, friends, and all elements of the universe. Like the previous area, it too is related to self-esteem. Take a slow, deep breath and as you exhale, focus on this beam of yellow light and say the following phrase to yourself: "I feel loved." Take one more deep breath and repeat this phrase again.

The Center of the Upper Chest: Green

The upper chest houses the heart, perhaps the most important organ in the body. The heart is symbolic of the emotion love, for it is through the heart that we share compassion with our fellow human beings and creatures of the planet, and even with the planet itself. Like a window, the metaphorical heart can be opened to share love or can be closed. The latter is often compared to a "hardened heart." Open the window of your heart and imagine an emerald green beam of light shining forth. This region of your body and this color represent your ability to share your feelings of warmth, happiness, compassion, and those aspects that comprise the emotion of love. Take a slow, deep breath and as you exhale, focus on this color green and say to yourself, "I choose love." Take one more deep breath and repeat this phrase again.

The Throat: Aqua Blue

Bring your attention to your throat. Imagine a soft blue beam of light emanating from your throat area and extending toward infinity. This area and this color represent your meaningful purpose in life or your life mission. For a moment, ponder what you think this might be for you right now. It may be very general, yet profound, or it may be a short-term goal you wish to accomplish. Think of the willpower and the drive necessary to accomplish this mission. Know that you have this resource within you. Focus on this mission and at the same time focus on the color blue. Take a deep breath and as you exhale, repeat this phrase: "I have a meaningful purpose to my life and I can do it." Take one more deep breath and repeat this phrase again.

The Center of the Forehead: Indigo Blue

This area of the forehead is sometimes referred to as the *third eye,* and it symbolizes wisdom and intuition. More clearly, it symbolizes wisdom stemming from the balance between the right and left hemispheres of the brain and the conscious and unconscious minds—the ability to access all mental faculties. Focus your attention on this area, just above your nose, in between your eyes. Using your imagination, see the color indigo blue emanate as a laser beam of light shooting straight toward infinity. As you see this color blue, think of your ability to balance your thinking skills to access your deepest wisdom. Take a slow, deep breath and as you exhale, repeat this phrase to yourself: "I feel balanced" or "I have inner wisdom." Take one more deep breath and repeat the phrase again.

The Crown of the Head: Violet

From the crown of your head, imagine emanating a beam of light the color violet or lavender. Regardless of which position your head is resting in, this beam of light always directs itself upward toward the heavens. This chakra was depicted as a halo over the head in the Renaissance period. This body region and the color associated with it represent your connection to the divine consciousness of the universe. To feel connected is a very important aspect of one's well-being. Focus on this color and think what it is like to feel a sense of connectedness and belonging. To be aware of this connection is to feel at one with the universe, to feel at peace with yourself. Take a slow, deep breath and as you exhale, visualize this color and say to yourself a phrase that reinforces a feeling of connectedness. It might be something like: "I am one with the world," "I am at peace with myself," or "I am one with God." Take one more deep breath and repeat the phrase again.

Finally, allow all these beams of light to grow in all directions so that soon they all merge together and you find yourself surrounded in a ball of brilliant white light.

Exercise 15.1

Exercise 15.2 Healing Water Meditation

New scientific discoveries reveal that water has the ability to hold intention and memory. As such, it can be a powerful means to deliver healing intentions. This meditation is based on the premise of mindfulness of water's healing potential.

1. Begin this meditation by filling a cup or glass with fresh water. Place it by your side or in front of you, as you sit with your back straight. Sit quietly and clear your mind of any and all random thoughts and nagging chit-chat, coming to a still place of peace.

2. Then, focus on your breathing to still both your mind and body. Take five slow, deep breaths. Feel a deep sense of relaxation with each exhalation.

3. Now, slowly reach for the glass of water and hold the glass in both hands, so that your hands surround the water. Taking another slow, deep breath, pause for a moment to reflect on the source of water in your glass. Let your mind flow backward toward the original source from whence this water came. Allow your mind to travel to the source—a mountain stream, a deep well, an underground aquifer, raindrops.

4. Slowly, shift your focus from the source of water to the many purposes of water, the gift of life. Water is used to cleanse and purify. It is used to hydrate and bring balance to that which craves balance. Water is a nutrient and is used as a source of sustenance, allowing life to flourish. Water is a symbol of the divine, and it is used to anoint and bless the vibration of divine spirit into dense matter. Think of all these and any other uses for this precious gift.

5. Holding the glass in both hands, bring the glass to your face and look at the water—first the surface, and then deep into the water. At room temperature, water is liquid, yet water can take many forms in the continuum of matter. Just as the glass holds water, so too does the water become a container to hold things. Water also amplifies our thoughts, feelings, and intentions.

6. In this meditation, allow the water in your hands to hold a special intention from your heart. Bring to your heart and mind a thought, prayer, or intention that surfaces regularly to your consciousness. Allow this healing intention (personal or global) to float on the surface of the water and then slowly dissolve into the water, like a drop of blue coloring, so that soon the entire glass of water holds this intention in every molecule.

7. Still holding the glass in both hands, bring the glass to your lips and slowly sip from the edge, taking some of this water into your body. As you do this, feel the water move over your tongue through your mouth and gently pass down your throat. Although you cannot see it, use your mind's eye to follow these drops of water into the heart of every cell in your body, replenishing the fluid that bathes your DNA.

8. When you are through with the mindfulness of this experience, slowly get up and walk outside and pour half of the remaining glass of water on the earthen soil, and as you do this, once again repeat the intention of your heart. Finally, place the glass of water in the sun to evaporate so that your healing intention may be carried by the four winds to be made manifest for the highest good of all concerned.

Exercise 15.3 Crystal Cave Meditation

There is an ancient proverb that says, "When the student is ready, the teacher will come." In truth, we are both the student and the teacher. To be "ready" means to quiet the mind. More specifically, it means to still the voice of the ego, so that the wisdom from the teacher can make itself known.

Seeking counsel from your intuition, the collective unconscious, or your higher self need not be a complicated process. It's simply an exercise in discipline and patience. The following exercise is a tool to be used when trying to gain clarity on an issue or become more grounded during any decision-making process. The crystal cave represents a magical metaphor of that "still place" in your mind where the teacher's wisdom can be heard clearly above the static noise of the conscious mind.

To begin this exercise, first focus your awareness on your breathing:

1. Feel the air come into your nose or mouth and travel down deep into your lungs. Feel your stomach extend out, then return, as you exhale. As you repeat this cycle of slow, deep breathing, become aware of how relaxed your body is with *each* exhalation.

2. Now, take a very slow, deep breath, as slow and as deep as you possibly can. Comfortably slow, comfortably deep. Then, follow that with one more breath, even slower and even deeper than before.

As you continue breathing comfortably . . .

1. Imagine that you are standing at the bottom of a short set of marble stairs, about ten steps in all. At the bottom, where you are, it is somewhat dark, but at the top of the stairs, you see a brilliant radiant light reaching down toward you. As you look up, you are immediately attracted toward the light, and . . .

2. You feel compelled to walk up the stairs, toward the light. But because the steps are rather large, you find that you can only take one step at a time. As you walk up the first step, you begin to feel a sense of inner peace within yourself that you have not felt for a long time. All judgments about yourself are suspended and you begin to accept yourself for *all* that you are. Now, take a slow, deep breath and exhale, and feel yourself step up to the next level.

3. As you move up toward the second step, you begin to feel a sense of inner peace between you and all of your family members. Whatever differences may exist, allow yourself to realize that they are unimportant now. So leave whatever frustrations you may have behind you as you progress up the next step. Once again, take a slow, deep breath, and as you exhale feel yourself step up to the next level.

4. On the third step, you begin to gain a sense of peace and resolution among all your friends and acquaintances. On this step, there is no resentment, no animosity—only compassion for everyone you have ever met, and this feels so good. Once again, leave whatever frustrations you have behind as you progress up the next step. As you do this, take a slow, comfortable, deep breath, and as you exhale, confidently feel yourself move up to the next level.

5. The fourth step brings a sense of calm and serenity within you and your higher self. As you continue up the stairs, you begin to notice that you feel yourself becoming much lighter. With each step toward the light, you feel your body become lighter and more relaxed. With this sense of lightness and peace, you almost feel yourself floating up the remaining steps—toward the top.

6. As you appear on the top step, you now find yourself surrounded in a brilliant golden-white light. Almost immediately, you feel yourself floating, up into the light. Each cell in your body radiates with this brilliant golden-white light, and this feels wonderful. In a moment's recognition, you immediately sense that you cannot distinguish yourself from the light. And once again, you feel an incredible sense of love, support, and nurturing from this source of radiance. Take a nice slow, deep, breath and breathe this light into your body.

7. Surrounded in light, you feel yourself floating down a hall of crystal glass, and the light that resides in you and all around you shines through the crystal glass, so that tiny rainbows appear everywhere—brilliant reds, deep oranges, bright yellows, lush greens, azure blues, and intense purples. The colors of these rainbows make you smile and you feel a sense of warmth, wonder, and awe as you float effortlessly through this hall toward what appears to be an opening into a crystal cave.

8. As you continue to float peacefully through this hall of crystal glass, you come upon a large room and you notice that it, too, is constructed of crystal glass prisms, each filled with tiny rainbows slowly dancing all around the room. As various colors of the rainbow filter through the glass crystal,

you see an area off to the left that has a sunken floor. You are drawn immediately to this area, and you soon find yourself sitting on a comfortable cushioned step, once again surrounded by the beauty of warm, dancing light all around you.

9. As quick as the mind can travel, you find yourself transported to this room in search of an answer. Deep in your heart, there is a question begging to be asked. There is some morsel of wisdom you yearn to have, to help you on your quest for self-improvement. *This* is why you have come here. Take a slow, deep breath and again feel a sense of warmth and comfort as you exhale.

10. Now, take a moment to look around the room. Intuitively, you feel the presence of someone nearby. As you gaze around, you notice that sitting next to you is a wise and friendly sage. It may be someone you fondly recognize immediately (male or female), or it may be someone you have never seen before, yet know and trust deep in your heart. Look into their face and deep into their eyes, and as you do, notice that you feel an immediate sense of recognition, an immediate sense of comfort and compassion coming from within this person directly toward you.

11. After you exchange smiles, you remember the question, the question to which you seek an answer. The essence of wisdom on the face of this sage radiates through to your mind. All you need do is think the question, and your voice will be heard. Now once again, take a slow, deep breath and find peace and comfort in the stillness. Then, listen very carefully for the answer. It will come as one of your own thoughts. Yet, at a deep level you will know that this insight has come from a place beyond the limits of your conscious mind. Sometimes, the answer comes quickly. Other times it is planted as a seed to germinate and grow at the most appropriate time of receptivity. With the question now posed, trust that the wisdom you seek is both accepted *and understood* at the deepest level. Please take a moment to quiet your mind now, and listen for the answer.

12. When you feel ready, thank this person with a thought, a smile, or perhaps even a wink. As you do, you then find yourself floating on a beam of light back through the hall of prism glass with multicolored rainbows. You enter through the passage of brilliant golden-white light and you come to the place where you now sit or lie.

    Take a deep breath and relax, contemplating the message you have received.

13. Take one more slow, comfortable deep breath and as you exhale bring yourself back to the awareness of the room in which you now find yourself. Become aware of the time of day, the day of the week, and perhaps what you have planned after you have completed this relaxation session.

When you feel ready, open your eyes to a soft gaze in front of you. If you wish, begin to slowly stretch your neck and shoulders, and then think to yourself about how great this sense of peace from the wisdom you have gained feels throughout your mind and body. And with confidence, you are ready to begin a new day.

Exercise 15.4 Celestial Heavens

Imagine that this evening is a warm summer night—neither hot nor humid, but comfortably warm. You step outside the back door and feel a slight breeze in the air, and it feels really nice against your face.

The sun has set, but it's still somewhat light. You look up in the sky and it is full of clouds—big, billowy clouds. The sun's last rays light up the clouds on the western horizon, and this light turns the gray clouds pink and orange for a few lingering moments. Tonight, the sky looks so inviting. As you stand at the back door, you think to yourself how nice it would be to grab a blanket and lie under the stars for a few hours. Then you think to yourself, "Hey, why not?" So you go back inside and grab a blanket, perhaps even a pillow, and then head back outside again.

After meandering a ways, you find a nice comfortable spot, far away from any city lights—your own private place to lie down and relax. You spread the blanket out and then lie down. Notice how good it feels to connect with the earth, and again you feel the summer breeze upon your face, and it feels good too.

From the time you first looked outside tonight to this very moment, you noticed that the sky has filled with more clouds, but you also notice that the winds have picked up and they quickly move the clouds from west to east across the night sky. Every now and then, you see what looks like an evening star peeking through the clouds. You look closely, but your mind begins to wander, and the star hides again.

Metaphorically speaking, clouds are like thoughts in your mind, and tonight these clouds represent the multitude of thoughts racing through your mind. The purpose of this meditation, this time looking up in the sky, is to clear your mind of excess thoughts, persistent, nagging thoughts, random thoughts so that your mind becomes as clear as the clearest night sky.

Specifically, these clouds overhead—these big, billowy clouds—are symbolic of any thoughts, issues, problems, or conflicts that you are facing in your life right now. As you see a cloud overhead, label it with whatever thought comes to mind. Take a nice, deep breath and as you exhale, let it go as you watch the wind carry the cloud away. In doing so, you allow yourself to detach from this thought or concern long enough to gain a better sense of clarity. Once again, take a nice, slow, deep breath and allow each cloud above to slowly disappear from view over the eastern horizon.

Every now and then you glimpse a star twinkling through the clouds. The first stars to appear in the night sky are typically our neighboring planets. Take a moment to focus on a star, but then notice it is quickly covered up as another cloud comes into view. As you see this next cloud come into view, bring to mind another stressor—some frustration or anxiety—label the cloud with it, and then watch it move across the horizon, fading from view. Once again, take a nice, slow, deep breath and allow this cloud and the thought it represents to slowly disappear from view, over the eastern horizon.

Every cloud that comes into view represents some problem or issue, but tonight, the cool wind acts like a broom to sweep away all these thoughts and concerns, leaving your mind clear and still. Allow the wind to carry your thoughts and concerns off to the horizon and beyond. Notice that as these clouds begin to move away from your field of vision, your body and mind become more and more relaxed. Once again, take a nice, slow, deep breath and allow the cloud overhead to slowly disappear from view over the eastern horizon.

Concentrate and look up in the sky. Tonight, and every night, the sky serves as a metaphor of your mind. As you gaze up to the heavens, you notice that above the layer of thick, billowy clouds is a very thin layer of cloud as well, so thin that you can faintly see the brightest stars shine through. This layer of clouds is also being pushed by the wind from west to east, and it moves high above your head. This layer of cloud represents any lingering thoughts, any random thoughts, or perhaps any excess energy that distracts your attention away from the celestial sea that it veils. Take a nice, deep, slow breath and allow this thin layer of clouds to slowly disappear over the horizon.

Above you now the sky is clear, and the stars are so near that you can practically reach out and touch them. As you gaze upward, you see in front of you the Milky Way stretched thick and wide across the sky, as if someone took a paint brush across the sky. As you focus on the stars, you begin to recognize familiar constellations: the Big Dipper, Orion, or perhaps the Pleiades.

Stars in the night sky are points of light that convey brilliance and wisdom. Take a moment to pick one star and focus your entire awareness on it. Once again, take a nice, deep, slow breath and as you exhale, feel a sense of deep peace throughout your mind and body, as deep as the celestial sky. Take one more slow, deep breath and this time as you exhale, allow your eyes to wander until they find another star to focus on. Again feel a deep sense of inner peace.

When you feel ready, close your eyes to this image and bring your awareness back to your body. Once again take a nice, slow, deep breath and feel a profound sense of relaxation throughout your mind and body.

Imagine yourself sitting up on the blanket, then standing up and grabbing the blanket and turning toward the direction of home. Soon you find yourself back on your back porch and then, in the blink of an eye, you are lying comfortably on your bed. Become aware of how relaxed you are, yet how energized you feel—refreshed and renewed.

When you feel ready, slowly open your eyes to a soft gaze in front of you. and bring yourself back to the awareness of the room you are now in. Remind yourself that although you feel relaxed, you do not feel sleepy or tired. In fact, you feel reenergized and renewed. On your next breath as you exhale, think to yourself the following phrase: "I am reenergized and renewed and inspired to continue whatever projects await me today."

CHAPTER

16

The Power of Mental Imagery and Visualization

*All this or something better now manifests for me in totally satisfying
and harmonious ways, for the highest good of all concerned.*
—Shakti Gawain

Ageless Wisdom of Imagery and Visualization

Plato once said that no thought exists without an image to accompany it. This insight is as true today as it was at the time he first said it over two millennia ago. The power of the mind is nothing less than phenomenal. When combined with the power of the human spirit, nothing, it seems, is impossible. Take, for example, Joe Simpson, who after falling several hundred feet only to shatter his right leg, descended single-handedly down Siula Grande in the Peruvian Andes and lived to tell about it in his book and subsequent movie, *Touching the Void*. By imagining himself moving painstakingly slow from point to point, he did the impossible and survived. Simpson is not alone in his efforts to harness the power of visualization, but his story is certainly one of the most dramatic.

Just as the mind can create positive images to accomplish the impossible, it can also manufacture images to immobilize our human potential as well. Perhaps with the proliferation of television and visual media to be found everywhere, visual images abound, thus accentuating your ability to create images (real or imagined) in your mind. The power of the mind to create images that can either heal or hurt is well founded throughout the history of humanity. Perhaps as no surprise, people unknowingly practice the art of visualization all the time, particularly imagining a series of worst-case scenarios with the anticipation of a stressful event. In the words of Albert Einstein, "No problem can be solved from the same consciousness that created it." Visualization and mental imagery require a different mind-set than the typical frenetic consciousness so prevalent today.

Visualization and Imagery

Although the terms *visualization* and *mental imagery* may seem like the same concept (and to many they are), those who specialize in the area of mind-body-spirit healing note a distinct difference, based on both the study of the mind and personal experience with scores of clients.

Visualization is the conscious direction of images on the screen of the mind's eye. Conscious intention is the hallmark of creative visualization. In the process of visualization, you are the writer, director, producer, and audience—all in one, which can become a very empowering experience. Conversely, *mental imagery* is best described as a series of images that bubble up from the unconscious mind with neither intent nor ego censorship. Mental imagery is often described as a spontaneous flow of thoughts originating from the unconscious mind. Uncensored spontaneity is the hallmark of mental imagery. Keeping in mind the wealth of wisdom contained in the depths of the unconscious mind, mental imagery can often prove to be far more effective than the work of the conscious mind alone.

The Art of Guided Visualization

Many people who find it hard to hold their concentration for prolonged periods of time find it easier to listen to someone else direct them through a visualization process. Focusing the mind for an extended period of time certainly requires discipline. Keeping your mind focused with the help of guided visualization CDs is one way to achieve the intended goal of relaxation or healing. Continued exposure to guided visualization CDs may also help you to augment your own imagination and creative abilities. As with any exposure to experiences that cultivate the powers of your mind, embellish all suggestions to your liking from the selected tracks and ignore any and all suggestions that you do not have a strong comfort level with.

Types of Visualization

Your imagination can take you wherever you wish to go, yet it seems that visualizations tend to fall into one of three categories.

1. **Tranquil scenes:** The epitome of a tranquil scene is a sublime beach with waves of aqua blue water slowly edging toward the shore. Tranquil scenes range from primeval forests to thick snowflakes falling from the sky. The sky is the limit when it comes to tranquil scenes. When looking to relax using this technique, imagine any scene that provides you with the deepest sense of relaxation. Exercise 16.1, "Solitude of a Mountain Lake," is an example of using a tranquil image as a metaphor to promote relaxation.

2. **Behavioral changes:** Mental imagery and visualization became mainstream several decades ago when coaches started using these techniques to enhance the sports performances of their star athletes. Under the name of *mental training,* athletes would rehearse their events again and again in their minds to gain an edge over their competition. Since then, and perhaps even before, visualization has been used as a core technique in the area of behavior modification, including smoking cessation as well as changes in eating behaviors.

3. **Internal healing body images:** Perhaps no where has the use of visualization been more dramatic than in the efforts to improve one's health status, from the repair of broken bones to the evaporation of tumors (both benign and malignant). Patients use both visualization and mental imagery to not only understand the illness, but make peace with it. Exercises 16.2 to 16.4 are examples of employing visualization and mental imagery to promote physical healing.

The Essential Components of Visualization

Both visualization and mental imagery employ the faculties of both conscious and unconscious minds, though visualization has a greater hand in the direction of the script. To gain the greatest benefit from guided visualization, it's best to understand how to coordinate the efforts of both conscious and unconscious minds. The following are essential aspects to consider to enhance your experience with this technique.

- **Present tense:** To the unconscious mind there is only one time zone: the present moment. Past memories and events as well as future events and aspects are all considered to be included in the present moment. Simply stated, the unconscious mind appears not to understand events as anything other than now! Therefore, as you craft your image, think in terms of bringing the image into the present moment as if you were experiencing it now.

- **Incorporate all five senses:** The stronger the image, the more real it becomes. Where appropriate, call to mind not only the power of your sense of sight, but also that of your senses of smell, touch, sound, and taste if possible. Make the image as real as you possibly know how.

- **Positive thoughts and intentions:** Just as the unconscious mind only understands one time zone, it also only understands positive thoughts. Words expressed negatively are translated into a positive framework. Therefore, to coordinate both conscious and unconscious minds toward a unified goal, construct your healing intention in a positive mind frame.

- **Emotional vibration:** New research on visualization and prayer indicates that thoughts alone produce no lasting effect. What really galvanizes the power of visualization is the emotion behind the thought. So as you begin to create the desired image, whether it be for a sense of tranquility, a positive behavior change, or the restoration of healing, generate a feeling of compassion, joy, bliss, or happiness with the image or series of images.

- **Detached outcomes:** Placing an expected outcome on the desired intention of each visualization is analogous to throwing down an anchor on a boat that is about to set sail. It halts any progress. Although it's human to have expectations, this, too, becomes an emotional vibration that negates the intended outcome. The ego projects strong expectations. For visualization to have the greatest effect, one must detach the ego from the outcome and simply let what happens, happen.

- **Attitude of gratitude:** Upon the completion of the visualization offer an expression of gratitude for the experience. An honest expression of gratitude fills the sails of every visualization with wind to transport it to the intended destination, wherever that may be.

How to Incorporate Imagery and Visualization into Your Life Routine

Although the practice of visualization can be as varied as the people doing it, here are some suggestions to get the most out of this process. In addition to the template previously mentioned (i.e., using the present tense, positive thoughts, emotional vibrations, detached outcomes, and the expression of an attitude of gratitude), there are other steps to enhance this process. If you intend to use this relaxation technique, you will find that like any other skill, the more you practice it, the better it will serve you. The beauty of visualization is that it can be done practically anywhere where you can sit or lie quietly with your eyes closed for several minutes.

The following are some time-honored aspects of the creative visualization process that can help augment your experience to the fullest extent.

Step 1: Relaxation. The strength of the brain's right hemisphere is best acknowledged in the presence of total relaxation. To create a desirable image, the mind must be clear of mental chit-chat and ego-based distractions. Loosen any tight-fitting clothing and find a comfortable place to unwind. Once you have minimized or eliminated all distractions, begin by taking a slow, deep breath and let all random thoughts leave your mind as you exhale.

Step 2: Concentration. A focused mind is a clear mind. Using your skills of concentration, focus your attention toward your breathing as a means to ensure a clear mind. If your mind wanders with distractions, acknowledge these thoughts and then focus your attention back to your breathing.

Step 3: Visualization. Next, combine a desired image with an intention and focus on this for several minutes. Again, if you find your mind wandering (and this will happen from time to time), merely redirect your attention to the desired image with a comfortable, slow, deep breath.

Step 4: Affirmation. Metaphorically speaking, a positive affirmation, used in tandem with visualization, is the postage needed to properly deliver your intended message. Moreover, combining an image with a word or phrase unites the energies of both the right and left brain for the best, desired result.

Stress Relief and Chronic Pain

Visualization holds the potential to offer immediate satisfaction for stress relief, by simply closing your eyes to the outside world. For this reason and many others, both mental imagery and visualization have been used extensively to help treat chronic pain. With the understanding that chronic pain is more than a physical ailment, mental imagery helps translates the language of the unconscious mind to provide insights for healing and restoration. Visualization empowers the conscious energy to create a new (healing) vibration of healing for whatever area of the body seeks it.

Best Benefits of Imagery and Visualization

In its simplest sense, visualization is like taking a mini-vacation, leaving all your cares and worries behind so you can come to a place of inner peace. The effects of visualization and mental imagery range from being mildly relaxing to profoundly enlightening depending on the particular image used, the frequency employed, and the conditions under which the visualization was experienced. Everyone can gain significant benefits from a single experience of guided visualization. You can too!

Additional Resources

Gawain, S. *Creative Visualization.* New York: Bantam Books, 1978.
Katra, J. *The Heart of the Mind.* Navato, CA: New World Library, 1999.
Locke, S. *The Healer Within.* New York: Mentor Books, 1986.
Roman, S. *Spiritual Growth: Being Your Higher Self.* Tiburon, CA: H.J. Kramer, 1989.
Simonton, O.C. *Getting Well Again.* New York: Bantam Books, 1978.
Targ, R., and Katra, J. *Miracles of Mind.* Navato, CA: New World Library, 1998.
Thondup, T. *The Healing Power of Mind.* Boston: Shambhala Books, 1996.

Exercise 16.1 Solitude of a Mountain Lake

Imagine yourself walking alone in the early morning, along a path of a primeval forest, through a gauntlet of towering pine trees. Each step you take is softly cushioned by a bed of golden brown needles. Quietness consumes these surroundings and then is broken by the melody of a songbird. As you stroll along at a leisurely pace, you focus on the sweet clean scent of the pines and evergreens, the coolness of the air, the warmth of the sun as it peeks through the trees, and the gentle breeze as it passes through the boughs of the pines and whispers past your ears.

Off in the distance, you hear the rush of water cascading over weathered rocks, babbling as it moves along. Yards ahead, a chipmunk perches on an old decaying birch stump along the side of the path, frozen momentarily to determine its next direction; then, in the blink of an eye, it disappears under the ground cover and all is silent again. As you continue to walk along this path, you see a clearing up ahead, and your pace picks up just a little to see what is up ahead. First boulders appear ahead, then behind them, a deep blue mountain lake emerges from beyond the rocks. You climb up on a boulder to secure a better view, and you find a comfortable spot carved out of the weathered stone to sit and quietly observe all the elements around you.

The shore of the lake is surrounded by a carpet of tall green grass and guarded by a host of trees: spruce, evergreen, pine, aspen, and birch. On top of one of the spruce trees, an eagle leaves his perch and spreads his wings to catch the remains of a thermal current, and gracefully glides over the lake. On the far side of the lake, off in the distance, dwarfing the tree line, is a rugged stone-face mountain. The first snows of autumn have dusted the fissures and crevasses, adding contrast to the rock's features. The color of the snow matches the one or two puffy white clouds and morning crescent moon that interrupt an otherwise cloudless day. A slight warm breeze begins to caress your cheeks and the backs of your hands as you direct your attention to the surface of the mountain lake.

The slight breeze sends tiny ripples across the surface of the lake. As you look at the water's surface, you realize that this body of water, this mountain lake, is just like your body—somewhat calm, yet yearning to be completely relaxed, completely calm. Focus your attention on the surface of the water. These ripples that you observe represent or symbolize any tensions, frustrations, or wandering thoughts that keep you from being completely relaxed. As you look at the surface of this mountain lake, slowly allow the ripples to dissipate, fade away, and disappear. To enhance this process, take a very slow, deep breath and feel the relaxation this brings to your body as you exhale. And as you exhale, slowly allow the ripples to fade away, giving way to a calm surface of water. As you continue to focus on this image, you see the surface of the lake becoming more and more calm—in fact, very placid, reflecting all that surrounds it.

As you focus on this image and realize that this body of water is like your body. Feel how relaxed you feel as you see the surface of the lake remain perfectly still, reflecting all that is around it. The water's surface reflects a mirror image of the green grass, the trees, the mountain face, and even the clouds and crescent moon. Your body is as relaxed as this body of water, this mountain lake. Try to lock in this feeling of calmness and etch this feeling into your memory bank so that you can call it up to your conscious mind when you get stressed or frustrated. Remember this image so that you can recall the serenity of this image that you have created to promote a deep sense of relaxation and to feel your body relax just by thinking of the solitude of this mountain lake.

Exercise 16.2 The Body Flame

Imagine, if you will, that the energy that you burn all day long is not just physical energy (such as calories). It's mental and emotional energy, as well. Imagine that this source of energy, which invigorates *every* cell, resides in the center of your body. The Japanese call this reservoir of energy the *Hara*. The Chinese refer to it as the *Danteein*. Although it cannot be measured by Western science at this time, this energy is essential to your well-being.

Take a moment now to locate the center of your body, and feel where this is—your center of gravity, the center of your entire body, and as you begin to focus on this area, realize that this is about an inch or two below your belly button.

It is believed that when this energy is too excessive (perhaps from a flurry of thoughts or unresolved emotions), you begin to feel frantic and overwhelmed, or sometimes just plain exhausted.

The Body Flame meditation, like the Breathing Clouds exercise, is a way to help clear your mind of excess thoughts and excess energy and return your mind and body to a profound sense of inner peace. As you do this meditation, as with all meditations, call to mind the power of your five senses and the power of your imagination and memory to draw forth the power of this visualization.

To begin this meditation, the best position is to lie comfortably flat on your back, keeping your spine aligned, from your head straight down to your hips. If you choose to sit, this will work as well.

Next, concentrate on your breathing by making each breath comfortably slow and comfortably deep. If your mind should happen to wander, gently guide it back to focus on your breathing.

If your eyes are not already closed, go ahead and close your eyes. Once again, locate the center of your body; then, using your mind's eye, call to mind an image of a flame hovering over this part of your body.

Metaphorically speaking, this flame is a symbol of your state of relaxation. It feeds off your body's energy. When your body has an abundance of energy—perhaps nervous thoughts or negative feelings—this flame will be quite tall, perhaps even like a blow torch. When you are completely relaxed, your flame will be quite small. This small flame is called the *maintenance flame*. It's like that which you would see as a pilot light in a gas stove. This is the desired size for complete relaxation.

So now, focus with your mind's eye, and take a look at the size of your body's flame. See its size relative to your body's level of energy. What does your flame look like? How big or small does it seem to you right now?

As you place all of your attention on the flame of your body, look at its color. Your body flame may be an intense, brilliant yellow-white color. As you look at this image, what color does your flame hold?

Once again with your mind's eye, take a look at the *shape* of your body's flame. Direct your attention to the base of the flame and notice, is the bottom round or oval shaped? How does it appear to you? As you focus your eyes toward the tip of the flame, notice that it comes to a jagged point.

You may even notice that your flame dances around a bit, or perhaps it remains still. As you look at this flame, *feel* it feed off the excess energy in your body, and let it burn off any excess energy that you wish to release to return to a complete sense of relaxation. Take a deep breath and let your flame burn off any excess energy you feel detracts from your ability to relax.

Once again, if you find your mind is distracted by wandering thoughts that pull your attention away from the image of the flame, gently redirect your attention to this image, and then allow your mind to send these thoughts and feelings from your head to your body's center and up through the flame.

As you continue to watch this image of the flame, feel your body slowly become more calm and relaxed. To help this out, take a nice, slow, comfortably deep breath. As you exhale, feel a greater sense of calm throughout your body.

Now look once again at the image of your flame. As your body becomes more tranquil, notice the flame decrease in height. Soon you will notice that your flame decreases in size, to about a quarter to one-half inch tall.

As you focus on the image of your body flame, once again notice its color, shape, and size. And, as you see the flame decrease in size, feel your body relax as you draw your attention to the relaxation effect of the maintenance flame.

There are times when this flame can be used to aid in the healing process of your physical body. By placing the flame over a specific part of your body, an area that is sore or experiencing pain, you allow the flame to feed off the excess energy of this area and restore a sense of peace to the organ or physiological system that is yearning for wholeness.

Now, please take several slow, deep breaths and as you exhale, allow your body flame to return to a sense of peace in this area. As you do this, feel peace reside here. When you feel ready, then slowly return the image of the flame to the center of your body.

Now, continue to focus your mind's eye on your body flame. When you feel completely relaxed, with your flame very small, notice how still it is. Then, when you feel you are at a point of complete relaxation, slowly allow this image to fade from your mind, but retain this feeling of relaxation, knowing that your mind is now clear, with fewer and fewer distractions.

To augment this relaxation process, please take one more slow, deep breath and then slowly bring yourself back to the awareness of the room you are in. Become aware of the time of day, the day of the week, and what you have planned after you have completed this relaxation session. When you feel ready, very slowly open your eyes to a soft gaze in front of you. If you would like, go ahead and stretch your arms and shoulders. Notice that although you feel relaxed, you don't feel tired or sleepy. You feel fully energized and revitalized, ready to do whatever you have planned for the rest of the day.

Exercise 16.2

Exercise 16.3   Body Colors and the Healing Light

The human body craves wholeness, and given the chance, the body will do all it can to return to a place of optimal health. In all its splendor, the body's innate ability to return to wholeness is a wonder to behold.

The word *health* comes from the root word *hal,* which means to be whole or holy. When we call upon the strength of the human spirit to work in unison with our mind and body, wholeness, expressed through inner peace, is achieved.

This meditation/visualization exercise calls upon the powers of the unconscious mind to awaken the innate healing powers of mind, body, and spirit so that you may return to that place of wholeness, that place of inner peace—wherever you may be.

As you do this meditation, as with all meditations, call to mind the power of your five senses and call to mind the power of your imagination and memory to draw forth the power of this visualization.

As with any type of visualization exercise, please feel free to augment, edit, and embellish the suggestions to make them vivid *and* the most empowering for you.

Imagine yourself lying in a warm, shallow pool of clear blue water. Visualize, through your mind's eye, that as you float effortlessly, your internal body reflects just one color, a brilliant white, as if you were observing a white silhouette in a pool of turquoise blue water. As you visualize this image, clearly picture a complete outline of your body, the contents of which are illuminated by the color white.

Now, focusing on this white silhouette, take a moment to carefully examine all parts and regions of your body, from your head down to your toes. As you do this, please search for any specific locations or regions of your body that feel tense, active, or perhaps express a sensation of pain. This can include any muscles, joints, organs, physiological systems (like the immune system or cardiovascular system), or any part of your body that seems less than whole, yet craves wholeness. For some, this might even include your mind, if by chance you find that a multitude of thoughts are constantly racing through your mind, with each thought competing for your attention.

Through this systematic scanning process, please locate one or perhaps several areas that, under stress and strain, have not been allowed to fully relax to the same capacity as the rest of your body.

For the moment, let's refer to these "active" areas as *hot spots,* because typically they *are* more metabolically active than all other areas that are more relaxed. As you locate a specific area of tension, allow yourself to envision that this area is symbolized by a strong, pulsating red light. Symbolically, the color red indicates a higher metabolic level of arousal or energy state; here, the same meaning can be quite literal.

Invite yourself to take a slow, deep breath and as you do, imagine that you are slowly inhaling *and* exhaling through an opening in this area. Follow this breath with one more, even slower, even deeper breath. As you breathe once more through this area, feel the flow of energy move through this region, as if a logjam floating on a river has been set free.

As you envision your body, represented by these two colors—a mass of white, with one, two, or perhaps several red pulsating areas—take a moment to specifically focus on the red pulsating lights. As you do this, through your conscious intention, invite these areas to become calm, as calm as the rest of your body.

With your mind's eye, imagine that this hot spot *slowly* begins to change color, transforming from a bright pulsating red light to a bright, but less intense orange color. Then take a nice, slow, deep breath and as you exhale watch the color change to orange. As you observe the color transform from red to orange, so too does the intensity of pulsation change, to a slower rate—symbolizing that indeed, the area is becoming more calm.

Once again, take a slow, deep breath and as you do, imagine that you are once again inhaling and exhaling through the region of your body acknowledged with a small pulsating orange light. Please follow this breath with one more, even slower, even deeper breath. Once again, as you breathe through this area, feel the flow of energy move through this region like a slow, yet strong flowing river of water.

Observe closely, as you look at and feel this area of tension or pain, become aware of the color orange and feel a deeper sense of calming beginning to occur in this region. The color orange is symbolic of change. The intention of this meditation *is* change—changing any areas of tension to a calm, tranquil sense of homeostasis, from stress to inner peace.

Now, with this calming sensation taking hold, begin to see the orange-colored light transform from bright orange to yellow. Once again take a slow, deep breath, and note the change as you exhale. The color yellow is symbolic of energy—in this case, a healing energy that enables the area in question to slowly return to homeostasis. As you observe the yellow color, note that the yellow light pulsates very infrequently, if at all. This means that this focus of your attention really is becoming more relaxed.

At your leisure, please take a slow, deep breath and as you do, imagine that you are inhaling and exhaling *through* this area. Follow this with one more even slower, even deeper breath. As you breathe once more through this area, feel the flow of energy move effortlessly through this region of your body.

Now, as you observe the area symbolized by a yellow light, you sense and feel that this area on which you have focused your attention is much more relaxed, more calm. Notice, as you observe the white silhouette of your body, that now all areas begin to match the sensation of calmness that you feel in the rest of your body.

As you look at this image of your entire body, you notice a beautiful reflection of white light. Once again please take a slow, deep breath and as you exhale, observe that the yellow area is now blending to become white with the brilliant white color that your internal body reflects. As you continue to look at this image you have created, you now see that your entire internal body image is one color—a brilliant white, radiating a calm light all around it. This color is symbolic of your level of complete relaxation and optimal health, and this image is one that you can recall to your consciousness at any time to invoke a sense of personal tranquility.

Please take a slow, deep breath and as you exhale, think to yourself this phrase: "I am calm and relaxed. I am whole!"

Now, once again, imagine your body lying comfortably and effortlessly in a shallow pool of warm water. Directly overhead, suspended about four to five feet above you, is a crystal bowl, filled with beautiful rays of light. These rays cascade down, like a fountain of water, over you. This crystal bowl contains an unending supply of golden-white light, a source of dynamic life force of energy. As this light pours over your body, it has the ability to stimulate and augment the healing process that *you* have initiated with your own ability to heal— through the color transformations from red to orange to yellow.

Using the power of your mind, slowly move this waterfall of luminescent energy over a specific part of your body that you feel needs the reinforcement of deep healing. With the power of intention, please allow the crystal bowl to tip its contents over this specific region of your body. Feel the warmth of this healing light as it continually pours into your body. More and more, allow the warmth of the healing light to move to the desired location and feel your body absorbing the light where it needs it the most.

As you do this, see the image of golden-white light within you and all around you. Take a moment to sense what this really feels like. Then, take a slow, deep breath and feel a deep sense of relaxation throughout your entire body. Once again, please repeat to yourself the phrase, "I am calm and relaxed; I am whole."

Notice now that you feel calm and relaxed, yet at the same time you feel wonderfully energized.

Take one final slow, deep breath and as you exhale, feel the sensation of relaxation envelop your whole body.

At your leisure, when you feel ready, slowly open your eyes to a soft glance in front of you. Take a moment to familiarize yourself with your surroundings, by thinking what you have planned once you finish this meditation. Realize that although you feel relaxed, you don't feel tired or sleepy—you feel fully energized and revitalized and ready to accomplish whatever task awaits you today.

Exercise 16.3

Exercise 16.4 — Healthy DNA Meditation: Reprogramming Your Life's Potential

It's been often said that we have a wealth of knowledge inside us. What was once a cute poetic proverb now seems to be a surprising reality. As scientists explore the wonders of our DNA, it appears that the two spiraling strands of sugar and protein molecules contain a vast source of information that would make even the National Library of Congress envious.

Research indicates that we only use 3 percent of our DNA. The rest seems to be inactive (scientist call the inactive part "junk"). One theory is that the inactive part of our DNA is like a blank space on a recordable CD-ROM. Using another metaphor, like a string of light bulbs that has not been plugged into a socket and is therefore deemed useless, it would appear that our DNA needs some attention to become activated, or as mystics described, to be woken up.

This meditation is an exploration into the wonders and potential of our DNA. Like other visualizations, this requires the use of your vivid imagination. As a reminder, please feel free to change these suggestions to make this exercise most comfortable for you. To begin . . .

1. Place yourself in a comfortably seated position, back straight, with your eyes closed. To become more relaxed, take a few deep breaths and as you exhale, remind yourself that you are becoming more calm and relaxed. Try repeating the following phrase to yourself on the next exhalation: "I am calm and relaxed." Take one more deep breath and repeat the phrase once again.

2. Now, imagine that you have the ability to look deep within your heart muscle, into the cells of the heart muscle itself. Using your mind's eye to travel deep into your heart tissue, focus on one specific cell and enlarge this cell so that a clear image is directly in front of you, as if you were watching this on a large movie screen. Take a deep breath and focus on this image.

3. Next, look deep into the cell and find the nucleus of the cell. Once you have found it, focus your attention on the nucleus. Then, enlarge the nucleus so that this cell structure is directly in front of you. Once you have this clear image, find the double helix, the spiral strand of DNA within the nucleus.

4. Focusing all your attention on the DNA, enlarge this structure so that it is now directly in front of you. If you wish, take time to notice the colors that comprise the two strands of DNA. Depending on your perspective, the strand of DNA may look like a spiral staircase, a ladder, or a twisted bridge. Take a moment to enter the image and travel around the DNA structure. You may notice that looking straight on from above, it may even resemble the taoist yin/yang symbol. Take a moment to look at this DNA strand from every possible angle, watching it rotate in motion.

5. As you look and study this double helix and all its many complexities, imagine that like a string of lights with 100 bulbs, there are only a few (3) that are actually lit. Using your imagination, create a light switch that, when turned on, causes all the lights to shine. Not only does each bulb extend a brilliant brightness, but upon closer examination of the double-stranded helix, there appears to be a beam of light energy that the two strands surround and actually embrace. The light from the DNA emanates out to the edge of the nucleus and then continues toward the cell membrane itself.

6. If it is true that the inactive part of the DNA molecule is similar to empty space on a CD-ROM, then this suggests that the space can be filled with information. From your highest source of integrity and intention, select a portion of the DNA strand into which to download information—more appropriately called wisdom based on unconditional love. This new program of information is now available for you to advance your own human potential.

7. Again using your imagination, think to yourself that just as one cell contains this vibrating DNA of light and wisdom, so do all cells in your body. Thus, every cell in the body now contains a double helix of DNA that emanates light, with all parts active for your highest good.

8. Now allow this image to fade from your mind's eye, but retain the feeling of light. Pay attention to the wisdom that comes to your conscious mind as you travel through the course of your day. Remember that repeated practice of this visualization will begin to enhance your access to the deep-seated wisdom within you.

CHAPTER

17

Soothing Sounds: Music to Relax By

Music is a moral law. It gives a soul to the universe, wings to the mind, flight to the imagination, a charm to sadness, gaiety and life to everything. It is the essence of order, and leads to all that is good, just and beautiful.

—Plato

Ageless Wisdom of Music Therapy

On a large drum lie several thousand fine grains of sand. Positioned around the drum sit approximately 20 people, each facing toward the center of the circle where the drum is placed. Upon the command of the leader, the entire group begins to chant a sacred Sanskrit mantra, a vibration known to instill a sense of harmony in all living things in its presence. The sound of "om" resonates throughout the room, and as it does so, the fine grains of sand lying randomly on the surface of the drum began to move. Like atoms in a molecule, the stationary position becomes a dance. As the grains move, they begin to form a pattern, a beautiful mandala-shaped labyrinth. With each repetition of the "om" chant, the lines become clearer.

The vibration of the chant "om" proves itself to be more than a cute new age exercise. The tone of healing reveals that it holds the power to create order from chaos, symmetry from randomness, and harmony from discordance—all with the intention to heal from one note of a musical scale. Long ago, mystics and healers held the inherent wisdom that, indeed, music possessed a very special power to restore a sense of wholeness to any individual in need of tranquility, from the stressed to the infirm. Even Plato suggested the merits of music as a panacea for ill health.

In the 1960s, Swiss physician Hans Jenny was so intrigued by the concept of sympathetic resonance that he began to study the relationship of sound to nearby objects. He coined the term *cyamantics* to describe this science. His research can be viewed from the collection of films he made to observe the effects of sound on a variety of substances, from water to oil. The images he recorded are nothing less than astonishing. It doesn't take much to make the leap from the effects of sound on sand particles or water droplets to the effects of sound on cell physiology. All living things are affected by sound vibrations. Music is the most obvious means of using vibrations to promote feelings of tranquility.

Sound is energy made audible. Unpleasant sounds are commonly referred to as noise. Sounds pleasing to the ear may fall into the category of music: a progression of musical tones that affects mind, body, spirit, and emotions. The field of physics (renowned for its interest in energy) lends great credence to the ageless wisdom of sound vibrations. Quantum physics reminds us that everything is energy; hence, the effect of vibrations on anything can be powerful. The power of music's healing (or harming) abilities goes far beyond the ability of the eardrum to convert sound waves into biochemical properties to which the nervous system will respond.

Cultures from every corner of the world have recognized the effect music has on people. Music can serve as a call to arms (marches by John Philip Sousa come to mind), and slow, peaceful melodies (e.g., Mozart's piano concerto in C minor) can sooth the savage breast. Today music therapy often conjures up images of people lying on a couch with headphones on to take their mind away from the rest of the world, yet by and large, music therapy includes a more active than passive role. Playing an instrument or singing is as much a part of good vibrations as simply listening to someone else make the music.

Over the years, several studies have been done to determine the most popular means to promote relaxation. The act of listening to music ranks at the top every time.

The Physics of Health: Entrainment and Sympathetic Resonance

Centuries ago, a young man set out to design a clock that used a pendulum and counterbalance as mechanical components for telling time. Although the first clock was impressive, it was during the creation of the second pendulum clock that Christian Huygens discovered more than a new way to build a mechanical clock. He discovered a law of physics called *entrainment.* As it turned out, the motion of the two pendulums initially were not in synchrony, but in a short period of time, they began to sway in motion like twin clocks. Entrainment is defined as the mutual phase locking of similar vibrations, where with two objects in close proximity, the object of weaker vibration will match or entrain to the object of stronger vibration. Entrainment is referred to in the field of physics as the law of the conservation of energy. Examples abound in nature, most notably the menstrual cycles of women who live or work together. Entrainment is also referred to as *sympathetic resonance.* Energy vibrations hold a greater influence over us than most people realize. Ancient shamans knew this and often used the power of the drumbeat to evoke entraining vibrations for more than just a ceremony. They were invoking a healing intention.

Every cell in our bodies maintains a vibration, as do many organs such as the brain and heart. Some vibrations are difficult to measure, yet vibrations for the heart and brain are much easier, as detected through an electrocardiogram (EKG) and electroencephalogram (EEG), respectively. Under ideal conditions, there is harmony among all vibrations housed in the human body, and this harmony is manifested as optimal health. Conversely, scientists know that cancer cells oscillate at a different (usually faster) vibration than normal healthy cells.

According to physicists who study energy and to experts who study the healing properties of sound, the vibration of homeostasis is identical to the vibration known as the *Schumann resonance.* The Schumann resonance is a mathematical number of oscillations determined by the circumference of the earth multiplied by the electromagnetic field. It's calculated to be 7.8 Hz. Perhaps it is no coincidence that 7.8 Hz is the same frequency detected in many sounds in nature, such as whale and dolphin songs and waterfalls. It would appear that like dolphin songs, music that is composed with this vibration instills a sense of relaxation that is unequalled by other methods.

As one might imagine, not all vibrations are healing. Some vibrations can be downright hazardous. In his landmark book *Cross Currents,* physician Robert Becker highlights the problems with ELFs (extremely low frequencies) and their consequences on human health. Powerful vibrations that are not in a harmonious chord with the 7.8-Hz frequency can entrain cells, organs, and living organism into a level of dissonance with devastating consequences. This underlies the problems of people who live near high-tension power lines who contract cancer or the rapid rate of brain tumors seen with frequent cell phone use.

Music Without Words

By some accounts, there are only two kinds of music in this world: that with words (lyrics) and that without words. In studies that have looked at the cognitive functions of either the right or left hemispheres of the brain, it has been revealed that each hemisphere specializes in a host of thought patterns and sensory stimulation processing.

The left hemisphere of the brain is the seat of analytical, rational, verbal, and linear thought processes. The right hemisphere of the brain, now well known for being the receptive, intuitive, and imaginative part, is most greatly influenced by music without words. Studies show that music without words produces a greater calming effect. The reason appears to be that when music with words is introduced, the analytical mind becomes activated by associating thoughts and memories with the interpretation of the lyrics. Rather than relaxing, this type of music is known to raise the resting heart rate and blood pressure rather than lower it. For this reason, music without words is the recommended choice to promote the greatest level of relaxation. There is no shortage of instrumental music in this classification, including but not limited to classical, jazz, new age, and what is now being called lifestyle music.

Tuning Out Bad Vibrations

Music therapy goes beyond simply turning on the CD player and flopping down on the couch for a few minutes. When you consider that all sound is vibration, then all vibrations lend themselves to the potential of either promoting relaxation or inhibiting the process completely. We can never get away from all sounds and repose in complete silence. However, there are some sounds (noise) that can become quite irritating, whether it's a loud car muffler from the car driving behind you to the cacophony of noise from blaring radios and televisions all over the house. You surely can minimize noisy disturbances that tend to add to a stressful mind. One way is by taking a proactive stance by closing windows, turning off equipment, or simply removing yourself from the area for a while. There is another option: white noise. *White noise* is any sound that you use to balance out the irritating noise that causes you stress. Music can do this quite nicely.

How to Incorporate Music Therapy into Your Life Routine

The easiest way to incorporate music therapy as a relaxation technique is to place a CD of calm, relaxing music into a CD player and either sit or lie down with your eyes closed and let the melody transport you to that magical place where troubles are not allowed. To do this most effectively, it's best to minimize all other distractions. The simplest way is to use headphones to block out all other noise (just be careful not to play the music too loud and damage your hearing). To have a more profound experience, close your eyes and allow yourself to float freely on a river of musical notes and watch on the screen of your mind's eye where each song takes you. If you are looking for new suggestions for relaxing music, consider the following list.

Top Ten Recommended CDs of Relaxing Music

I am often asked to make recommendations of relaxing music. These ten CDs are what I (and many others) consider to be *the* classics to soothe the savage beast, breast, or anything else that's stressed in your house. This is slow music for fast times. If you don't find these in your favorite music store, they can be special ordered. Consider making your own compilation of cuts from these CDs as your personal music prescription.

Artist	CD Title	Instrumentation
Eversound Series	*One Quiet Night**	Various instruments
Jim Wilson	*Northern Seascapes*	Solo piano
Michael Hoppé	*The Poet*	Solo cello
Michael Hoppé	*The Dreamer*	Solo flute
Secret Garden	*White Stones*	Violin and piano

* *One Quiet Night* is a compilation from the Eversound Music collection that I was invited to put together as a sample of the best relaxation music on this label. This music has received rave reviews as wonderful music to promote relaxation.

Bruce Becvar	*Forever Blue Sky*	Solo guitar
David Lanz	*Christophori's Dream*	Solo Piano
Chris Spheeris	*Eros*	Solo guitar
Yanni	*In My Time*	Solo piano
Sean Harkness	*Aloft*	Solo guitar

Developing Your Mastery of Music Therapy

Of all the qualities that are used to determine the effectiveness of music as a means to promote relaxation, your perception of the music (like or dislike) is at the top of the list. The most calming music to one person may be akin to fingernails on a chalk board to another set of ears. Developing your mastery means taking the time to cultivate your tastes and build a music collection that nurtures that sense of peace in you. If you are like most people, you may find that over time your taste in music expands to include types of music that at an earlier age you wouldn't be caught dead listening to. The bottom line is that it doesn't matter what the experts think or recommend—it only matters what you prefer. One thing that is common among people looking to add music therapy to their collection of relaxation techniques is a hunger to add more music to their library.

Stress Relief and Chronic Pain

Music as vibration has a tremendous influence on mind, body, spirit, and emotions. The right music (your perception is a key factor) can melt stress away. Music as vibration also holds the potential for coping with and minimizing chronic pain in ways that many people still don't understand. The answer appears to be through the power of entrainment.

Best Benefits of Music Therapy

Living in the digital age of MP3 technology (and whatever else may come onto the scene shortly), it becomes easy to forget that for millennia music was the sole creation of live performances by people playing a variety of instruments. Music therapy is so much more than simply listening to music; it includes playing a musical instrument and singing as well.

The benefits of music therapy are many, but two stand out among the rest. First, listening to music has the potential to act as a diversion tactic to steer the focus of your attention away from that which stresses you to a distant place where thoughts and worries are left far behind. Music, like a magic carpet, has a capacity to transport you to distant lands and memories. Anyone who has listened to a Mozart concerto or Beethoven's Fifth Symphony knows the power that music has to shift one's focus of attention. In the words of contemporary composer Michael Hoppé, "Music lifts the veil of anxiety to view a place where love is stored."

The other benefit of music, although initially more subtle, becomes more dynamic well after the music has ended. As sound vibrations, music imparts a healing vibration that returns mind, body, and spirit to a deeper level of homeostasis. In either case, the healing power of music allows one to pause in the midst of stress long enough to catch one's breath.

Additional Resources

Becker, R. *Cross Currents*. New York: Tarcher/Putnam, 1999.
Campbell, D. *The Mozart Effect*. New York: Avon Books, 1997.
Campbell, D. *Music: Physician for Times to Come*. Wheaton IL: Quest Books, 1991.
Gaynor, M. *The Healing Power of Sound*. Boston: Shambhala Press, 2002.
Goldman, J. *Healing Sounds*. Rockport, MA: Element Books, 1997.
Merritt, S. *Mind, Music and Imagery*. Santa Rosa, CA: Aslan Publishing, 1996.
Spear, D.Z. *Ears of the Angels*. Carlsbad, CA: Hay House, 2002.

Exercise 17.1 Good Vibrations: From Sound to Music

The following are some exercises to engage more fully in the practice of music therapy.

Make (Mix) Your Own Music CD Prescription

Today's technology makes it very easy for you to compile your favorite instrumental songs and burn them onto a CD. Here is a suggestion: Make a list of 12 to 16 of your favorite instrumental pieces and write them down. Be sure to include not only a variety of styles (e.g., classical, new age, jazz) but also a variety of instrumentation (e.g., piano, guitar, violin, cello). Next, consider burning a few extra copies: one for the car when you get stuck in traffic, one for the office when things there go haywire, and one for home to listen to late at night to help you unwind.

Finding the Lost Chord

Not everyone is blessed with a great singing voice, but you don't have to have one to do this exercise. Using the diagram on page 20 to remind yourself of the location of the chakras, find a nice quiet place (preferably where no one will hear you) and simply voice the word *Om* (Ohhmmmmmmmmmmmmm). Carry the note for about 30 seconds, starting with the root chakra, then taking a slight pause, and then moving up through the line of chakras. (This may feel really weird, but that's why you have closed the door.) Try repeating this cycle about three to four times. You can also find CDs with the om chant and merely sing along. Synchronicity has an *Om* CD (1-800-926-2033), as does Jonathan Goldman, whose CD is called *Chakra Chants.*

A variation of this exercise is to sing the scale (doe, ray, mee, fah, so, la, tee, doe), starting with the lowest note and continuing up the scale through each of the seven notes (seven notes—seven chakras).

Music and Visualization

For this exercise, find a CD with instrumental music. That listed as New Age works the best. (Two suggestions: John Serrier's *And the Stars Go With You* or Raphael's *Music to Disappear In.*) Hit the Play button, turn the lights down low, lie down on your back, and close your eyes, listening to the piece (or pieces) of music that you have selected. Allow your mind to wander and begin to observe whatever images appear on the screen of your mind's eye. Note the colors, symbols, energies, and so forth and merely observe where your mind takes you. Allow the music to help you paint a picture. As you do this, it's essential not to judge what you visualize, but rather to simply observe and enjoy! Another option is to listen to a hemi-sync CD (The Monroe Institute), a specially designed instrumental music CD that entrains the theta waves of each brain hemisphere for the ultimate music therapy experience. (www.hemi-Sync.com).

The Musical Sounds of Nature

Nature provides an incredible soundtrack. In this exercise, you are invited to listen to the actual sounds of nature (e.g., a thunderstorm, waterfall, ocean surf, bird songs) or find a CD with these recorded sounds. Give yourself about 30 minutes to listen to the natural sounds and simply allow your mind to wander wherever it will, without any judgment or reservations.

CHAPTER

18

Self-Hypnosis and Autogenics

Open your mind to the power of self-suggestion.
—Johannes Schultz

Ageless Wisdom of Self-Hypnosis

For decades, if not centuries, Western science held the belief that the mind, as powerful as it was, could not control the autonomic nervous system. Aspects of human physiology, including heart rate, blood pressure, breathing, blood distribution, and other parameters, were thought to be totally under the influence of regions of the brain that were not influenced by conscious thought. All of this changed dramatically in the early 20th century when Western scientists traveled to the Himalayan region of India to observe yogis who appeared to display mystical powers over human physiology. The ability to sit comfortably on a bed of nails paled in comparison to the ability to control one's breathing, heart rate, and blood flow.

The average person breathes 14 to 16 times per minute. When completely relaxed, the average person can take perhaps as few as 6 breaths per minute. These yogis could comfortably breathe less than once per minute. Moreover, they could decrease their heart rates to less than 20 beats per minute. For all intents and purposes they appeared dead. These feats were thought to be humanly impossible. Perhaps even more amazing was the ability of certain yogis to redistribute the flow of blood entirely to the right side of the body, leaving the left side stone cold. Punctures to the skin produced no bleeding.

In the 1960s, Elmer and Alyse Green, from the Menniger Clinic, traveled to India to conduct scientific investigations of these talented yogis. They even convinced one yogi, Swami Rama, to come back and be studied under laboratory conditions. Results revealed that these changes were neither magic nor the ploy of adept conjurers. These yogis, who had cultivated a wealth of mental discipline, were indeed able to defy the autonomic nervous system and consciously influence a host of physiological parameters. They not only redefined the word *homeostasis,* but opened the door to a view of consciousness that had only been hinted at before, sowing the seeds for a new field of study: psychoneuroimmunology.

It's well known that in a relaxed state, the mind is more receptive to suggestions; either those you give to yourself, or those you hear from someone else's voice. The receptivity to the power of suggestion is more commonly known as *hypnosis.* Most likely, everyone has seen or heard of people volunteering to be hypnotized on stage by an entertainer. Through the use of hypnosis, participants perform ludicrous acts that appear to defy reality. However, long before some magician thought to use hypnosis as part of his or her Las Vegas act, the power of suggestion, through the use of guided hypnosis, had been used for centuries—perhaps longer. In the late 1700s Anton Mesmer combined the use of hypnotic suggestion (and magnets) as a means to heal people from a host of serious diseases. Today the word *mesmerized* is used to suggest a trancelike state of bewilderment.

In 1939 two German physicians, Johannes Schultz and Wolfgang Luthe, combined the use of hypnosis and relaxation to create what is commonly known today as *autogenic training* or *self-regulation:* the ability to follow a series of self-suggestions to promote a deep sense of relaxation. This technique did not go unnoticed by magicians either. Houdini, and many others who followed in his footsteps, was known for using the power of self-suggestion and self-regulation to perform many of his escape tricks and illusions. Perhaps it goes without saying that you would have to be very relaxed to be handcuffed in a straitjacket and submerged under water and then escape—unscathed!

The Power of Suggestion

Some people shudder at the mention of hypnosis, but in truth, people give themselves suggestions all the time. Usually it's the ego doing the suggesting—directing people to watch out for this, or avoid that. The ego is a master at the power of suggestion and becomes even more so during times of stress. The real power of human potential comes not from the ego, however, but a deeper source of strength hidden in the unconscious mind, often censored by the ego. In a relaxed state, the ego is disarmed. Self-guided suggestions (or even those provided by others, such as a therapist on guided imagery CDs) allow you to unite the power of the conscious and unconscious minds to achieve states of physiological homeostasis that are not possible when the ego is standing guard. As a rule, people are most open to the power of suggestion when they are relaxed. This is the promise of self-regulation. Exercise 18.1 directs you to try this technique.

The Art of Self-Regulation

The secret to autogenic training is to make your arms, hands, legs, and feet feel comfortably warm and heavy. The warmth and heaviness come from the flow of blood that you consciously direct to whatever region on which you intend to focus your awareness. In a resting state, the majority (80 percent) of your body's blood resides in your gastrointestinal (GI) tract. The other 20 percent circulates throughout the body to provide oxygen and a host of nutrients for metabolic functions. By consciously directing the flow of blood from your body's core to your arms and hands or your legs and feet, you begin to send a message to the autonomic nervous system to constrict the blood vessels in your stomach area and dilate the blood vessels in either the arms or the legs, thus allowing the movement of blood to these areas.

Because muscles are not normally saturated with blood in a resting state, the autogenic effect (similar to the feeling when sitting in a Jacuzzi) is very relaxing. To initiate this technique, all you need do is give yourself a series of suggestions to have either your arms and hand, or legs and feet (some even suggest trying the back of your head), feel warm and heavy. If you wish, you can add to this suggestion a visualization of the flow of blood directed to the desired areas.

How to Incorporate Autogenics into Your Life Routine

Lie on your back in a comfortable position, with your arms by your side. Take a moment to focus your awareness on your breathing, following the flow of air in through your nostrils and down deep into your lungs, and simply relax. This is the first stage of autogenics. Exercise 18.2 guides you through an entire autogenics session.

Many people who use autogenics feel that it is a great technique to use to fall asleep at night. For this reason, autogenics is a technique to use late at night, or perhaps on weekend mornings when there is no rush to get out of bed. When done properly, this technique takes about 15 to 30 minutes, and like most skills, the more you practice it, the easier it becomes. It is an easy technique to use for muscle soreness. It has also been used by patients (with the help of their physicians) who are undergoing surgery. They experience fewer complications with healing.

Developing Your Mastery of Autogenic Training

To experience the best benefits of autogenic training, please consider following these guidelines:

- Be sure to minimize all distractions, such as blaring radios, televisions, and cell phones.
- Find a quite place to lie down (it's best to try this technique lying down, but it can be done sitting as well).
- Get comfortable, loosening any tight-fitting clothing. Begin to focus on your breathing. Begin to pay close attention to your body's physiology and your heart rate.
- Follow the directions in Exercise 18.2. You can read through these directions first and then call to mind the progression of steps for either the arms, legs, or head.

Stress Relief and Chronic Pain

When people take the time to learn the premise of autogenic training, they find it to be one of the most powerful means of relieving the symptoms of physical stress. It also is a favorite for people with insomnia and people suffering from Raynaud's disease. Autogenic training is often used in tandem with clinical biofeedback (see Chapter 23), and is found to be very useful as a means to control not only sensations of pain, but in some cases the causes of it as well.

Best Benefits of Autogenics

The immediate effect of autogenics is similar to a muscle massage. Like a dry sponge, tight muscles have very poor blood flow due to constricted blood vessels and capillaries. The practice of autogenics allows for a greater distribution of blood flow to the intended area, helping to saturate the muscles with blood and, in a sense, massaging them from the inside. Metaphorically speaking, the dry sponge becomes saturated, making the tissue more pliable and relaxed. The neural endings in the muscles decrease their firing. This, in turn, sends a message to the brain to relax. The long-term effects of autogenic training give one a sense of profound relaxation through autosuggestion. It also provides a sense of empowerment to know that there are some things you truly have control over, and this tends to carry over into other areas of your life.

Additional Resources

Alman, B., and Lambrou, P. *Self-Hypnosis: The Complete Manual for Health and Self-Change,* 2nd ed. New York: Brunner/Mazel, 1991.

Blair, F.R. *Instant Self-Hypnosis.* New York: Sourcebooks, 2004.

Green, E., and Green, A. *Beyond Biofeedback.* New York: Delacorte Press, 1977.

Exercise 18.1 The Power of Self-Suggestion

The following is a brief exercise to assist you in uniting the powers of your conscious and unconscious minds by giving yourself your own suggestions to follow as a means to promote a sense of relaxation. Please first create and then read through the suggestions so that you have a strong comfort level with them. Then assume a comfortable position and talk yourself through these suggestions. Remember that in a relaxed state you are more open to suggestions, particularly those you give yourself. After giving some thought to one or more behaviors you might wish to change, write these down as well so they can be used in a relaxed state.

Suggestions for Relaxation

Example: "My body is calm and relaxed."

1. _____

2. _____

3. _____

4. _____

Suggestions for Self-Improvement and Confidence

Example: "I can do anything!"

1. _____

2. _____

3. _____

4. _____

Exercise 18.2 The Direct Approach of Autogenics

Autogenic training has both a direct and indirect approach to relaxation. The direct approach is a more detailed visual interpretation than simple general instructions to feel warm and heavy. In this exercise, a slight variation on the original technique offers added instructions for those who need more understanding of how the physiological changes occur. In the direct approach, the specific mechanisms involved in warmth and heaviness are focused on to initiate a stronger sense of relaxation. Here, you start out with diaphragmatic breathing to induce relaxation. When mind and body become relaxed through this technique, the mind becomes more receptive to additional thoughts (warmth and heaviness), and thus the selected awareness process is enhanced.

The length of time required for this approach will vary. To begin, you may want to work on only one body region, such as the arms and hands. With proficiency, you can add to the duration of each session. The following instructions can be read prior to your session, or they can be read to you by a friend while you are performing this technique. Assume a comfortable position and become as relaxed as possible.

Instructions

1. First, concentrate on your breathing. Feel the air come in through your nose or mouth and down into your lungs, and feel your stomach rise and then fall as you exhale the air through your mouth.

2. Take a comfortably slow, deep breath, feeling the air enter the lower chambers of your lungs. Feel your stomach rise slowly with the intake of air, and then slowly descend as the air leaves your lungs. Repeat this, making the breath even slower and deeper. With each exhalation, feel how relaxed your body has become.

3. Focus on your heartbeat. Listen to and feel your heart beating in your chest. As you concentrate on this, allow a longer pause after each heartbeat. Just by allowing the thought of your heart relaxing, you can make it do so. Allow a longer pause after each beat. Now, to help relax the heart muscle, take one more slow, deep breath and as you exhale feel how relaxed your heart has become. Again consciously choose to place a longer pause after each heartbeat.

4. Take a moment to realize that in the resting state you are now in, your body's core receives the greatest percentage (80 percent) of blood, most of it going to the gastrointestinal tract. While the body's core is receiving a great supply of blood, the periphery—arms and legs—receive only a maintenance supply.

5. Be aware that when your muscles are saturated with blood, they become very relaxed and pliable, like a wet sponge. Now, think to yourself that you would like to recreate the feeling of relaxation in the muscles of your arms and hands.

6. Allow the blood to move from the body's core up to your shoulders and down toward your arms and hands. As you think and desire this, you will begin to constrict the blood vessels of your stomach area while at the same time dilating those of your arms and hands.

7. With each breath you take, with each beat of your heart, allow the flow of blood to move from your stomach area to your arms and hands.

8. You will begin to notice that as you allow this movement of blood from your core to your arms and hands, they begin to feel slightly heavy. They feel heavy because they are not quite used to the sensation of additional blood flow to this region. You will also notice that your arms and particularly your hands feel warm, especially your palms and fingers, since they have the greatest number of temperature receptors.

9. With each breath and each beat of your heart, allow the blood to continue to move from your stomach area toward your arms and hands. Feel how comfortable your arms and hands have become. They feel warm and heavy, and very relaxed. As the muscles become saturated with blood, stiffness dissipates and relaxation ensues.

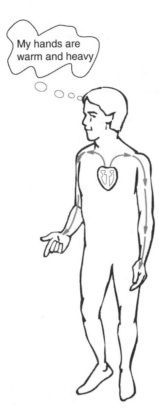

Figure 18.1

10. Soon you will notice that your arms feel increasingly heavy, so much so that should you want to move them you couldn't because they feel immobilized. You feel as if they were making indentations in the floor or chair frame. Your arms and hands feel so relaxed they just don't want to move.

11. With each breath and each beat of your heart, continue to send the flow of blood to your arms and hands. Feel the warmth spread from your arms all the way down to your palms and fingers.

12. Take a long, slow, deep breath and gauge how relaxed your whole body feels as you exhale. Sense how relaxed your arms and hands feel.

13. Now, take one more slow, deep breath, and as you exhale allow the flow of blood to return to your stomach area. Reverse the flow of blood from your arms and hands back to your body's core. By thinking this, you now allow the blood vessels of the arms and hands to constrict, shunting the blood back to the GI tract. At the same time, you allow the blood vessels of the stomach area to dilate and receive the flow of blood you have sent to it.

14. As the blood returns, you may notice that your arms begin to feel a little lighter, but the sensation of warmth still lingers.

15. With each breath you take, with each beat of your heart, allow the flow of blood to return to where it came from.

16. Again, concentrate on your breathing. Feel the air come in through your nose or mouth, down into your lungs, and feel your stomach rise and then descend as you exhale the air through your mouth.

17. Now, take a comfortably slow, deep breath and feel the air enter the lower chambers of your lungs. Feel your stomach rise slowly with the intake of air, and slowly descend as the air leaves your lungs. Do this again, making the breath even slower and deeper. With each exhalation, become more aware of how relaxed your body has become.

18. Next, focus again on the beat of your heart. Listen to and feel your heart beating in your chest. As you concentrate on this, allow a longer pause between heartbeats. Just by allowing the thought of your heart relaxing, you can make it do so. Think to allow a longer pause between beats. To help relax the heart muscle, take one more slow, deep breath, and feel how relaxed your heart has become as you exhale. Again, place a longer pause after each heartbeat.

19. Again, take a moment to realize that in the resting state you are now in, your body's core contains the greatest percentage of your blood supply, roughly 80 percent.

20. Think to yourself that when your muscles are saturated with blood, they become very relaxed and pliable like a wet sponge. Now become consciously aware that you desire to recreate that feeling of relaxation in the muscles of your legs and feet.

21. Allow the blood from your stomach area to move down toward your legs and feet. As you think and desire this, the blood vessels of your stomach area will begin to constrict, while at the same time those of your legs and feet will begin to dilate. This constriction process in your body's core will begin to shunt blood to your thighs, hamstrings, calves, and feet, where the dilating vessels will be able to receive more blood.

22. With each breath you take, with each beat of your heat, allow the flow of blood to move from your stomach area down toward your legs and feet.

23. You will begin to notice that as you allow this movement of blood from your body's core to your legs and feet, both your legs and feet begin to feel slightly heavy. This heaviness increases with each breath and each heartbeat. They feel very heavy because muscles in this region are not used to the sensation of additional blood flow. You will also notice that your legs and particularly your feet feel warm, especially the heels of your feet and your toes, as they have the greatest number of temperature receptors.

24. With each breath and each beat of your heart, allow the blood to continue to move from your stomach area to your legs and feet. Feel how comfortable your thighs and calves are. They feel warm, comfortably heavy, and very relaxed. As the muscles become saturated with blood, stiffness dissipates and relaxation ensues.

25. Be aware that your legs now feel increasingly heavy, so much so that you want to move them but they feel immobilized. You feel as if each leg has sunk under its weight into the floor. Your legs and feet feel so relaxed they don't want to move.

26. With each breath and each beat of your heart, continue to send the flow of blood to legs and feet. Feel the warmth spread from your stomach area all the way down to your toes.

27. Take a long, slow, deep breath and gauge how relaxed your whole body feels as you exhale. Feel how relaxed your legs and feet feel.

28. Now, take one more slow, deep breath and as you exhale, allow the flow of blood to return to your stomach area. Reverse the flow of blood from your legs and feet back to your body's core. By thinking this, you allow the blood vessels of the legs and feet to constrict, shunting the blood back to the GI tract. At the same time, you allow the blood vessels of the stomach area to dilate and receive the flow of blood you are sending to it.

29. As the blood returns, you will notice that your legs are beginning to feel a little lighter, but the sensations of warmth linger, especially in your feet and toes.

30. With each breath you take, with each beat of your heart, allow the flow of blood to return to where it came from.

31. As your body returns to a resting state, feel the sensation of relaxation throughout. Although you feel relaxed, you don't feel tired or sleepy. You feel alert and energized.

32. When you feel ready, open your eyes and stretch the muscles of your arms, shoulders, and legs.

CHAPTER

19

Massage Therapy

Without adequate tactile input, the human organism will die. Touch is one of the principal elements necessary for the successful development and functional organization of the central nervous system, and is as vital to our existence as food, water, and breath.
—Ken Dychtwald

Ageless Wisdom of Massage Therapy

Muscle tension, above all else, is *the* symptom of stress! Although tense muscles don't necessarily place people in the hospital like cancer and heart disease do, muscle tension is the number one symptom of stress. At the mere hint of stress, the nervous system releases epinephrine and norepinephrine to prepare the body for fight or flight. Every muscle responds to the call, resulting in various levels of muscle contraction. Whether the muscles tense for seconds, minutes, or days, the cumulative effects can be pronounced. You don't have to be on the run to experience soreness. Muscles can easily tense in a sitting position in front of a computer screen, behind a driving wheel, or even standing in line at the grocery store. Over time, slight contractions lead to an imbalance in opposing muscle groups, resulting in poor posture, structural imbalance, lower-back pain, and a host of other problems.

Dan began the process of deep tissue massage on a client lying on a massage table. With low lighting, a scented candle burning, and soft instrumental music playing in the background, the environment exuded relaxation. Curious about the types of people he works on, I asked what percentage of his clientele come to him because of stress. His reply: "100%! All of them."

According to historical records, the practice of massage therapy dates back to ancient Egypt, but most likely muscle massage is as old as time itself. Throughout the ages the demands of strenuous physical work have resulted in extreme muscle soreness, stiffness, and pain. Muscle massage offered an obvious answer to this age-old symptom. Even a life of leisure has its moments of stress, and the pampering of kings, queens, and leaders of various royal lineage was not without its practice of muscle massage either. A quick glance at the names of various types of massage indicates the worldwide appeal of this technique.

Today, muscle massage is one of many modalities in the family of massage therapy known as *bodywork,* which includes Swedish massage, Thai massage, shiatsu, Rolfing, and many, many others. Interestingly, one needn't actually be touched to experience the effects of muscle relaxation. Additional "touch" therapies include pet therapy, hydrotherapy, stone therapy, aromatherapy, and energy healing.

Massage therapy is now a bona fide therapeutic practice certified through the American Massage Therapy Association (AMTA). Certification typically requires a six-month program with over 500 hours of classroom instruction in an approved school and three years of professional experience. Since the inception of the AMTA in 1943, the popularity of massage has mushroomed, particularly in the past decade. There are now over 250 approved massage therapy schools nationwide and over 49,000 certified members. Students are taught a variety of massage styles and then typically specialize in one or two as they begin their practice.

Let's take an in-depth look at the family of modalities that constitute the field of bodywork.

Types of Bodywork

Swedish Massage

Swedish massage is the most commonly known type of massage in the United States. Created decades ago by gymnast Peter Heinrik Ling, this style of massage emphasizes both decreased muscle tension and increased circulation to the muscle group worked upon. Swedish massage includes a number of movements such as effleurage (long stroking), petrissage (rolling or squeezing), and friction (deep kneading), all of which attempt to relax the specific muscle fiber. As with most types of massage, the therapist greets you and then leaves the room so that you may disrobe and lie comfortably under a sheet on the massage table. Upon reentering the room, the therapist may begin the session at the head or feet.

Shiatsu

Based on the Oriental concept of energy or chi, shiatsu (also known as acupressure) is a massage style that works to unblock the flow of chi or life force energy that travels through the body's energy meridian system. Direct pressure is placed on a specific meridian point to release, unblock, or decongest the flow of energy, thus bringing the body's flow of energy back into balance. The word *shiatsu* translates as "finger pressure"; however, fingers, knuckles, and even elbows may be used in this process. Although shiatsu is used as a means to promote relaxation, it is also known to help relieve sinus problems, TMJD, tension headaches, and nausea. Some dentists now use various shiatsu points for their patients.

Rolfing or Structural Integration

Muscles may contract, but it's the fascia that holds the muscles together. *Fascia,* the connective tissue of your body that is composed primarily of collagen, can become restricted due to chronic muscle tension, resulting in a distortion to one's spine and skeletal structure. Structural integration is known in the field of bodywork as "deep tissue" massage. The purpose is to help realign the body into its most correct posture by working to release the constriction of fascia.

The concept of structural integration was first put forth by cell biologist Ida Rolf in the early 20th century. She developed a technique, called *Rolfing,* to realign the body's ideal skeletal structure. The massage therapist applies deep pressure along the lines of muscle tissue to release constricted fascia. Those who have had a single session (or the entire ten-session treatment) will tell you that while it's being done, this type of deep tissue work is anything but relaxing. In fact, it can be downright painful. However, these same people will also tell you that the effects of Rolfing are phenomenal because chronic pain disappears with deep tissue work. It should be noted that deep tissue work is also done with a style of bodywork called *myofascial release* and some types of osteopathic manipulation.

Sports Massage

Amateur and professional athletes alike spend a lot of time flexing and contracting muscles. It's the nature of their work. In the quest for the elusive gold medal, Olympic coaches searched for ways to quicken the pace of recovery and muscle restoration after extended bouts of arduous training. Muscle massage was proved to be one way to augment the recovery process, by flushing out waste products (lactic acid) and increasing circulation to tired muscles in the recovery stage of postexercise. Sports massage developed as a combination of a few other types of massage, including the kneading motions of Swedish massage, the deep tissue work of structural integration, and the finger pressure of shiatsu. Sports massage is not exclusively for Olympic athletes. Anyone can benefit from a good sports massage, including the weekend warrior.

Reflexology

At first glance, reflexology appears to be nothing more than a simple foot massage. Looks can be deceiving. The art of reflexology dates back to ancient Egypt, and what appears to be a foot massage is really a means to provide relaxation to the entire body. The science of reflexology is based on the concept of a hologram in which the foot is a template for the entire body. Virtually all the body's organs are mapped out on the foot's imprint, which includes the toes, sole, and heel. The purpose of reflexology is not only to massage the muscles of the foot, but also to provide a reciprocal healing to various organs that correspond to areas of the foot being massaged. You don't have to understand (or believe) in the holographic concept of reflexology to appreciate a good foot massage.

Thai Massage

Thai massage is believed to date back to the dynasty of Thai King Rama III one thousand years ago. In an effort to ensure the legacy of this type of bodywork, he had his healers etch diagrams of the human body with energy lines in stone as texts for future healers. Thai massage is perhaps best described as a complex sequence of soft tissue pressure (massage) combined with stretching, twisting, and joint manipulations. With manipulations, pressure is used to achieve stretching and twisting that requires several different positions to achieve the desired result of alignment, flexibility, and relaxation. Proper leverage is essential for this style of bodywork, and typically a small effort by the practitioner results in a large effect for the client. It is not uncommon for the bodyworker to twist, pull, push, and rotate segments of body parts and joints for the optimal effect.

The session is typically divided into zones (e.g., feet and legs, legs and back, chest and abdomen, arms and hands, neck and face), and the session will include the client both lying down and sitting. It is also not uncommon for the bodyworker to use his or her hands, elbows, feet, and knees for the specific leverage desired. Like acupressure, Thai massage acknowledges working with the body's energy patterns to establish a correct alignment for the optimal energy flow. Each technique in Thai massage is designed to stimulate and access the flow of intrinsic (subtle) energies by allowing the release of blocked energies that inhibit a sense of balance for mind, body, and spirit. Although it may look and feel painful, the peaceful nature of Thai massage is based on the principles of Buddhist compassion and, like a good yoga session, it actually feels quite refreshing.

Other Touch Therapies

Not all touch therapies involve a massage therapist, nor do they involve muscle manipulation. Interestingly, they can produce the same end result. The following are just a few of the more common examples of touch therapy. Unlike most modalities of bodywork, which may require a therapist, some of these can be self-directed.

Stone Therapy

Stone therapy is a type of bodywork in which smooth river stones are either heated or, in some cases, cooled and placed on various regions of the body to promote a deep sense of relaxation. Specifically, these regions align with the energy centers of the body (chakras). Some types of stone therapy go one step further and are used by the therapist as a tool to augment deeper or harder muscle contact.

Pet Therapy

Rubbing the stomach of a dog or the head of a cat may seem like a far cry from a full body massage, but the connection to an animal can be equally profound and relaxing. Research studies reveal that pet owners appear to have less stress, showing signs of decreased resting heart rate, blood pressure, and muscle tension. Soft fur or even feathers are not only soothing to the touch of human skin, but appear to decrease firing of muscle neurons, which, in turn, decreases muscle tension. What never seems to be mentioned in the clinical studies involving pet therapy is the emotional component. Unconditional love is also known to allay the worst frustrations and anxieties.

Hydrotherapy

If you have ever stepped into a hot bubbling Jacuzzi and lingered for several minutes, then you know how relaxing this type of touch therapy can be. Warm water draws blood from the body's core to the periphery. Because the muscles of the arms and legs are part of this periphery, they become engulfed in blood. Unlike during a bout of exercise, where working muscle capillaries are rich in blood as a means to provide nutrients for energy metabolism, in a resting state the muscles become very relaxed, in essence experiencing the same effect as a muscle massage. Even without the air jets, a warm bath can produce the similar effects.

Aromatherapy

Like the name suggests, aromatherapy uses the smells of pleasant fragrances such as lavender, peppermint, rose, and vanilla to promote a sense of relaxation. Specific fragrances target the olfactory nerve to decrease the neural firing in muscles, replacing it with the parasympathetic response associated with relaxation. Although the use of essential oils from plants and flowers has been known for eons, it has taken on a new appeal with the broad interest in complementary medicine. Lavender is often used in maternity wards when mothers are going into labor. The scent of vanilla is often used to relax people who are nervous while entering the tunnel of the MRI machine. Some massage therapists combine the use of aromatherapy with their practice of bodywork to produce a deeper sense of relaxation, in some cases applying a scented lotion directly to the skin.

Energy Work

Therapeutic touch, healing touch, Reiki, polarity healing, zero balancing, Qi Gong, and bio-energy are all types of energy work that combine the use of the human energy field, chakras, and meridians to promote a balance in one's life force of energy. Ironically, with most of these therapies there is no direct touching at all. The work is done at the more subtle energy levels of the human energy field, yet changes produced through the subtle energy systems are quite profound. Initially one might feel a sense of heat to a particular region, but generally what most people feel is an improved sense of well-being.

How to Incorporate Massage Therapy into Your Life Routine

The following are some suggestions that may help you include this incredible relaxation technique in your stress management repertoire.

Selecting a Massage Therapist

Although the art of self-massage (see the next section) can feel good, nothing beats having a full body massage, which typically takes about one and a half hours. Across the country, the cost of a massage varies from $50 to $100 per session, depending on the locale. One might think that all massages are similar; however, no two massage therapists are alike. Before you make an appointment, determine which type of massage you prefer. Some like deep tissue work; others don't. The best way to select a massage therapist is to ask your friends and colleagues for a recommendation. Shop around to see who is good and who is available. Really good massage therapists tend to be booked up; however, you might consider asking to be called for their first cancellation.

As more and more massage schools open up across the country and more people consider massage therapy as a new vocation, these students need practice. Massage therapy schools offer massage therapy sessions at reduced rates so their students can learn the trade. It's my opinion based on personal experience that students tend to be more attentive while learning the skill and for this reason do an excellent job.

The Art of Self-Massage

Giving yourself a massage can be a welcome relief to tired, achy muscles overworked from sitting all day at a computer station or completing a strenuous workout. Performing a variation of a Swedish massage (kneading and stroking) can prove quite effective in reducing muscle tension. If you have a friend, spouse, roommate, or partner who can help you with the neck and shoulders, consider asking him or her for help with the promise of returning the favor.

Stress Relief and Chronic Pain

With muscle tension being the number one symptom of stress, bodywork of any kind is desirable. Its popularity over the millennia speaks to its effectiveness. Not all chronic pain is structural (muscles, fascia, ligaments, and bones), but a large percentage is. For this reason, muscle massage is considered to be paramount in the effort to reduce the symptoms of chronic pain. Different types of massage will vary with regard to their long-term effectiveness, yet all forms of bodywork are considered beneficial.

Best Benefits of Progressive Massage Therapy and Bodywork

The benefits of any type of bodywork can be felt immediately. Specific changes include decreased muscle tension and increased relaxation. In an age of high-tech virtual communication, more and more people have less direct contact with others. The consequences can be feelings of isolation and depression. Human touch is proven unequivocally to be essential for health and well-being. The long-term effects go well beyond the time spent lying on a massage table.

Additional Resources

Lundberg, P. *The Book of Massage*. New York: Fireside Books, 2003.
Schatz, B. *Soft Tissue Massage for Pain Relief*. Charlottesville, VA: Hampton Road Press, 2001.
Widdowson, R. *Head Massage*. London: Hamlyn Sterling, 2003.
Wills, P. *The Reflexology Manual*. Rochester, VT: Healing Art Press, 1995.

CHAPTER

20

Hatha Yoga

You have to learn to listen to your body, going with it and not against it.
You will be amazed to discover that, if you are kind to your body,
it will respond in an incredible way.
—Vanda Scaravelli

Ageless Wisdom of Yoga

One of the most ancient practices of stress management comes from the Asian continent and is often described as a 6,000-year-old science of self-mastery. The Sanskrit word *yoga* means "union." Specifically, yoga refers to the integration, balance, and harmony of mind and body. The sage known as Patanjali is given credit for recording the specific postures, known as *asanas* (ah-san-ahs), that assist in the process of augmenting this union of mind (*ha*) and body (*tha*). Although there are many types of yoga, including karma yoga and kundalini yoga, hatha yoga is by far the most popular style in the Western world. The fact that today hatha yoga is practiced by millions of people throughout the world indicates how ageless the wisdom of this union really is, and that the importance of maintaining this union in an increasingly stress-filled world has been recognized.

What appears to be a series of simple flexibility exercises that work the legs, lower back, neck and shoulders, and arms is really a progression of conscious movements, in combination with one's breath, designed to discipline the mind and ego. The purpose is to fully integrate a higher sense of conscious awareness in all movements, actions, and behaviors throughout the course of any given day. The subtle theme of hatha yoga is that by learning to become more flexible with your physical body, in turn you become more flexible with your thoughts and emotions in each and every situation that you encounter in your collective environment.

The Omega Institute, well respected for decades among health educators for offering adult education classes in all aspects of mind-body-spirit healing, cites yoga as a powerful psycho-spiritual discipline that has the intention of integrating all aspects of one's human experience. Practitioners of hatha yoga would certainly agree, saying that the simple practice appears to transform the human body into a vessel capable of great vitality and longevity. Practitioners would also be the first to tell you that although hatha yoga is derived from the Hindu culture, it is not, repeat *not*, a religion; it's merely a philosophy of living your life in balance.

Pranayama: The Art of Breathing

In the practice of hatha yoga, conscious breathing plays a vital role in the process of uniting mind, body, and spirit. Breathing, or *pranayama,* influenced by the diaphragm is the current of life force that circulates the flow of universal energy throughout the body. The word *prana* means "breath," and the word *yama* translates to "pause." Unlike the common practice of thoracic (upper chest) breathing, pranayama invites a conscious effort of the entire pulmonary system, including the nose, throat, lungs, intercostal muscles, and diaphragm.

Each yoga asana is composed of a contraction phase and a release phase, in which muscles in a specific region of focus are slowly stretched and relaxed. As the muscles are stretched, air is drawn into the lungs by the diaphragm. As the muscles begin the relaxation phase of the asana, one exhales. When first learning these positions, trying to coordinate the pranayama with the asanas may seem challenging, but with practice, the coordination becomes second nature.

The Art of Conscious Stretching

Desk work, computer work, prolonged driving, and even walking in high-heeled shoes tend to promote an unnatural state of contracted muscles. Eventually the body adapts to these positions and various muscles remain contracted, causing stiffness and soreness. Moreover, tensed muscles tend to distort one's posture along the spinal column, which eventually leads to chronic pain in the lower back, hips, and shoulder region. The asanas used in the practice of hatha yoga are designed to help provide a full range of motion to all joints and promote correct posture in the vertebral column.

The art of conscious stretching is a practice to stretch the intended muscle group long enough, without pain, to allow for the full restoration of one's structural integrity. Conscious stretching means to complete the posture without ego. Most, if not all, asansa have Sanskrit names, with Western counterparts, such as Tasasana (Mountain Pose) or Matsyasana (Fish Pose). Without a doubt, Shavasana (Corpse Pose) is by far the most relaxing posture, and the one everyone cannot wait to do at the end of yoga class.

How to Incorporate Hatha Yoga into Your Life Routine

Exercise 20.1, "Salute to the Sun," guides you through a short series of yoga asanas to try on your own. The following are some tips and suggestions to consider when incorporating this relaxation technique as a part of your lifestyle routine.

- Maintaining a practice of hatha yoga on your own is possible, and those who make it a practice tend to do some routine (long or short) nearly every day. Motivation and time can run low in a busy day, which is why yoga classes have become very popular in this country. If you choose to attend a class, ask around to find the best fit for your schedule and personality. Despite the new certification requirements, no two yoga classes are exactly alike. Many yoga studios offer a drop-in fee, which is an excellent way to sample various classes.

- Hatha yoga means to unite mind and body. The ultimate goal of yoga is to do so by lowering the walls of the ego (the censor of the conscious mind). Whereas most athletic endeavors have a competitive edge to them, hatha yoga does not. It doesn't matter that your attempts at an asana don't equal those of an instructor, classmates, or pictures in a book. Pain is not a goal in yoga. Although reaching and stretching are encouraged, pain is not. Know your limits and avoid pain.

- It is best not to perform any yoga asanas on a full stomach. Yoga instructors suggest that you allow one to two hours between eating and a yoga workout, particularly if you attend a Bikram yoga class in which the room is intentionally set at a high temperature.

- Wear loose-fitting clothing and avoid wearing jewelry (watches, earrings, necklaces, bracelets, etc.).

- Find a quiet place to practice. A well-lit, well-ventilated room is ideal. A thin yoga mat is recommended for several standing positions, but is not necessary.

- Early morning is believed to be the preferred time for conscious awareness; however, afternoon and evening are when the body is most limber. Yoga postures tend to have a greater relaxation effect after a long, busy day. Find a time that best fits your schedule.

- The underlying premise of hatha yoga is balance. It is highly recommended that when a posture is done on one side of your body (e.g., right knee to chest), you should repeat it on the other side (e.g., left knee to chest) to maintain a sense of balance.

- Many yoga sessions begin with the Salute to the Sun (Exercise 20.1). If you are new to yoga, this might be a great way to incorporate this into your session.

- Breathing is a central part of hatha yoga. Practice your breathing (pranayama) and try not to hold your breath at any one point.

- Meditation is not a requirement of yoga, but it's a nice complement to a yoga session. Most classes end with students lying on their backs on the floor in Shavasana (Corpse Pose), which is the relaxation pose. Some instructors will offer a contemplative meditation at this time. You can do this on your own as well.

Stress Relief and Chronic Pain

Hatha yoga, for most people, is considered primarily as a preventive and maintenance health exercise. However, it has long been recognized for its ability to restore a sense of peace and tranquility to the most hectic lifestyle. Moreover, the nature of hatha yoga is to provide balance to musculature on each side of the body, providing symmetry to muscle groups that are often imbalanced from stress, leading to chronic pain, particularly lower-back, neck, and shoulder pain. Many case studies report tremendous success in the cessation of chronic pain through a practice of yoga.

Best Benefits of Hatha Yoga

Hatha yoga is more than simply stretching your muscles and feeling limber. Hatha yoga is a philosophy of life: a means of consciously living your life in balance and harmony. This philosophy goes beyond postures to include healthy eating, a practice of meditation, maintaining a strong ethical nature, and treating all people with respect.

One session of yoga can make your body feel great! Tight muscles become more flexible, and closing a session in the Corpse Pose is always a nice way to feel relaxed. People who maintain a regular practice of yoga (three or more times per week) find themselves to be not only more flexible with their body, but also more flexible in their thinking. They claim to sleep better, eat better, have fewer emotional mood swings, and feel an overall positive sense of well-being. By honoring the aspects of balance and integration through a progression of asanas, hatha yoga is believed to help augment the balance and integration of the brain's right and left hemispheres, thus promoting a sense of relaxed awareness. More recently, hatha yoga has been used by many to help alleviate chronic problems such as lower-back pain, neck and shoulder pain, and carpal tunnel syndrome.

Additional Resources

Devi, N.J. *The Healing Path of Yoga.* New York: Three Rivers Press, 2000.
Farhi, D. *Yoga, Mind, Body, Spirit.* New York: Owl Books, 2000.
Finger, A. *Introduction to Yoga.* New York: Three Rivers Press, 2000.
Francina, S. *The New Yoga for People Over 50.* Deerfield Beach, FL: Health Communications, 1997.
Ward, S.W. *Yoga for the Young at Heart.* Navato, CA: New World Library, 2002.
Weintraub, A., and Cope, S. *Yoga for Depression.* New York: Broadway Books, 2003.

Exercise 20.1 Salute to the Sun (Surya Namaskar)

The Salute to the Sun is a very symbolic series of asanas. It is traditionally performed at the beginning and end of each yoga session. Surya Namaskar began as a form of meditation worship wherein one would start the day by facing east and performing the series of movements in order to maintain harmony throughout the day. Today it is recognized as an excellent exercise to stretch and limber muscles throughout the entire body, but particularly the spine and legs. Runners and joggers may recognize a few of these stretches, as they are excellent flexibility exercises for hamstrings and calf muscles.

The Salute to the Sun should be performed slowly, and every effort should be made to maintain balance through each posture. Once the movements become more natural, the exercise can be done more rapidly. Each posture is counterbalanced in the next asana. A complete Salute to the Sun consists of two sequences. In the first cycle, lead with the right foot in positions 4 and 9, and in the second, lead with the left. It makes no difference what direction you face when doing this exercise; however, facing east marks symbolic awareness of the beginning of the life of each new day.

Instructions

Preposition: Stand with your feet shoulder-width apart, spine completely aligned, and weight evenly distributed on both feet. Hold hands straight above head, palms facing out, with arms fully extended.

Position 1 (Figs. 20.1 and 20.2): Raise your arms in a wide circular motion over the head and then slowly down in front of the face to the midpoint of the chest. Hold palms together and exhale.

Figure 20.1   Figure 20.2

Position 2 (Fig. 20.3): Raise your arms directly over your head, pushing from the waist, keeping legs straight and back slightly arched. As you do this, slowly inhale and look up to the sky.

Figure 20.3

Figure 20.4

Position 3 (Fig. 20.4):   Leading with your hands, reach to your toes, exhaling as you lower your head to your knees. Keep your back comfortably straight and slightly bent. (Tight hamstrings will decrease the length of your reach. Reach only as far as it is comfortably possible.)

Figure 20.5

Position 4 (Fig. 20.5):   Place your palms on the floor, then bring your right foot between your hands. Extend the left leg behind you, and lower your knee to the floor. Inhale as you extend the leg, arch your back, and look up to the sky.

Figure 20.6

Position 5 (Fig. 20.6):   Bring the right foot back to meet the left, and exhale. Raise your hips and buttocks high, keeping your head down and eyes directed toward your feet. Arms should be fully extended.

Figure 20.7

Position 6 (Fig. 20.7):   Lower your knees to the floor, followed by your chest and then your forehead. Hips should be slightly bent and raised off the floor. Breath is slowly exhaled throughout.

Figure 20.8

Position 7 (Fig. 20.8):   Bring your hips to the floor, fully extending your legs behind you. Then inhale while placing your hands directly beneath your shoulders and raising your chest. Look up to the sky, and arch your head and back slightly.

Figure 20.9

Position 8 (Fig. 20.9):   Raise hips and buttocks high off the floor, keeping your palms and feet flat on the floor. As you do so, exhale. Keep your head down, eyes directly toward your feet, and your arms fully extended.

Figure 20.10

Position 9 (Fig. 20.10):   Place your left foot between your hands, extend your right leg back, and place the knee on the floor as you inhale. Arch your back and head slightly, looking up to the sky.

Figure 20.11

Position 10 (Fig. 20.11):   Bring your feet together, shoulder-width apart, with arms extended and hands reaching toward feet. Keep your back straight, and knees slightly bent. As you bring your head to your knees, exhale.

Figure 20.12

Position 11 (Fig. 20.12):   Reach with your hands overhead, and slowly inhale. Extend your head back to look up to the sky, arching the back slightly.

Figure 20.13

Position 12 (Fig. 20.13):   Lower your arms to mid-chest height, palms facing together, and exhale.

Now repeat the entire exercise, this time leading with the right foot in positions 5 and 10. Upon completion, turn your attention inward to observe any and all physical sensations.

21

Nutrition: Eating for a Healthy Immune System

We got a chance yesterday to see exactly what the major food industry groups want for American consumers. They want ignorance.
—Editorial, *New York Times*

Ageless Wisdom of Healthy Eating

Since the beginning of time, food has played an essential, if not critical, role in the survival of the human species. Over the ages, food was hunted, gathered, and grown not only for nutrients and energy but also for health and the restoration of health from disease and illness. Plants in the form of fruits, vegetables, legumes, and herbs were critical to one's diet. Additionally, food is a great pacifier. There is no denying that certain foods can exalt the senses to a state of euphoria in a way that no other means can. Combined with great company, eating is known as one of the greatest means to happiness.

For all these reasons, it's not an understatement to say that nutrition is taken very seriously because life depends on it. In essence, food is considered to be the first course of action to take to maintain health and well-being. Ironically, today much of the food available is the cause of much disease and illness, rather than a means to prevent a decline in one's health. At no time in the history of America has the food choice been so great, yet the quality of food, loaded with chemicals, been so questionable. For millennia, nutrition was first and foremost a health issue; however, today health concerns are grossly outweighed by economic and political concerns. One need only be reminded of how cows (known herbivores) became mad in the first place. They were fed rendered parts of other cows, lambs, and chicken feces, all mixed in with their grain cereal.

In the past two decades a large uncontrolled experiment has been conducted on the American population through the introduction of synthetic substances into food production. With the introduction of synthetic hormones, antibiotics, pesticides, herbicides, fungicides, fertilizers, artificial sweeteners, artificial fats, food brighteners, and most recently genetically modified foods, Americans have seen a corresponding rise in a variety of chronic diseases. Some foods contain so many chemicals that there is literally no place for them on the food guide pyramid, yet people consume vast quantities of them every day. A case in point occurred in 2001 when Kellogg's corn flakes and Taco John taco shells were recalled due to the amount of pesticides found in them. Genetically modified foods are considered so unnatural that the body doesn't know what to do with them. 2004 saw the first case of mad cow disease in the United States, something Americans were assured would never happen.

In 1995 the American Cancer Society (ACS) stated that although the death rate due to cancer had decreased due to early detection, one of every three people would contract cancer in his or her lifetime. They also stated that 60% (more than half) of all cases of cancer could be eliminated if people would choose a healthier diet. Apparently, people's concern for taste has won out over their concern for health in the 24-7 fast-paced American lifestyle. The ACS might as well have been shouting in the wind, as their warning seems to have gone unheeded.

In an effort to promote shelf life and increase profits, the major food corporations concoct ingenious ways to keep food looking and tasting fresh. We now know that chemical preservatives, hydrogenated fats, and scores of other synthetic components used in the process of food production certainly prolong shelf life, but appear to do absolutely nothing to promote health. Instead, they compromise health. Today, synthetic foods are considered a stressor to the body—specifically, to the immune system.

Even if there weren't such an influx of synthetic foods, there are a series of problems that occur regarding nutrition and stress. Each problem itself is easy to rectify; however, as these problems mount, their combined effects pose a greater danger to the integrity of your health. Metaphorically speaking, there are four dominos that tumble in a progression to a stressed lifestyle, the result of which significantly compromises one's physiology.

Stress Domino 1

Under the physiological demands of the stress response, the body's requirement for energy increases, regardless if the actions of fight or flight are used. In simple terms, more glucose is released into the bloodstream as a source of immediate energy. Second, more free fatty acids are released, just in case they are needed for long-term energy. The net result of these and other metabolic reactions to the stress response is a depletion of both macronutrients (carbohydrates, fats, and proteins) and micronutrients (vitamins, minerals). As the micronutrients are depleted, the efficiency of the metabolic response becomes compromised until they are replaced.

Stress Domino 2

Sadly, when people are stressed, good eating habits are the first thing to be ignored in a hectic schedule. Home-cooked meals are replaced with convenient fast foods. As was noted in the book *Fast Food Nation,* these foods are processed for taste, not nutrition. The vast majority of these foods contain what is known in nutrition circles as "empty calories," meaning they have little or no nutritional value. The consequence of bad eating habits is that the nutrients depleted during prolonged periods of stress are not replaced. Hence, the body's physiological systems operate less efficiently. Many systems are compromised, including the immune system and the reproductive system. Under compromised conditions, the body tries to compensate, but over time even these backup systems fail. The end result is a host of physiological problems that lead to poor health.

Stress Domino 3

As if it's not bad enough that valuable nutrients are depleted during prolonged stress and many of these nutrients are not replaced, many of the fast foods, junk foods, and convenient foods contain substances that act on the nervous system to keep the stress response elevated. These include the following:
- **Caffeine:** Coffee, teas, soda, and chocolate contain a constituent found in caffeine called methylated xanthines, a substance known to trigger the release of epinephrine and norepinephrine, which in turn increase heart rate, blood pressure, and other metabolic activities in the preparation for fight or flight.
- **Refined sugar:** Research suggests that refined sugar can have a similar effect on the nervous system as caffeine. It's no secret that processed foods are high in refined sugar. High-fructose corn syrup and table sugar are two examples.

- **Refined flour:** As with refined sugar, refined flour appears to affect the nervous system and in some cases the adrenal (stress) gland.
- **Salt (sodium):** Salt is known to retain water. Water retention tends to increase blood pressure. Although only one teaspoon of salt is recommended per day, processed food is loaded with salt to appease the taste buds. Stress plus sodium equals high blood pressure.

Stress Domino 4

A new word has entered the American lexicon regarding the proliferation of toxic chemical residues found in the body. The word is *bio-burden,* and it describes the amounts of toxic chemical substances that are found in the body's blood and tissue samples, including mother's milk. Not only do processed foods contain a plethora of chemicals, but the skin also absorbs chemicals via the use of makeup, shampoos, hair dyes, deodorants, sun block, and other substances applied topically to the skin and absorbed. Studies on the effects of these substances are not conclusive with humans, but in animal studies the results are disturbing. Suffice it to say that even in trace amounts these chemical residues become a stressor to the body's physiology and immune system, presenting a challenge to the integrity of one's overall health and well-being.

A Word About Water

Although it contains no calories, water is often acknowledged as *the* most important nutrient. In simple terms, we would die quickly (a matter of days) without it. Although the average person does drink a fair amount of beverages, most people do not consume enough water. Instead, coffee, teas, and soft drinks act as diuretics, resulting in a moderate state of dehydration. If you are thirsty, most likely you are already showing signs of dehydration.

Signs of dehydration include sluggishness, fatigue, headaches, low energy, and poor appetite. Not only does this stress the body's physiology, but it may increase emotional stress regarding other life issues. Many proponents of rehydration suggest eight glasses of water per day, but the real test to see if you are drinking enough water is to check the color of your urine. Near-clear urine is the goal. A good goal is to drink a glass of water soon after you awaken because the body has gone roughly eight hours without any fluids.

Best Benefits of Healthy Eating

The benefits of healthy eating are too numerous to mention, but suffice it to say that sound nutritional practices play a crucial role in nearly every aspect of health, from eyesight to kidney function. Moreover, poor nutritional habits add to the critical mass of stress that people face each day. Although it's true that the human body has an amazing ability to adapt to the stress placed on it, there are limits. For this reason, perpetual poor eating habits tend to result in chronic illnesses rather than acute problems. The good news is that the body, by and large, has the great gift of resiliency, meaning that by making healthy changes in your diet, the body has a better chance to begin and sustain the healing process. Today, healthy eating requires a slight sense of vigilance with regard to the food industry. All the while, you could drive yourself nuts trying to avoid all the pot holes in the national food chain. For this reason it's best to be cautious, but not neurotic, about your food choices.

How to Incorporate the Practice of Healthy Eating into Your Life Routine

Hippocrates, the father of modern medicine, once said, "Let food be your medicine and let medicine be your food." Unfortunately today, rather than eating food as medicine, the vast majority of people eat food as poison. Like a river into which toxins have been dumped, the human body can only take so much before signs of disease and illness manifest. The following is a list of suggestions to tip the scales back into balance and promote a sense of health and well-being.

- **Consume a good supply of antioxidants.** Antioxidants fight the damage of free radicals that destroy cell membranes, DNA, RNA, and mitochondria. Antioxidants can be found in foods containing beta-carotene, vitamin C, vitamin E, and the mineral selenium. If you were to take a look at the eating habits of indigenous tribes around the world, you would notice that the greatest amount of calories in their diet come from vegetables. Vegetables not only contain a rich supply of vitamins, minerals, and fiber, but also contain a wonderful supply of antioxidants, nature's antidote to free radicals. Research in the field of nutrition has begun to reveal that antioxidants can be found in a variety of natural food sources, including vegetables, fruits, and herbs.

- **Consume a good supply of fiber** (30–40 grams per day with organic vegetables). Fiber helps clean the colon of toxic materials that might otherwise be absorbed into the bloodstream. The average American eats about 5 to 8 grams of fiber, far below the recommended amount. There is not a lot of fiber in iceberg lettuce, but there is plenty to be found in dark-green leafy veggies, citrus fruits, and legumes. Fiber also helps regulate the elimination process of your bowels. Under the best conditions, the typical transit time from mouth to rectum is about 12 to 18 hours. Experts suggest that there should be one bowel movement per meal. For the average person who eats three meals a day, this would mean three bowel movements; however, many people confide to their physicians that their average is more like one per day. Waste that doesn't get removed becomes toxic to the colon and affects the whole body. Colon cancer is the third most prevalent type of cancer in America.

- **Drink plenty of fresh, clean (filtered) water.** As was mentioned earlier, water acts as a transport system to remove toxic waste, produced by each cell, to the kidneys, where it can be excreted. Dehydration tends to compromise the body's ability to remove toxic waste. Toxins that are not flushed out cause damage of all kinds at the cellular level.

  An article in *National Geographic* stated that only 1 percent of the world's water is drinkable. News reports suggest that fresh water will become the issue of the decade (the United Nations has even suggested that wars will be fought over water). Toxicologists have noted that agricultural runoff from industrial farms into our national waterways has infiltrated our water supply. Moreover, water specialists have noted an increase in pharmaceutical by-products (Zoloft, Prozac, birth control pills, etc.) in our drinking water, which may be related to a score of health problems. As you can see, water safety is already an issue. In addition, water filtration plants use huge amounts of chlorine and fluoride as water treatment procedures, all of which ends up in our tap water. For this reason it is a great idea to install your own water filtration system as a means to purify the water you drink.

  Bottled water may sound like a good idea; however, supplies of bottled water are stored in warehouses for prolonged periods of time, allowing the chemicals from plastic residue to seep into the water. Water stored in hard (nonbendable) plastic is the only recommended water product, suggesting you may wish to bring your own bottled water with you. A good way to determine if you are drinking enough water is the excretion of near-clear urine.

- **Decrease consumption of pesticides, fungicides, and herbicides, which are toxic and may be carcinogenic (eat organic foods whenever possible).** Current research reveals that we consume large amounts of synthetic estrogens from the foods we eat. Synthetic estrogens are used in a host of agricultural products such as fertilizers, pesticides, fungicides, and herbicides. (They are also found in animal food products because these substances are used in animal feed.) These toxins are not simply found on the exterior of fruits and veggies to be washed off, but are also taken up by the root system and deposited in the stems, leaves, and fruits of these plants. Once consumed, it's the role of the liver to filter out toxins, yet the liver can only do so much, and those toxins that slip back into the bloodstream are transported to fatty tissue.

Long before the word *organic* was introduced to the American lexicon, the word *natural* conveyed a sense of the pristine nature of foods that were undisturbed by the agricultural complex. Today the word *natural* has become a marketing term and rarely means what the word originally described. Today, the difference between organic and natural is this: "100% organic" means that the soil in which the plants are grown must be clean of synthetic chemicals for a period of three years, and that the crops grown on the soil must only be exposed to natural fertilizers (seaweeds) and pesticides. In 2001, Congress passed legislation requiring that certified organic food be labeled as such. Be sure to read your food labels.

- **Consume an adequate intake of complete proteins.** To ensure the intake of all essential amino acids (white blood cells are composed of amino acids from protein sources), it is necessary to consume complete proteins. There are eight amino acids that the body cannot produce and must therefore obtain from outside food sources. Foods such as meats, fish, poultry, and eggs contain all the essential amino acids (hence the term complete), whereas many grains and legumes do not. If you are not a vegetarian, this really isn't a concern, but if you are, it is important to know how to complement your protein sources to ensure you are getting all the essential amino acids. Because amino acids are used for the production of enzymes, hormones, and the entire family of white blood cells, it is imperative to consume adequate amounts of protein in your diet. Again, 100% organic foods are the preferred source.

- **Decrease consumption of all processed foods (e.g., junk food, fast food).** Here are two little-known facts: Not only does most food travel a distance of 1,500 miles from farm to store, but the average amount of time that packaged food remains on the grocery store shelf is about three to six days, depending on your locale. If you were to check the expiration date on these packages, however, you would find that the suggested shelf life is projected in years. What allows these products to endure this long? If you read the labels, you would find a long list of preservatives comprised mainly of chemicals (none of which appear on any food guide pyramid).

  Once again, the role of the liver is to filter these out of the system, but the liver can only do so much. Most people's livers are overtaxed. Many of these chemicals enter the bloodstream to cause havoc in the body. Once in the bloodstream, it becomes the job of the immune system to destroy or remove them, but an overtaxed immune system can only do so much as well. For this reason, it is best to minimize or avoid processed foods altogether. As the expression goes, "Think outside the box," particularly with processed foods, to avoid overconsumption of additives and preservatives that your body really doesn't need.

- **Decrease or avoid the consumption of antibiotics and hormones.** Perhaps it's no coincidence that the rise in cancer corresponds to the rise of many unnatural chemicals found in our foods today. One topic of concern is the proliferation of pharmacological substances found in our protein sources today. To stop the spread of disease among cattle, chicken, turkeys, and even fish farmed in hatcheries, these animals are given massive amounts of hormones and antibiotics. Although some chemicals pass through, many of them are stored in the animals' muscle tissue, which is then eaten by unsuspecting consumers, whether it's bought in the grocery store or served on a plate in a restaurant. Antibiotics can have an adverse effect on the intestinal flora in your GI tract (killing the much-needed friendly bacteria called *acidophilus*). A significant decrease in acidophilus lays the groundwork for the yeast infection caused by *Candida. Candida*, it should be noted, is suggested by some to be the underlying cause of fibromyalgia and chronic fatigue syndrome.

- **Consume a good supply and balance of omega-3s (cold-water fish and flax seed oil) and omega-6s (vegetable oils).** There are two essential fatty acids that the body cannot produce and must consume from outside sources. Ironically, there is no mention of these two essential fatty acids on the current food guide pyramid. Although the merits of omega-3 oils have been known for decades, surprisingly few people are aware that omega-3 is used in the synthesis of prostaglandins, whose primary role is as an anti-inflammatory agent. Long ago, cold-water fish were considered brain food. What was once considered an old wives' tale now turns out to be quite true, as omega-3s are considered an essential aspect of brain tissue (which is composed mostly of fatty tissue). The American diet is heavy in omega-6s and virtually nonexistent in omega-3s. The suggested balance between these two is a ratio of 2:1 (omega-6 to omega-3).

- **Decrease intake of saturated fats (meat and dairy products).** Current research suggests that a diet high in saturated fat is associated with higher levels of cholesterol. But here is another interesting fact. When fats are digested and transported to the liver, they cannot travel via the bloodstream until they get to the liver. Instead, they have to be transported via the lymphatic system. In his book *Spontaneous Healing,* Andrew Weil states that a diet high in fats tends to preoccupy the immune system with energy devoted to this, thus decreasing the efficiency of the immune system. Balance is the key.

- **Decrease or avoid intake of transfatty acids (partially hydrogenated oils).** Fats that are liquid at room temperature are called *lipids.* Lipids are prone to becoming rancid when they are subjected to heat and light. Researchers figured out a way to decrease rancidity by changing the molecular structure of lipids to make them solid at room temperature. The process is known as *hydrogenation,* and today these fats are known as *partially hydrogenated oils* or *transfatty acids.* Transfatty acids are anything but natural. The current joke about transfatty acids is that the reason they prolong shelf life is that bacteria won't go near them. We should be as smart. Transfatty acids tend to destroy cell membranes by blocking the gates that allow nutrients to go in and waste products to leave. When cells become toxic, cancer is not far behind. Transfatty acids, found in most baked goods such as cereal, cookies, and tortilla shells, are associated with both coronary heart disease and cancer, and perhaps scores of other diseases we don't know yet. They act like free radicals and should be avoided at all costs.

- **Eat a variety of food colors (fruits and vegetables with bioflavinoids).** In Eastern traditions, it is suggested to eat foods (fruits and veggies) with a wide variety of colors. Not only does food provide energy, but the colors also provide energy to the body's core energy centers (chakras). Known as the *rainbow diet,* food colors are thought to play an important role in the vitality and health of the organs associated with each chakra region: cranberry juice for urinary tract infection, tomatoes for prostate health, bilberries for the eyes, and so forth. In the mid- to late 1990s, food researchers discovered that bioflavinoids, a nonnutrient associated with food color, contained an active ingredient to help prevent cancer. The real message here is to eat a good variety of fruits and vegetables (organic whenever possible).

- **Consume a good balance of foods with proper pH.** The body's acid/alkaline balance is very delicate. Although it had been assumed that by the time food particles have been digested for absorption, they do not disturb this balance, this assumption is now being questioned. Recent discoveries suggest that cancerous tumors are more likely to grow in an acidic environment. Many processed and pasteurized foods are noted as being acidic, thus tipping the scales toward a body more prone to cancer. Proponents of raw foods (fruits and veggies) suggest that this type of diet helps the body regain its balance toward the magic number 7 on the acid/alkaline scale. This might be something to consider for those people who have cancer.

- **Replenish nutrients consumed by the stress response.** The stress response (fight or flight) demands energy, in the form of both carbohydrates (glucose) and fats (lipids). If you are experiencing chronic stress, more than likely you are using and possibly depleting a host of essential nutrients. To have these nutrients available for use, a whole series of metabolic reactions are necessary, which require vitamins and minerals. The following are believed to be involved with energy metabolism and thus need to be replaced on a regular basis under stress: B complex (B_6, B_{12}) vitamin C, magnesium, chromium, copper, iron, and zinc.

- **Decrease consumption of simple sugars.** It is believed that the average person consumes two to three times his or her body weight in refined sugar each year. Perhaps it's human nature to have a sweet tooth; however, as the saying goes, everything in moderation. A diet high in refined sugar sets the stage for many health problems. Aside from overtaxing the pancreas to regulate blood sugar levels with the release of insulin, it is suggested that cancer cells thrive on a high-simple-sugar diet. Some reports suggest that refined sugar also decreases white blood cell count. All of this implies that a diet high in refined sugar is a threat to your immune system.

- **Decrease or avoid excitotoxins.** As noted in the critically acclaimed book *Excitotoxins,* aspartame and monosodium glutamate (MSG) inhibit brain function by crossing the blood–brain barrier to affect cognitive functions, including response time, decision-making, attention span, and memory. Pilots for several national airlines are forbidden to drink any beverage or food (even gum) containing aspartame (Nutrasweet). Current research reveals that when not refrigerated, the two amino acids that combine to form this artificial sweetener go through a chemical reaction resulting in the formation of formaldehyde. In laboratory studies, formaldehyde is shown to compromise the integrity of the immune system. MSG is also cited as an excitotoxin. Due to agreements made with the Food and Drug Administration (FDA), MSG is not listed on food labels as "monosodium glutamate." Rather, it is simply listed as "spice." Read the labels and avoid excitotoxins!

- **Moderate your consumption of alcohol.** A high intake of alcohol (more than two glasses per day) is said to compromise liver and immune function. Current studies reveal that excessive alcohol consumption decreases the efficiency of the immune system, thus making one more vulnerable to the effects of bacteria, viruses, and other pathogens that make their way into the body. Although studies show that red wine can increase levels of HDLs (the good cholesterol) in your blood, moderation is the key to good health.

- **Prepare food in the best way possible.** Even though you may think you are getting an adequate amount of vitamins and minerals, you may be losing these nutrients depending on how you cook your foods. Many vitamins are destroyed with high amounts of heat, which is why microwave ovens are not recommended. Veggies should be steamed, not cooked in water, because the water-soluble vitamins and minerals are leached out and then thrown down the drain. A new health food trend these days is the raw food diet, with an emphasis on eating vegetables and fruits uncooked so that the full array of vitamins, minerals, and enzymes is available to the human body for absorption.

- **Eat organic produce and free-range meats whenever possible.** Because of the increasing presence of hormones and antibiotics in beef, chicken, and other sources of animal products, it is highly recommended to eat animal products without these. The term *free range* was introduced to convey a sense that animals were free to roam and eat natural vegetation. Check with your butcher, because this is not always the case. With the introduction of mad cow disease and chronic wasting disease in the past few years, eating organic has taken on a whole new importance. Buffalo is a good choice, because to date, this is one animal that hasn't been tinkered with.

- **Avoid genetically modified organisms (GMOs), which are known to promote allergy problems.** For centuries farmers have experimented with plants through grafts and cross-fertilization to come up with new variations of plant species, from fruits (seedless oranges) to flowers (the variegated tulip). It wasn't until the late 1990s that scientists began to pull genes from one species (e.g., flounder) and place them in the DNA of another (e.g., tomato), hence playing God with our food supply. We now have super-tomatoes that can withstand a cold frost. The problem comes when people with an allergy to one food (e.g., nuts) find themselves having an acute allergic reaction to a food they previously were able to eat (e.g., corn) because of genetic engineering. A dramatic rise in food allergies has been linked to a corresponding influx of genetically modified foods. Current estimates suggest that over half of the food bought in your local grocery store is genetically modified, yet due to political overtures by food corporations to the FDA, you will never see this on a food label. GMOs are a burden to the immune system, which doesn't recognize these unnatural concoctions. Allergic reactions are a message from your immune system that something is terribly amiss. Again, organic foods are your safest bet.

- **Use herbal therapies to boost the immune system.** Long before the Bayer company patented aspirin, herbs were (and in many countries still are) the primary source of healing to bring the body back to a sense of homeostasis. Today pharmaceutical companies are spending millions to replicate the active ingredients of various herbs, yet traditional herbalists will tell you that the best results occur by going directly to the plant itself. If that's not possible, consider tinctures or teas.

   Herbs that are known to help boost or activate the immune system include astragalus; shiitake, maitake, and reishi mushrooms; tumeric; and echinacea. Milk thistle is also good for helping the liver cleanse toxins from the body; in this day and age, everyone could use milk thistle.

   Linda Whitedove is a traditional herbalist in Boulder, Colorado, and a consultant for Home Grown Herbals. She is also the first herbalist hired by her local hospital in the Department of Integrative Medicine to work alongside physicians. As a guest speaker in my nutrition course, Linda had this to say about the connection between herbs and chronic illness: "Not long ago, people used many herbs and spices when preparing foods, such as rosemary, oregano, thyme, coriander, cilantro, and basil. It was the essential oils in these plants which contain many healing properties. Today most people eat out, or eat processed foods. The only natural additive they're getting is sodium and that's not even a spice. My recommendation is to cook more of your own meals and reintroduce the use of more fresh spices."

Best Benefits of Sound Nutritional Habits

After reading this chapter you may wonder if any food is safe to eat. The answer is yes! In today's market, organic foods offer the best source of healthy nutrients for the body. Remember, the body is resilient and desires a state of wholeness. Given the chance, it will do all it can to return to a state of wholeness. This means that you can still enjoy an ice cream cone every now and then. If, however, you or a loved one is diagnosed with a chronic disease, you may wish to pull in the reins and guide your eating habits with several of the suggestions provided in this chapter. Here is a final tip to help keep your body in balance: Consider eating one meal a day for your immune system.

Additional Resources

Blaylock, E. *Excitotoxins: The Taste That Kills.* Santa Fe: Health Press, 1994.
Lyman, H. *The Mad Cowboy.* New York: Scribner, 2001.
Robins, J. *The Food Revolution.* Berkeley, CA: Conari Press, 2001.
Rountree, R., and Colman, C. *Immunotics.* New York: Putnam Books, 2000.
Scholsser, E. *Fast Food Nation.* Boston: Houghton Mifflin, 2001.
Simon, C. *Cancer and Nutrition.* Garden City, NY: Avery Publishing, 1994.
Somer, E. *Food and Mood,* 2nd ed. New York: Owl Books, 1999.
Teitel, M., and Wilson, K. *Genetically Engineered Food.* Rochester, VT: Park Street Press, 1999.
Weil, A. *Eating Well for Optimal Health.* New York: Knopf Books, 2000.
Weil, A. *Spontaneous Healing.* New York: Knopf Books, 1995.

Exercise 21.1 Stress-Related Eating Behaviors

Please read the following statements and circle the appropriate answer. Then tally the total to determine your score from the key.

	4 = Always	3 = Often	2 = Sometimes	1 = Rarely	0 = Never

1.	I tend to skip breakfast on a regular basis.	4	3	2	1	0
2.	On average, two or three meals are prepared outside the home.	4	3	2	1	0
3.	I drink more than one cup of coffee or tea a day.	4	3	2	1	0
4.	I tend to drink more than one soda/pop per day.	4	3	2	1	0
5.	I commonly snack between meals.	4	3	2	1	0
6.	When in a hurry, I usually eat at fast food places.	4	3	2	1	0
7.	I tend to snack while watching television.	4	3	2	1	0
8.	I tend to put salt on my food before tasting it.	4	4	2	1	0
9.	I drink fewer than eight glasses of water a day.	4	3	2	1	0
10.	I tend to satisfy my sweet tooth daily.	4	3	2	1	0
11.	When preparing meals at home, I usually don't cook from scratch.	4	3	2	1	0
12.	Honestly, my eating habits lean toward fast, junk, processed foods.	4	3	2	1	0
13.	I eat fewer than 4 to 5 servings of fresh vegetables per day.	4	3	2	1	0
14.	I drink at least one glass of wine, beer, or other alcohol a day.	4	3	2	1	0
15.	My meals are eaten sporadically throughout the day rather than at regularly scheduled times.	4	3	2	1	0
16.	I don't usually cook with fresh herbs and spices.	4	3	2	1	0
17.	I usually don't make a habit of eating organic fruits and veggies.	4	3	2	1	0
18.	My biggest meal of the day is usually eaten after 7:00 P.M.	4	3	2	1	0
19.	For the most part, my vitamins and minerals come from the foods I eat.	4	3	2	1	0
20.	Artificial sweeteners are in many of the foods I eat.	4	3	2	1	0

Total Score

Score   A score of more than 20 points indicates that your eating behaviors are not conducive to reducing stress. A score of more than 30 suggests that your eating habits may seriously compromise the integrity of your immune system.

Exercise 21.2 The Rainbow Diet

Food color is more important than having a nice presentation on your dinner plate. Each color holds a specific vibration in the spectrum of light. When this is combined with the nutrient value of food, it can help to enhance the health of the physical body. In the science of subtle energies, each of the body's primary chakras is associated with a specific color (see the following chart). It is thought that eating fruits and vegetables associated with the color of various chakras provides healthy energy to that specific region. For example, women with urinary tract infections (root chakra) are recommended to drink cranberry juice (red). Diabetics with macular problems are recommended to eat blueberries and take the herb bilberry (blue). Moreover, recent research suggests that the active ingredients that give fruits and vegetables their color are bioflavinoids, which are now thought to help prevent cancer. Regardless of Eastern philosophies or Western science, the bottom line is to eat a good variety of fruits and vegetables.

The following list identifies the seven chakras, their respective body regions, and the color associated with each chakra or region. List five fruits, veggies, or herbs for each color.

Chakra	Body Region	Color	Food Choices
7. Crown	Pineal	Purple	_____ _____ _____
6. Brow	Pituitary	Indigo	_____ _____
5. Throat	Thymus	Aqua blue	_____ _____ _____
4. Heart	Heart	Green	_____ _____ _____
3. Solar plexus	Adrenals	Yellow	_____ _____ _____
2. Navel	Spleen	Orange	_____ _____ _____
1. Root	Gonads	Red	_____ _____ _____

Exercise 21.2

CHAPTER

22

Physical Exercise: Flushing Out the Stress Hormones

How much happiness is gained and how much misery escaped
by frequent and challenging exertion of the body.
—Anonymous

Ageless Wisdom of Physical Exercise

In his book *The Best Alternative Medicine,* acclaimed stress management expert Kenneth Pelletier notes that the term *alternative medicine* encompasses over 600 modalities, from acupuncture to zero balancing. Of all these modalities, physical exercise has been the most researched to prove its efficacy in promoting health and well-being. Pelletier goes so far as to say that "Exercise is more important for health than the most exotic forms of CAM, and a great many forms of Western conventional medicine."

The field of exercise physiology is relatively new as an academic discipline when compared with the fields of mathematics and physics, yet the information garnered from over six decades of research has proven to be invaluable with regard to physical health and longevity. The bottom line is that physical exercise is essential for health and well-being.

In the early 1970s coronary heart disease made headline news as the nation's number one killer. Sadly, more than three decades later, coronary heart disease is still ranked as the number one killer in the United States. At times, it appears that Americans have grown numb to these statistics. Today, exercise formulas can be found on cereal boxes and infomercials, yet despite the best efforts by health care educators and practioners, not only has coronary heart disease remained the leading cause of death, but Americans have grown fatter and more sedentary and have contracted a whole host of chronic diseases that were unknown 30 years ago, such as Epstein-Barr (chronic fatigue syndrome) and fibromyalgia.

What we now know about exercise is that the body needs periodic bouts of physical stress to maintain a proper level of health in every physiological system, including the cardiovascular system, the immune system, the nervous system, and the digestive system. Ironically, physical exercise is a form of stress: In no uncertain terms, physical exercise is the fulfillment of the fight-or-flight response. In the course of exercise, there is an increase in heart rate, blood pressure, respiration, perspiration, and muscle tension. The physical demands for energy metabolism initiate a cascade of hormones and enzymes for energy production.

Physical exercise isn't the fountain of youth, but it does do something that other relaxation techniques don't do as well. Under stress your body produces a flood of stress hormones, including cortisol, vasopressin, and aldosterone. Because these same hormones are produced during exercise, they are used for their intended purpose rather than causing ultimate wear and tear on the body. Furthermore, upon the completion of your workout, exercise acts to flush these hormones out of the body. Perhaps the best effect of exercise is what is known as the *parasympathetic rebound effect,* in which, after exercise, heart rate, blood pressure, and breathing cycles return to a lower resting rate than before exercise. In a day and age where physical threats are few and far between, the actual need to run or fight may seem rather antiquated. Nothing could be further from the truth. Mental, emotional, and spiritual stressors have replaced physical stressors, and although you cannot really run away from these problems, cardiovascular exercise has proven to be a valuable means to deal with these kinds of problems as well. Simply by bringing the body back into balance, the other components are positively affected.

Energy Balance

It is hard to walk by the checkout stand at the local grocer and not notice the latest fad diet grabbing the headlines. Low protein, high protein, low carb, low fat, high density, low toxins, low calories—the list is nearly endless. Quite frankly, there is no one diet for everyone, and research reveals that diets have a rather poor success rate. This much we know about diets: To maintain your weight, the number of calories consumed must equal the number of calories expended. Weight loss comes from fewer calories eaten than expended, and weight gain comes from more calories eaten than burned. This is the science behind what is referred to as *energy balance.* The body in all its amazing wonder and wisdom knows enough to store calories that may be needed later for fight or flight.

The simple truth is that excess carbohydrates that are not broken down into glucose and used for energy are stored as fat (adipose tissue, or what some people refer to as *cellulite*). Moreover, protein that is not used for refurbishing cell structure and other metabolic demands, such as hormone and enzyme synthesis, is also stored as fat. Fats and lipids that are not needed for metabolic demands are also stored as adipose tissue. Given the supersize mentality of our fast food nation and the sedentary lifestyle of the couch potato culture, it's no wonder that obesity is such a problem. The bottom line is that there is a huge imbalance in the energy balance.

Cortisol and Weight Gain

Is there a connection between chronic stress and obesity? Perhaps! There is new speculation that cortisol, a hormone released from the adrenal gland during the stress response, may be related to the steady accumulation of body fat in one's lifetime. Given the amount of chronic stressors each American experiences today, and the incredible rate of obesity, there may indeed be a connection. As discussed in Chapter 2, cortisol is responsible for a number of metabolic activities for fight or flight, including ensuring the release of glucose and free fatty acids into the blood for short- and long-term energy. If a person chooses not to fight or flee (anaerobic or aerobic exercise), watching hours of television instead, then the body may redistribute these energy nutrients as adipose tissue (fat). Additional speculation suggests that cortisol may be a principal hormone for regulating appetite under stress to ensure that there is an adequate supply of both short- and long-term energy. It is well known that stress (acute and chronic) raises the blood sugar levels of type II diabetics, hence making an exercise program all the more important for this target population.

A training program that includes regular cardiovascular exercise helps to ensure that the hormones synthesized and released as a result of chronic stress are used for their intended purpose and then flushed out of the system with other metabolic waste products. Exercise also burns calories, making this a desired health package for everyone. It's no secret that the marketplace is becoming flooded with drugs and herbal products to minimize or block the effect of cortisol on appetite and weight gain. However, drugs and supplements can have several side effects, throwing your body's biochemistry out of balance. When performed correctly, the short- and long-term effects of exercise restore balance to mind, body, and spirit with no harmful side effects—and exercise is free.

The Mind-Body-Spirit Connection

From cereal boxes to infomercials, physical exercise is promoted as the best way to maintain physical fitness. Although this is quite true, there is a whole other side to exercise that receives far less notoriety, yet is equally important: the impact of exercise, specifically cardiovascular exercise, on the mind. Ask anyone who has maintained a cardiovascular fitness program for any length of time and they will tell you that what first began as a fitness regimen soon became a mental health program. Rhythmical activities such as running, swimming, walking, or bike riding not only allow for emotional catharsis but also become a type of meditation. The continuous deep breathing cycle, repetitive physical motion, or perhaps both act as a mantra for increased concentration and awareness, thus giving the mind a sense of peace as well. With greater mental clarity comes greater access to the right-brain cognitive skills. Imagination, acceptance, receptivity, intuition, and other right-brain functions are highly accessible, making an aerobic activity session truly a holistic modality.

There are even more benefits. When the phrase "runner's high" was first coined, nonrunners thought this was a marketing strategy to win them over. It took science a while to catch up with psychology, but evidence now reveals that the brain produces a series of neurochemicals called *neuropeptides* with a unique opiate-like quality. The beta-endorphin was named as the primary chemical agent that produces a euphoric sensation when one is running, swimming, walking, or performing any other activity with the proper intensity, frequency, and duration.

How to Incorporate Physical Exercise into Your Life Routine

In simple terms, there are two types of exercise: anaerobic and aerobic. Although these terms have become household words to some, a quick review is necessary. *Anaerobic exercise* involves short, intense bursts of energy that typically last no longer than a few minutes, usually less. Because the supply of both blood and oxygen is deficient, muscle contractions are the result of stored energy in the muscle by way of a chemical process known as ADP. The word *aerobic* means "in the presence of oxygen," and the energy demands from this type of work require oxygen, delivered by the blood, for muscle contraction. Because the redistribution of blood from the body's core (GI tract) to the periphery (arms and legs) takes about five minutes, the first part of an aerobic workout involves some anaerobic work.

Examples of anaerobic work include weight lifting, sprints, and isometric exercises. Aerobic exercise, also referred to as "cardio" exercise, includes jogging, walking, swimming, cycling, spinning, and any other activity in which the supply of oxygen meets the demand of the work involved. Using a stress metaphor, anaerobic work is used in the fight response, whereas aerobic work is employed in the flight response. Ideally, a well-balanced or holistic exercise program includes a combination of both anaerobic work (muscle strength) and aerobic work (cardiovascular endurance). Exercises 22.1 and 22.2 are provided to assist you in putting together a cardiovascular fitness program.

The All-or-None Conditioning Principle

It's no secret that laziness is a force to be reckoned with in the American lifestyle. Given the chance, most people would rather sit and rest than get up and exercise. Mark Twain once said, "When I feel the urge to exercise, I lay down till it goes away." Sadly, his thought on this matter is not unique. Perhaps for this reason, researchers in the field of exercise physiology have studied the dynamics of exercise to determine the minimal amount required to gain the coveted health benefits. The dynamics involved include four factors: intensity, frequency, duration of exercise, and mode of exercise. To gain the best benefits of exercise, one must employ all of these or receive none of the benefits, hence the name all-or-none conditioning principle.

Intensity. Intensity is the challenge placed on the specific physiological system being worked (e.g., cardiovascular, musculoskeletal). Intensity of exercise is typically expressed as one's target heart rate for cardiovascular work (75% of one's maximal heart rate), whereas pounds, reps (repetitions), and sets are the means to determine the level of intensity for muscle strength.

Frequency. Frequency is determined by the number of workouts per week. The minimum recommended number of workouts per week is three, with usually a day of rest in between.

Duration. Duration is measured by the amount of time spent exercising. The minimum duration per workout is 20 minutes, or 30 minutes if you add a 5-minute warm-up and a 5-minute cool-down period.

Mode of Exercise. Different types of exercise are designed to challenge different physiological systems of the body. Weight training will not enhance one's cardiovascular endurance very well, nor will jogging develop muscle strength, although it will help tone muscles. The mode of exercise is specific for the benefits you wish to gain.

Phases of a Workout. Regardless of which mode of exercise you choose to do, experts agree that every workout should follow the progression of these three steps:

1. **Warm-up period:** A period of five to ten minutes during which blood flow is allowed to redistribute to the large muscle groups, followed by light stretching. When you start breaking a sweat, then a proper warm-up has been achieved.

2. **Stimulus period:** A period of 20 minutes (or more) in which the intensity of the activity is reached and maintained for the duration of the exercise period.

3. **Cool-down period:** A five- to ten-minute period of decreased intensity that allows for a gradual shift in the flow of blood from the large muscle groups to the body's core. Most exercise physiologists insist that this is as crucial as the stimulus period, for without a proper cool down, complications may arise with the cardiovascular system.

A Word About Soreness and Injuries

In exercise circles, there are two kinds of pain: good pain and bad pain. Good pain (a dull pain) is when muscles are sore; the soreness comes from lack of use, and typically disappears within hours to a day or so. Bad pain (sharp pain) is a sensation generating from the joints and doesn't lessen in a few hours. Sprains, strains, and fractures fall in this category. This type of pain may require medical attention.

Additional Tips for a Successful Exercise Program

- **Start cautiously and progress moderately with your exercise routine.** The biggest problem with exercise programs is that people do too much too soon, resulting in injuries. For this reason, sage advice reminds people to start slow and work their way up to the routine they wish to maintain. Most people begin exercise programs not to keep their heart or bones healthy, but to lose weight. Although exercise is a great means to do so, the simple truth is that pounds don't disappear overnight. The recommended amount of weight loss, so that it stays off, is about one to two pounds per week. Typically, anything more than this is due to water loss and will return with rehydration.

- **Select an activity you really enjoy.** Because obesity (not to mention coronary heart disease) is such a concern in American culture, the focus of attention is on cardiovascular exercise, and for a good reason. The good news is that there are many different types of cardiovascular exercise, including walking. It's best to pick an activity that you like or think you like and begin with that. It's also important to have a backup activity in the event that an injury prevents you from continuing with your original activity or you simply get bored with the sport. Most people quit their exercise programs out of boredom, so variety is also a good aspect to consider.

- **Select a specific time of day to exercise.** A routine is essential for maintaining a healthy exercise program. Selecting a specific time each day to exercise (even if you only do it three times per week) helps create healthy boundaries. Some people consider exercise a lower priority than work, and hence when work piles up, the workout gets canceled at a time when it's probably the most important. Establish healthy boundaries with your exercise routine and stick to them.

- **Exercise with the best clothes and equipment.** You don't have to spend a lot of money for exercise equipment (although many people do). Perhaps the most important thing is a good pair of workout shoes. Although it might seem that spending $100 on a pair of running shoes is outrageous, consider that a pair of good shoes is really an insurance policy against injuries. It's worth the extra money to ensure that you don't get hurt during a workout. If you begin to get sharp joint pain, the first thing to consider is a new pair of exercise shoes.

- **Initiate a support exercise group.** Let's face it, exercise is work, and it's easy to quit work when you're working out by yourself. It's harder to back out when you have made a commitment with others to do it together. Working out with a friend makes the time go by quicker, and camaraderie can be a great motivation to stay with your program. If you are having a hard time getting or staying motivated, consider inviting some friends to join you.

- **Set personal fitness goals for yourself.** Even the best exercise routines can become monotonous without a goal to obtain. Some people use road races as personal goals. Others set personal health goals (e.g., lower cholesterol, lower resting heart rate). Having a personal goal serves as great intrinsic motivation to get out of the house when other things seem to distract you from exercising.

- **Take care of and prevent injuries.** An injury can become a stressor quite quickly. If you are using exercise to reduce stress, this is the last thing you want to have happen. If you feel joint soreness at any time during an exercise period, this is the time to stop. If you feel a general soreness after a workout (which is to be expected), then give yourself a day's rest before starting exercising again.

Your Body's Natural Rhythm

Your body runs on a natural clock. Science calls this clock *circadian rhythms,* and it has been the topic of much interest over the past 100 years. We know that the body not only craves exercise and relaxation, but also craves a routine schedule. Apparently, eating, sleeping, doing exercise, and other lifestyle habits tend to throw off the clock. When the clock is thrown off, our health suffers. Living out of a routine becomes a chronological stress. Exercise 22.3 invites you to check your circadian rhythms to determine if they promote or detract from your health.

Developing Your Mastery of Exercise as a Relaxation Technique

Exercise as a relaxation technique is one of the best ways to bring balance back into your life. Walking is the most underrated activity, and almost everyone can walk. Any other sports require some skill, yet skills increase with practice. Although the best benefits of a single bout of exercise can be felt almost immediately, research shows that it takes about six to eight weeks to notice the more significant changes, such as weight loss, decreased cholesterol, and so forth. To really gain the full effects of physical exercise, your exercise routine must be as much a part of your life as taking a shower and brushing your teeth.

Best Benefits of Physical Exercise

If you could take all the benefits of physical exercise and manufacture it into a pill, it would be the most popular pharmaceutical in the world. But you cannot. Our bodies were designed for exercise. They were not designed to sit in front of a computer screen all day or a television all night. Physical exercise is actually good stress for the body; the body requires it to keep things in balance. By not exercising, the cardiovascular system becomes less efficient, bones begin to demineralize, energy balance is compromised, and several other metabolic processes become unbalanced.

The benefits of exercise have to be gained from the actual work of exercise, and exercise is work, but the payoffs are incredible. Here is a short list of the beneficial effects of exercise:

- Increased immune system function

- Increased quality of sleep

- Decreased resting heart rate and blood pressure

- Increased mental alertness and concentration skills

- A decrease of the aging process

Additional Resources

Anderson, B. *Stretching*. Bolinas, CA: Shelter Publications, 1980.

Bingham, J. *No Need for Speed: A Beginner's Guide to the Joy of Running*. Emmaus, PA: Rodale Press, 2002.

Green, B. *Get with the Program*. New York: Simon & Schuster, 2002.

Kowalchik, C. *The Complete Book of Running for Women*. New York: Pocket Books, 1999.

Meyers, C. *Walking: A Complete Guide to the Complete Exercise*. New York: Random House, 1992.

Pelletier, K. *The Best Alternative Medicine: What Works? What Does Not?* New York: Simon & Schuster, 2000.

Exercise 22.1 Determining Your Target Heart Rate

Using the formula below, calculate your estimated target heart rate. Typically, target heart rate is 75% of one's maximal heart rate. The number 220 is a constant estimate for everyone. If your fitness level is poor, consider an initial target heart rate to be 65%. Once you have estimated your target heart rate for your cardiovascular workout, check your heart rate by taking your pulse to see if indeed you are within the target range of intensity that will produce the beneficial effects of regular rhythmical exercise.

Predicted Target Heart Rate Formula

220 (Constant)

− Age

_____

=

_____

=

× 0.75 (Intensity)

_____

=   (Your target heart rate for cardiovascular exercise)
÷ 6 for a 10-second count

Example

220 − 20 = 200 × 0.75 = 150 beats/min
÷ 6 = 25 beats/min for a 10-second count

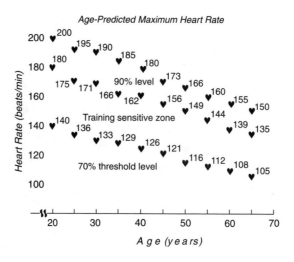

Exercise 22.2 Personal Fitness Program Training Log

Week of: _____

Target heart rate: _____

Exercise Schedule	Sun	Mon	Tue	Wed	Thu	Fri	Sat
Date:							
Time:							
Exercise mode (e.g., cardio, weights, flexibility stretching, etc.)							
Warm-up period (minutes)							
Warm-up exercises							
Intensity (e.g., heart rate)							
Duration of exercise period							
Cool-down period							
Cool-down exercises							
Personal comments							
Other:							

Exercise 22.2

Exercise 22.3 Your Circadian Rhythms

Your body runs on a 24+ hour clock, based on the earth spinning on its axis around the sun. Research shows that people who keep to a regular schedule tend to be healthier (fewer colds, flus, etc.) than those whose lifestyle behaviors tend to be more erratic, because these tend to stress your body. In this exercise you are asked to monitor your lifestyle behaviors based on the time of day that these occur for the period of a full week.

Week of _____

Circadian Rhythms	Sun	Mon	Tue	Wed	Thu	Fri	Sat
Time you awake each morning							
Time you go to bed							
Time you fall asleep							
Time that you eat breakfast							
Time that you eat lunch							
Time that you eat dinner							
Times that you snack							
Time of bowel movements							
Time that you exercise							
Time that you have sex							
Other regular activities							
Other regular activities							

Observations   What observations can you make from charting your body functions?

_____

_____

_____

_____

_____

_____

_____

_____

CHAPTER

23

Additional Relaxation Techniques

That the birds fly overhead, this you cannot stop.
That the birds make a nest in your hair, this you can prevent.
—Ancient Chinese proverb

Tai Chi: Poetry in Motion

There is a life force of subtle energy that surrounds and permeates us all. This energy goes by many names. The Chinese call it *chi*. To move in unison with this energy is to move as freely as running water. A congestion or distortion of one's life energy ultimately leads to disease and illness. Therefore, the goal in life is to be in harmony with the flow of chi, because this promotes tranquility and a sense of being one with the universe. This is the essence of Tai Chi, a moving meditation that dates back to ancient China. It provides a means to create and maintain this harmony and balance with the vital life force of universal energy and the natural world of which we are very much a part.

The words *Tai Chi* can best be translated to mean the "Supreme Ultimate," a symbolic representation of balance, power, and enlightenment. Although it is often called the softest of the martial arts, those who study this art form know that above all else, it is a discipline that unites mind, body, and spirit. The art of self-defense comes much later, if at all. Mental, emotional, and spiritual stress can block the flow of chi through the body. It is the progression of moves consciously executed with precision and finesse in the practice of Tai Chi that works to unblock and regulate the life force of universal energy, hence restoring health. To see Tai Chi practiced by a master is nothing less than poetry in motion, which is why it is often called a moving meditation. The majority of people who practice Tai Chi perform it not as a means of self-defense, but rather as an exercise to promote health and vitality.

The underlying premise of Tai Chi is to learn to move with the flow of energy rather than fight or resist it. In everyday life this philosophy translates to the concept of going with the flow of things you cannot control, rather than wasting or depleting your personal energy. The philosophy of Tai Chi is based on the taoist concept of yin/yang, where opposites come together to form a whole (e.g., soft/hard, masculine/feminine, hot/cold). However, any good Tai Chi instructor will tell you that the taoist path is not one of extremes, but rather the middle road where one strives to live in balance and harmony with all aspects of one's life.

To learn this relaxation technique correctly, it is best to find a teacher whose philosophy of Tai Chi matches yours (e.g., self-defense vs. healthy vitality). Books or videos may serve as a good supplement, but they rarely provide a sound method of quality instruction. As any good Tai Chi instructor will tell you, once you have learned the sequence of steps, it will take years, if not decades, to fully master them. If you have an interest or curiosity regarding this technique, consider checking your yellow page directory or newspaper community listings, or do an Internet search for classes in your area. When you find a course, ask if you can observe or participate in one class to get a feel for the instructor and decide from there if you wish to continue.

Progressive Muscular Relaxation: Decreasing Muscle Tension

Nearly all relaxation techniques, from massage and meditation to yoga and Tai Chi, trace their origins back to the ancient cultures of Asia. One exception is the technique known as progressive muscular relaxation (PMR), which was created by an American physician several decades ago. As a physician, Edmund Jacobson noted that virtually all his patients who were sick appeared to have one common symptom: muscle tension. So concerned was he about this phenomenon that he decided to create a muscle relaxation technique that would help alleviate tense muscles and possibly restore one to health.

Jacobson designed a systematic approach to reducing muscle tension, whereby a person begins at the top of his or her head and isolates a specific muscle group. He or she then begins a process of tensing and relaxing each muscle group, moving from head to toe, so that the individual can recognize the difference between tension and relaxation. By doing so, the desired effect is to be aware of muscle tension that may exist and work to release it through progressive relaxation. Progressive muscular relaxation has proven to be a beneficial technique for people with insomnia, TMJD, and even those who wish to quit smoking. Exercise 23.1 is a modified example of this technique.

Clinical Biofeedback: Technology as a Mirror

As we have seen throughout this book, the mind holds an incredible power to influence the body—in both positive and negative ways. Clinical biofeedback is a technique that enhances the mind's power of healing through the assistance of technology, which simply amplifies one or more of the body's physiological parameters so the mind can get a better picture of what is going on inside. Through the wonderful complexities of biochemistry, the human body gives off a number of vibrations of electrical impulses. Monitoring various physiological indices such as heart rate, blood pressure, muscle tension, brain waves, body temperature, and blood flow allows technology to mirror specific aspects of human physiology. In doing so, the mind can intercept these stress-prone areas (e.g., muscle tension) and help the body return to a deeper state of homeostasis.

Through the use of electrodes, transducer, a television monitor, and a certified biofeedback specialist, an individual is taught to observe an aspect or area of his or her body and then, through self-regulation, consciously decrease activity to this area with the help of the television monitor (or stereo speakers).

Clinical biofeedback has been instrumental in helping people treat and heal a range of physical problems in which stress manifests, such as tension headaches, migraine headaches, lower-back pain, TMJD, hypertension, Raynaud's disease, and many, many others. For this reason it is regarded as one of the premier modalities of complementary medicine. If this is something you wish to explore, consider locating a certified biofeedback specialist in your area.

Additional Resources

Huang, A. *Complete Tai Chi*. Boston: Tuttle Publishing, 1993.
The Journey to Wild Divine: The Passage (a biofeedback video game). The Wild Divine Project. 1-866-594-WILD. www.wilddivine.com.

Exercise 23.1 Progressive Muscular Relaxation

The following exercise is a slight variation of Jacobson's original technique, which divides muscle contractions into three intensities—100, 50, and 5 percent—of five seconds' duration, followed by the relaxation phase of five to ten seconds' duration after each contraction. By sensing the differences between muscle contraction intensities, you become more aware of your muscle-tension levels over the course of a day. The instructions here are written to be read yourself before you perform the technique, or to be read by a friend or colleague while you perform the exercise. Included are three muscle groups (the face, neck and shoulders, and hands); however, you can expand this to include your abdominal area, upper legs, buttocks, calf muscles, and feet as well. Before you begin, find a comfortable position (preferably on your back on a carpeted floor), loosen any constrictive clothing, kick off your shoes, take several slow, comfortable, deep breaths, and simply begin to unwind.

Face

1. Tense the muscles of the forehead and eyes, as if you were pulling all your facial muscles to the center of your nose (Fig. 23.1). Pull really tight, as tight as you can, and hold it. Feel the tension you create in these muscles, especially the forehead and eyes. Now relax and exhale. Feel the absence of tension in these muscles, how loose and calm they feel. Try to compare this feeling of relaxation with the tension just produced.

2. Now, contract the same muscles, but this time at 50 percent the intensity, and hold it. Then relax and exhale. Feel how relaxed those muscles are. Compare this feeling to that during the last contraction. This comparison should make the muscles even more relaxed.

3. Finally, contract the same facial muscles slightly, at only 5 percent intensity. This is like feeling a slight warm breeze on your forehead and cheeks. Hold it. And relax. Take a comfortably slow and deep breath and, as you exhale, feel how relaxed the muscles are.

Figure 23.1

Shoulders

1. Concentrate on the muscles of your shoulders and isolate these from the surrounding neck and upper arm muscles. Take a moment to sense the muscles of the deltoid region. Notice any degree of residual tension. (The shoulder muscles can harbor a lot of undetected muscle tension, resulting in stiffness. Quite literally, your shoulders carry the weight of all your thoughts, the weight of your world.) Now consciously tense the muscles of your shoulders really tight, as tight as you can, and hold it, even tighter, and hold it (Fig. 23.2). Now relax these muscles and sense the tension disappear completely. Sense the difference between how these muscles feel now and how they felt during contraction.

2. Once again, contract these same muscles, but this time at half the intensity. Hold the tension, keep holding; now completely relax these muscles. Sense how relaxed your shoulder muscles are. Compare this feeling with what you felt at 100 percent intensity.

3. Finally, contract these same muscles at only 5 percent, only just sensing clothing touching your shoulder muscles. Hold it, keep holding, and relax. Release any remaining tension so that these muscles are completely loose and relaxed. Feel just how relaxed these muscles are. To enhance this feeling of relaxation, take a comfortably slow, deep breath and sense how relaxed your shoulder muscles have become.

Figure 23.2

Hands and Forearms

1.   Concentrate on the muscles of your hands and forearms. Take a moment to feel these muscles, including your fingers, palms, and wrists. Notice the slightest bit of tension. Now consciously tense the muscles of each hand and forearm really tight by making a fist, as tight as you can, and hold it as if you were hanging on for dear life. Make it even tighter, and hold it. Now release the tension and relax these muscles. Sense the tension disappear completely. Open the palm of each hand slowly, extend your fingers, and let them recoil just a bit. Sense the difference between how relaxed these muscles feel now compared with what you just experienced at 100 percent contraction. They should feel very relaxed.

2.   Now contract these same muscles at a 50 percent contraction. Hold the tension, keep holding, and relax again. Sense how relaxed these muscles are. Compare this feeling of relaxation with what you just felt.

3.   Now, contract these same muscles at only 5 percent, like holding an empty eggshell in the palm of your hand. Now hold it, keep holding, and relax. Release any remaining tension so that these muscles are completely relaxed. Feel just how relaxed these muscles have become. To enhance this feeling of relaxation, take a comfortably slow, deep breath and sense how relaxed your forearm and hand muscles have become.

When you are done, lie comfortably for several moments and sense how your body feels. Take several slow, deep breaths and begin to retain this feeling of deep relaxation throughout your body. When you feel ready, slowly make yourself aware of your surroundings. Then open your eyes to a soft gaze in front of you. If you wish, you can begin to stretch your arms and hands. When you feel ready, sit up and bring yourself back to the full awareness of the room where you find yourself.

PART IV

Designing Your Personal Relaxation Program

CHAPTER

24

Designing Your Personal Relaxation Program

There is an old joke shared among behavioral psychologists that goes like this: "How many psychologists does it take to change a light bulb? Answer: One, but the light bulb really has to want to change." Making changes in our life, whether they be small corrections or a complete about-face, requires more than just an exposure to the concepts, it requires a burning desire and steady discipline, so that the change becomes permanent and not just a passing fancy. Experts who study behavior change note that although people may want an immediate complete makeover, changes that really last begin one habit at a time, until it is fully mastered and incorporated into one's daily routine. This approach may take a little longer, yet the results are more successful because they become part of who you are.

By now, having read this entire book or even just a few chapters, you most likely have a pretty good idea of what aspects of your life need fine-tuning to bring you back to a place of balance. Although you may have already started on some aspects of reducing the stress in your life and working to resolve issues that trigger feelings of anger or fear, it's always a good idea to look at the bigger picture. Exercise 24.1, "Mandala for Personal Health," invites you to organize your stress-relief habits so that all aspects—mind, body, spirit, and emotions—are equally addressed in your strategy to maintain personal balance.

Additional Resources

Mind-Body-Spirit Organizations

Institute of Noetic Sciences, www.noetic.org.
International Society for the Study of Subtle Energies and Energy Medicine, www.issseem.org.
The Omega Institute, www.eomega.org.
The National Wellness Institute, www.nationalwellness.org.
American Holistic Nursing Association, www.ahna.org.
American Holistic Medical Association, www.holisticmedicine.org.

Energy Healing

Wirkus, Mietek. *Bioenergy Healer.* 303-652-1691.
Eden, Donna. *Energy Healing.* Innersource. 800-835-8332.
Hurwitz, Wendy. *Medical Intuitive.* 212-877-2031.

Exercise 24.1 Mandala for Personal Health: Your Holistic Stress Management Strategy

This mandala exercise invites you use this symbol of wholeness as both a reminder of your true self and a compass to help get you there, should you lose your way in the course of daily events and circumstances that tend to cloud your vision and perspective. Using the mandala below, first write your name in the center. Next, keeping in mind that many activities cross the lines between these quadrants, write in each respective quadrant your ideas, skills, techniques, exercises, and habits that allow you to achieve inner peace through the integration, balance, and harmony of mind, body, spirit, and emotions. For example, let's take the quadrant for physical well-being. You might consider writing down ideas for your personal exercise program, new or improved eating habits, sleep habits, and perhaps even acupuncture and a massage. List those things that you either currently do or wish to include in your life routine. When you finish, place the mandala in a place where you can see it regularly, to serve as a reminder to guide you to your optimal health potential. You may also consider doing a larger version by cutting out color photographs and words from magazines to bring this mandala to a whole new level.

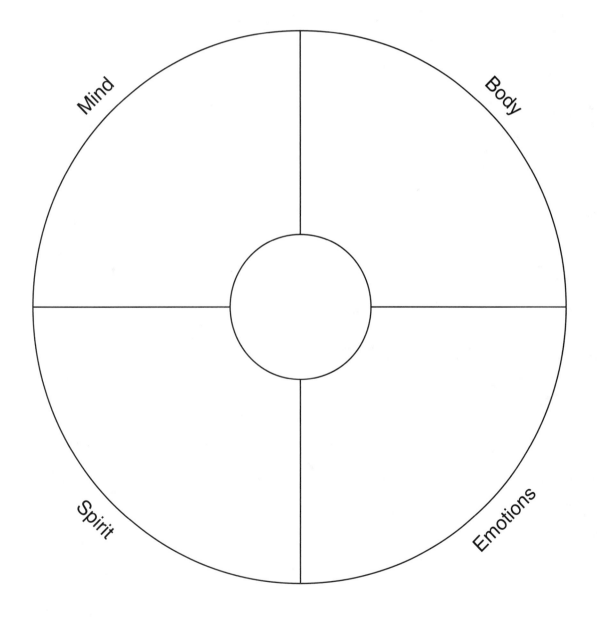